Sheffield Hallam University
Learning and IT Services
Adsetts Centre City Cam
Sheffield S1 1WS

101 985 871 0

D1324547

STOCK

SHEFFIELD HALLAM UNIVERSITY
LEARNING CENTRE
WITHDRAWN FROM STOCK

Studies in War, Society, and the Military

General Editors

Peter Maslowski
University of Nebraska–Lincoln

David Graff
Kansas State University

Reina Pennington
Norwich University

Editorial Board

D'Ann Campbell
*Director of Government and Foundation
Relations, U.S. Coast Guard Foundation*

Mark A. Clodfelter
National War College

Brooks D. Simpson
Arizona State University

Roger J. Spiller
*George C. Marshall Professor Military History
U.S. Army Command
and General Staff College (retired)*

Timothy H. E. Travers
University of Calgary

Arthur Waldron
*Lauder Professor of International Relations
University of Pennsylvania*

DAVID RAUB SNYDER

Sex Crimes under the Wehrmacht

UNIVERSITY OF NEBRASKA PRESS   LINCOLN & LONDON

SHEFFIELD HALLAM UNIVERSITY
WL
364.1530943
SN
ADSETTS LEARNING CENTRE

© 2007 by the Board of Regents
of the University of Nebraska
All rights reserved
Manufactured in the
United States of America

Library of Congress Cataloging-
in-Publication Data

Snyder, David Raub, 1964–
Sex crimes under the Wehrmacht /
David Raub Snyder.
p.   cm.—(Studies in war, society,
and the military)
Includes bibliographical references
and index.
ISBN-13: 978-0-8032-4332-3
(hardcover: alk. paper)
ISBN-13: 978-0-8032-2507-7
(paperback: alk. paper)
1. Sex crimes—Germany—History—
20th century.   2. Military courts—
Germany—History—20th century.
3. National socialism and justice—
Germany.   I. Title.
HV6569.G3S68   2007
364.15'3094309043—dc20
2006032915

For my parents

Contents

Acknowledgments

I would like to express my appreciation and thanks to Professors Peter Maslowski and Alan Steinweis for their support, advice, and interest in my work. I also owe a debt of gratitude to my friends and colleagues in Germany. Hans Georg Dilgard, the head of the Central Documentation Agency in Aachen-Kornelimünster, made my time in the archive not just productive but also a genuinely pleasant experience. I would also like to thank my archivist, Michael Krüger, as well as Herr Ronald Meentz for extending their helping (and friendly) hands. Professor Klaus Schwabe and Dr. Christoph Rass were most helpful during my time in Aachen and I am very grateful to have had their assistance and guidance. I also owe a debt of gratitude to Heather Lundine, Ann Baker, Linnea Fredrickson, and the rest of the staff at the University of Nebraska Press. My editor, Sandy Crump, also deserves recognition for her patience and professionalism. Her assistance and input have been invaluable.

Finally, my wife, Heather, and my children, Malcolm, Margaret, and David, sacrificed greatly during the research and writing of this book.

This project began as an investigation into the Wehrmacht's role as an agent of social conformity under National Socialism. Assuming that courts-martial would have been the ultimate arbiter of appropriate behavior in the Wehrmacht, I turned my attention to the relevant secondary literature. Although scholars have devoted considerable attention to desertion, insubordination, and other military obstructive acts, the literature is largely silent about nonmilitary offenses, offenses that the civilian penal code threatened with punishment.

Although homosexuality under the swastika has attracted the attention of scholars, no book-length studies have been written on the Wehrmacht's treatment of homosexuals. Franz Seidler devotes forty pages to homosexuality in *Prostitution, Homosexualität, Selbstverstümmelung* (Prostitution, homosexuality, self-inflicted wounds), but he approaches the issue from the problems homosexuality posed for the army medical services rather than the military leadership. In fact, in the pages that Seidler devotes to homosexuality, only ten pages deal directly with the Wehrmacht, with the remainder focusing on other issues such as homosexuality and the SS or Hitler Youth.[1] Beyond this example, one must search the secondary literature diligently for a mere mention of sexuality and the Wehrmacht.[2]

Scholars of sexuality may discuss the Wehrmacht, but more often than not they do so tangentially or by generalized extension from their work on civilian issues. For example, Susan Brownmiller, in her landmark study *Against Our Will: Men, Women, and Rape*, provides an analysis of sexual assault during the Second World War, with nine pages devoted to the Wehrmacht. She contends that Nazism's exaggeration of values that "normal society held to be masculine" and Hitler's perception that the Bolshevik masses were "weak and feminine" naturally made rape an ideal means of repression. "It was not surprising," concludes Brownmiller, "that the ideology of rape burst into perfect flower as Hitler's armies goose-stepped over the face of Europe."[3] She reaches this conclusion, however, apparently on the basis of generalizations regarding National Socialism rather than on the basis of documentation.

Quoting testimony given before the International Military Tribunal, Brownmiller also concludes that rape had been not only an ideal means of repression but also a "routine" weapon of terror employed by the Wehrmacht.[4] Enumerating various sexual crimes committed by German soldiers during the war, Brownmiller mistakenly equates these specific atrocities with an expressed policy. Despite the Wehrmacht's complicity in Hitler's racial war of annihilation against the Soviet Union, sexual assault had not been an expressed component of the annihilation strategy. In fact, the Wehrmacht identified sexual assault as one of the few crimes against Soviet civilians that merited prosecution. Of course, the prosecution and punishment of sexual assaults had been based not on compassion for Soviet civilians but instead on the Wehrmacht's desire to maintain discipline and prevent the spread of sexually transmitted diseases.

In preparation for the assault on the Soviet Union, the army's commander-in-chief demanded in June 1941 that military judicial action be taken in all cases where "discipline was threatened and there was a risk of degeneration of the troops, especially in the case of sexual offenses."[5] This does not mean that German soldiers never committed rape crimes in the east or that the military judicial authorities prosecuted every case that came to their attention. However, drawing conclusions about the Wehrmacht's strategy on the basis of atrocities reported at Nuremburg and National Socialism's inherent characteristics has led, at least in this case, to an unsubstantiated generalization. Brownmiller admits that Allied soldiers raped with "gusto," but this does not prove that the Allies employed rape as part of their expressed military strategy.[6]

Although the Wehrmacht's role as an agent of social conformity still remains subtly below the surface, this project ultimately became an investigation into the German army's prosecution and punishment of sex offenders during the Second World War. The text aims to restore balance to the historiography of Wehrmachtjustiz, which has generally focused on military offenses, and to contribute to the historiography of sexuality and the Third Reich. By examining the Wehrmacht's treatment of sex offenders, the text might also generate further interest and research into three groups often ignored by scholars, especially military historians: gays, women, and children.

Organization

Part I, "The Military Administration of Justice: Organization, Structures, and Methods," is based primarily on the secondary literature and published documents yet is nevertheless informed by military judicial records examined at the German Federal Archives Central Documentation Agency (Bundesarchiv-Zentralnachweistelle) in Aachen-Kornelimünster. Chapter 1 outlines the controversy and current debate that surrounds Nazi Germany's military judiciary. Especially heated and tendentious among German scholars, the military administration of justice under Hitler has become a divisive topic. Anyone hoping to be quickly educated on sexuality and the Wehrmacht will be disappointed, as this aspect of the Wehrmacht's history has yet to be told. Chapter 2 examines the developments in the military judicial sphere between the Nazi seizure of power and the beginning of the Second World War in 1939. It also delineates the military judicial machinery and the individual components within the military administration of justice under Hitler. Chapter 3 describes the modifications made to the military judicial system after 1939 as the Wehrmacht adapted the military judiciary to meet the demands of total war. To provide a basis for understanding the fates of the individuals who became ensnared in the military judicial machinery (and who are the subject of part II), chapter 4 examines the Wehrmacht's special penal formations and unique parole system.

Part II, "Sex under the Swastika: The Regime, the Wehrmacht, and the Case Files," begins with a brief discussion, in chapter 5, of the military judicial case files housed at the Central Documentation Agency. The case files represent the bulk of the primary sources scrutinized for this investigation, and they provide valuable insight into the everyday reality of Wehrmachtjustiz. Each case file contains documents pertaining to a specific military judicial inquiry or court martial, providing a paper trail from the pretrial investigation to conviction and incarceration, and, when applicable, parole. More than four hundred of these files from dozens of different courts were sampled from the Central Documentation Agency's collection. Unless otherwise noted, any mention of the case files refers to these documents.

Chapter 6 addresses the plight of homosexuals during the Third Reich, and examines the military judiciary's handling of individuals committing homosexual "offenses." Both gay men and heterosexuals committed such infractions. Following the same approach as chapter 6, chapter 7 addresses rape and sexual assault, and chapter 8 investigates child molestation and incest. Chapter 9 provides a tentative analysis of racial defilement (sexual contact between "Aryans" and Jews) and the taboo topic of bestiality. Finally, chapter 10 discusses the role of alcohol in sexual misconduct and the courts' application of the penal codes governing crimes committed by those with diminished mental capacity. Chapter 11 briefly summarizes the inescapable conclusions that should be drawn from this investigation.

Unless otherwise noted, all translations appearing in this book are my own, and I take full responsibility for any errors or omissions.

Sex Crimes under the Wehrmacht

PART ONE

The Military Administration of Justice

ORGANIZATION, STRUCTURES, AND METHODS

CHAPTER ONE

The Historiography of Wehrmachtjustiz

With few exceptions, scholars have portrayed National Socialist Germany's military judiciary (*Wehrmachtjustiz*) as a monolithic entity, an organization that must be wholly condemned or wholly praised. The apologists, led by former Wehrmacht jurist Erich Schwinge, depict Nazi Germany's military judiciary as a haven for non-Nazi jurists and even as a center of resistance to Adolf Hitler. Hoping to escape the destruction of judicial independence occurring in the civil courts, jurists of conscience, according to the apologists, flocked to the military. Protected by the (allegedly) politically neutral Wehrmacht, they battled to maintain constitutional processes and the rule of law.

Critics, on the other hand, characterize the military judiciary as a compliant tool of the regime or as Hitler's willing and self-motivated partner, dispensing terror-justice in support of National Socialist goals. Manfred Messerschmidt and Fritz Wüllner have contributed the most damning account, which portrays Hitler's military jurists as agents for the *Volksgemeinschaft*'s purification. According to the critics, the jurists imposed death sentences for the most trivial offenses and stabilized the regime until its final collapse.

The truth, however, most likely lies somewhere in between. The complexity of any large organization and, indeed, the complexity of the German military judicial process render sweeping generalizations and blanket assessments a risky enterprise. With more than one thousand courts and thousands of jurists, the potential for wide variations in the law's application should not be underestimated.

On the other hand, given that the National Socialist military judiciary imposed an unprecedented number of death sentences, its draconian nature cannot honestly be disputed. Messerschmidt and Wüllner estimate that military courts sentenced at least thirty thousand German soldiers, sailors, and airmen to death during the Second World War.[1] Erich Schwinge, even after attempts to minimize the number through disingenuous omissions and deceptive calculations, concludes that the courts condemned ten thousand to twelve thousand soldiers to death, fifteen times the number of death sentences imposed by U.S. military courts.[2] Much more at issue, then, is the motivation behind the military jurists' merciless application of the law.

For their analyses of Wehrmachtjustiz, scholars have focused primarily on desertion and *Wehrkraftzersetzung*, which translates loosely as "subversion of fighting power." "Subversive" acts included evasion of military service, defeatist expressions, and comments critical of the political or military leadership. Convictions for desertion and Wehrkraftzersetzung produced the vast majority of death sentences, and their assessment obviously is crucial to understanding Wehrmachtjustiz. Although infrequently motivated by purely political considerations, desertion and Wehrkraftzersetzung nevertheless represent the rejection of Hitler's main foreign political goal, the conquest of living space (*Lebensraum*), and scholars therefore classify these offenses as political in nature. As posed by Manfred Messerschmidt, whatever the deserters' motives, "They collectively have weakened objectively the NS-system [the National Socialist system], they have committed the political offense as such—the breach of loyalty."[3]

But what about offenses that violated the regime's social goals? Before concluding that Wehrmacht jurists acted as agents for the Volksgemeinschaft's purification, would not an analysis of their handling of offenses that violated the regime's social goals be important? Sexual offenses made up only a small fraction of the cases tried before military courts, and scholars have generally ignored them. However, an objective assessment of Wehrmachtjustiz must include an analysis of its treatment of homosexuals, rapists, child molesters, and other sex offenders, and such an analysis may indeed provide valuable insight into the military judiciary's true nature.

Little scholarly work was done on Wehrmachtjustiz until the 1980s. Unlike the civilian administration of justice—which had been tainted by the activities of the People's Court and its fanatic chief, Roland Freisler—the military judiciary escaped criticism for many years after the war.[4] Most Germans perceived the military judiciary the way they perceived the Wehrmacht itself in the first decades following the war, as having been politically neutral and performing its task, albeit reluctantly. Personal accounts by leading military jurists such as Christian von Hammerstein, chief of the Air Force Legal Division (Rechtsabteilung der Luftwaffe) from 1939 to 1945, and Admiral Max Bastian, of the Reich Supreme Military Court (Reichskriegsgericht), lauded the military jurists' resistance to party encroachments and established the myth of a benign military judiciary under Hitler.[5]

In addition, neither the International Military Tribunal (IMT) nor West German courts after 1949 convicted a single presiding military jurist for the perversion of justice or complicity in the regime's crimes.[6] This too nourished the public's belief in the myth. The execution of Dr. Karl Sack, who was the army's chief justice (Chef der Heeresrechtsabteilung) from October 1, 1942, to September 8, 1944, for his role in the failed attempt to assassinate Hitler on July 20, 1944, also reinforced the legend of a military judiciary in resistance.[7]

The first significant breach in the mythical image of a benign military judiciary occurred in the 1960s with the publication of Otto Hennicke's essay "Auszüge aus der Wehrmachtkriminalstatistik" (Excerpts from the Wehrmacht Criminal Statistics).[8] An East German historian, Hennicke had access to the official statistics compiled by the combined office for the Army Administration of Justice (Amtsgruppe Heeresrechtswesen) from the war's outbreak in 1939 until mid-1944.[9] These statistics, until Germany's reunification, were stored at the German Military Archive in Potsdam in the German Democratic Republic. Hennicke, extrapolating for data that went unrecorded during the war's last ten months, concluded that German military courts imposed 25,500 death sentences (16,000 against servicemen) during the war.[10] The large number of death sentences, he concludes, can be explained only by the judicial terror employed to counter decreasing support for the regime after 1943.[11] Many in the Federal Republic of Germany characterized Hennicke's efforts as Marxist/antifascist propaganda, but his statistical analysis provided the first evidence of the military judiciary's draconian nature under the swastika.

Although Hennicke opened the door, it took the publication of Erich Schwinge's *Die deutsche Militärjustiz in der Zeit des Nationalsozialismus* (German military justice in the time of National Socialism) in 1977 to provoke serious scholarly interest in Wehrmachtjustiz in the Federal Republic of Germany. The twisted road leading to the publication of this controversial account began in 1962 when the

Institute for Contemporary History in Munich commissioned Otto Peter Schweling, a former Luftwaffe jurist, to write an analysis of Wehrmachtjustiz for the institute's planned book series on the administration of justice under National Socialism.

The institute considered the thousand-page manuscript, which Schweling completed in 1966, as conceptually inadequate. Even after the manuscript was revised, the institute believed that it gave the impression of a "half-finished product" that failed to evaluate the memoirs of former jurists. The institute also found the selection of sources "too one-sided" and "too small," and said that many sources were insufficiently documented. Furthermore, it said that Schweling had ignored many easily accessible documents that could have been used to shed light on "internal events in the higher agencies of Wehrmachtjustiz" as well as the origins of important ordinances and decrees, which remained "insufficiently" evaluated. For example, Schweling's analysis did not address the role of Wehrmacht jurists in the formulation of the Barbarossa Jurisdiction Decree and the Commissar Order. In the end, the institute decided that Schweling's study appeared too apologetic and portrayed Wehrmachtjustiz and National Socialism as two independent and opposing phenomena—entities that neither influenced each other nor shared any common interests.[12] After years of acrimonious negotiation with the author, the institute definitively rejected the manuscript in 1976, a year after Schweling's death.[13]

After Schweling died, university law professor and former Wehrmacht jurist Erich Schwinge represented the author's interests before the institute. When the manuscript was finally rejected, Schwinge supplemented and edited it for publication with another press. The completed work appeared in 1977 and was quickly accepted among lay readers (and not a few historians) as the standard and authoritative work on Wehrmachtjustiz.

Based on his analysis of a thousand case files randomly selected from the collection housed at the German Federal Archives Central Documentation Agency, Schwinge characterizes Wehrmachtjustiz as mild rather than harsh, especially with regard to offenses that did not injure military order and discipline.[14] According to Schwinge, the nearly ten thousand death sentences documented in the official Wehrmacht Criminal Statistics cannot be blamed on judicial terror; rather, they can be attributed only to the war's length and its ferocity after June 1941. In other words, the barbarous nature of the conflict in the east prompted a large number of soldiers to desert, a crime that the armed forces of all belligerents during the Second World War threatened with death.[15] "If desertion increases to a high level," Schwinge reflects, "then in all nations' armed forces will the number of death sentences increase."[16]

Furthermore, nearly half of the condemned received clemency or were paroled to the front. The number of death sentences actually carried out, Schwinge asserts, was not appreciably higher per capita than the number of death sentences imposed by the French army in the First World War.[17] With approximately 57 percent of all convicted soldiers receiving an early parole, Schwinge concludes that Wehrmacht jurists were merciful rather than bloodthirsty.[18]

According to Schwinge, none of the fourteen men occupying the top positions in Wehrmachtjustiz before and during the war were convinced Nazis. The majority of the jurists sitting on the bench, he concludes, consciously resisted the regime's efforts to undermine constitutionality and the legal process.[19]

The controversy over Schweling's original manuscript and Schwinge's published version stirred interest within a small circle of historians, and a number of scholarly works began to appear in the 1980s. Manfred Messerschmidt and Fritz Wüllner, however, must be credited with single-handedly destroying the legend of a politically neutral and merciful military judiciary. *Die Wehrmachtjustiz im Dienste des Nationalsozialismus* (The military administration of justice in the service of National Socialism), published in 1987 (and now considered the standard and most authoritative account of Wehrmachtjustiz), took direct aim at Schwinge's interpretation. The authors characterize Schwinge's analysis as not only inaccurate but also a deliberate attempt at deception.

According to Messerschmidt and Wüllner, Schwinge's sample of one thousand case files cannot be considered representative "under any circumstances," especially with regard to the number of death sentences. Wartime regulations required that, after the execution of death sentences imposed by army courts, the case files had to be sent to the army's Potsdam archive. The Allies completely destroyed this facility during a bombing mission against Berlin in the spring of 1945. Because the majority of death sentences had been carried out and the case files documenting these deaths were destroyed, the death sentences documented in the Central Documentation Agency's collection therefore represent only a fraction of the actual total. Schwinge, as a former military jurist, would certainly have known these facts. Indeed, not one of the twelve death sentences handed down by army courts in Schwinge's case file sample was carried out, while all three death sentences imposed by naval courts in the sample were carried out.[20]

Through extensive scrutiny of punishment lists (*Straflisten*), which survived in much greater numbers than the case files, Messerschmidt and Wüllner demonstrate that the official Wehrmacht Criminal Statistics are much more incomplete than previously assumed. Schwinge used the official statistics in all his calculations, characterizing them as undoubtedly accurate, complete, and authoritative.[21] Messerschmidt and Wüllner document many instances in which data went unrecorded in the official statistics because of either delays in communications or the destruction of documents by enemy action. By factoring these delays and loss factors into the statistics, as well as adjusting their totals to take into account the geometric progression of crimes during the war, they estimate that the number of convictions during the war amounted to between 1.3 million and 1.5 million, rather than the approximately seven hundred thousand documented in the official statistics and cited by Schwinge.[22]

Messerschmidt and Wüllner also conclude that the number of servicemen condemned to death was thirty thousand, not 9,700 as cited in the official statistics.[23] Furthermore, even if 40 percent (a percentage that Messerschmidt and Wüllner deem too high) of the condemned had been granted clemency, this was not, as Schwinge suggests, the result of an act of mercy by compassionate jurists. These soldiers were sent to parole and penal units, which, according to Messerschmidt and Wüllner, meant almost certain death. In other words, there was nothing merciful about clemency. Schwinge's assertion that jurists passed death sentences to satisfy the political leadership, but then compassionately granted clemency as an act of mercy, is therefore a distortion of the truth.

Wehrmacht jurists, Messerschmidt and Wüllner maintain, willingly formulated the orders that Hitler demanded for his war of annihilation against the Soviet Union (the Barbarossa Jurisdiction Decree and the Commissar Order). The jurists also participated obligingly in preparing the Wartime Penal Code (Kriegssonderstrafrechtsverordnung) and the Wartime Judicial Procedure Code (Kriegsstrafverfahrensordnung) in 1938 for the intensification and streamlining of the wartime military judicial process. According to Messerschmidt and Wüllner, the codes allowed Wehrmachtjustiz to proceed with extreme vigor and harshness against the most trivial offenses, and Wehrmacht courts used these tools extensively of their own accord. They did not have to be coerced or steered from above. Indeed, the authors estimate that thirty thousand soldiers, sailors, and airmen received the death penalty and that perhaps twenty-two thousand servicemen had their death sentences carried out.[24]

Finally, contrary to Schwinge's assertion that the military judiciary was a center of resistance to the political leadership, Messerschmidt and Wüllner contend that military jurists conducted "conscious ideological cooperation." Hitler's military jurists, they argue, agreed fully with the National Socialist conception of the law. Not only did they perceive themselves as agents for the Volksgemeinschaft's purification, they also worked diligently to stabilize the regime until the last days of the war.[25]

Although it is considered the standard work on Wehrmachtjustiz today, Messerschmidt and Wüllner's account has its faults. The authors proceed from the questionable assumption that because legal theorists and commentators filled contemporary professional journals with commentaries promoting a system of justice based on National Socialist ideology, the men sitting on the bench adjudicated according to these precepts and did so out of conviction. It would be more surprising, however, to find commentaries, journal articles, and speeches from the period in question that failed to support the regime, its policies, and its goals.[26]

The authors also emphasize the ideological invective and Nazi insults hurled at defendants by judges, as recorded in court transcripts.[27] The adoption of Nazi phrases and vocabulary, however, cannot be considered definitive proof of the jurists' attitudes. It can be demonstrated very easily that the National Socialist vernacular had a tendency to creep into military judicial documents. Commanding officers were required to vouch for a judge's political reliability in performance evaluations, and in the jurists' personnel files the officers reported that every jurist under review "at all times and without reservation supports the National Socialist state and represents it actively."[28] This phrase seldom varied, and the officers simply recapitulated the question as posed on the standard questionnaire.

In addition, Nazi insults and ideological invective are the exception rather than the rule in the case files of sex offenders. This begs the question of why jurists would have been prone to hurl National Socialist slurs and insults at deserters and "subversives," who were at the center of Messerschmidt's and Wüllner's account, but not at individuals whose crimes had not demonstrated any unwillingness to fight, opposition to the war, or resistance to the regime, such as sex offenders.

Messerschmidt and Wüllner condemn Schwinge for his "number acrobatics," but at times they too are quite agile with numbers. Although they document cases of missing data in the official statistics, they do not substantiate their estimated loss factor of 20 percent for the entire war. Large numbers of military judicial documents undoubtedly were delayed, lost, or destroyed during the war. Lost documents, however, do not automatically translate into missing data because redundant sources for the relevant statistical information existed.[29] It is possible that, at times, losses could have reached the level suggested by the authors, but the assumption of a constant 20 percent loss factor for the entire war cannot be justified.[30]

Finally, the authors fail to address adequately the military judiciary's development over time and its adaptation to the demands of total war, most importantly the evolution of the Wehrmacht's penal and parole system. This is not to suggest that wartime necessity justified draconian punishments. However, by proceeding from the assumption that Wehrmachtjustiz operated solely according to ideology, the authors neglect the practical reality of the military judiciary as an instrument of war. One would be mistaken to assume (and many scholars do) that a fanatic Nazi would want every nonconformist, "criminal element," or deserter to be shot, but that a normal, highly professional Christian military officer would rarely, if ever, deem death an appropriate punishment. Again, the military judiciary was an instrument of war that the Wehrmacht considered necessary for the achievement of its strategic tasks.

As an instrument of war, the individual courts were subordinated to a military officer, the *Gerichtsherr*, the commander possessing supreme legal authority over the court attached to his unit. Messerschmidt and Wüllner trivialize his role in the military administration of justice.[31] Depicting the Gerichtsherr as a passive decision maker at the mercy of the jurists, they imply that he had neither any interest in the law as an instrument of command authority nor any opinion on what punishment a crime deserved. The case files, however, reveal that commanding officers had very specific ideas on crime and punishment; and they dominated not just the sentencing and parole phases but also the entire military judicial process.

Despite these criticisms, Messerschmidt and Wüllner effectively demonstrate that Schwinge's account is at least unreliable and at most intentionally deceptive. The authors' work brought Wehrmachtjustiz into the historical mainstream and inspired further research on the topic.

Following his collaboration with Manfred Messerschmidt, Fritz Wüllner published another book, *Die NS-Militärjustiz und das Elend der Geschichtsschreibung* (National Socialist military justice and the deplorable state of the historiography), in 1991. Unfortunately, a powerful bias undermines the credibility of the book, and many of his conclusions remain wholly unsubstantiated. He contends, for example, that "no single document" exists indicating that any soldier atoned his entire sentence and returned to a regular unit as a free soldier.[32] Selected from a wide variety of courts, however, the case files used in this study most emphatically refute this contention.

Although Wüllner's conclusions and interpretations are questionable, he nevertheless provides much valuable factual information regarding the mechanics of the military judicial process, including the Wehrmacht's penal institutions and parole formations. He is also quite accurate in characterizing the Wehrmacht's parole system as a "sword of Damocles."[33] Paroled soldiers had to serve in units actually engaged at the front in order to prove themselves "before the enemy" (*vor dem Feind*).[34] Thus, parolees were exposed to enemy fire for the war's duration. Yet if an individual was rendered unfit for combat through battlefield injuries, illnesses, or accidents, his parole had to be revoked, and he was returned to the Wehrmacht's penal institutions' harsh conditions.[35] Thus, Wüllner's "sword of Damocles" is an apt description.

Collectively, the secondary literature suffers from several deficiencies. Its most basic flaw is that it attempts to prove (or disprove) Wehrmachtjustiz's constitutionality. The pervasiveness of this issue can probably best be explained as a natural reaction to former jurists' claims that they maintained constitutional processes and legal guarantees under National Socialism. This debate, however, is predicated on the assumption that Nazi Germany's military judiciary was equivalent to the civilian administration of justice before 1933. But it decidedly was not.

The National Socialist military judicial system's origins can be traced to the Prussian mercenary armies of the old regime. Adopted upon unification in 1871, the Prussian system, despite modifications during the first half of the nineteenth century, functioned basically as it had during the eighteenth century. Although Social Democrats condemned Imperial Germany's military judicial process as unconstitutional after 1871, the military judiciary's regulations and processes remained largely unchanged until the empire's collapse in 1918.[36] The Weimar Constitution suspended military jurisdiction (except on board ship), but after 1933 the Nazi regime reestablished military jurisdiction firmly on the basis of the Military Penal Code (Militärstrafgesetzbuch) of 1872. Under the code, courts-martial functioned essentially as they had under Frederick I.[37]

The Imperial German military judiciary had been designed as an instrument to be used by the political and military leadership for the attainment of the state's foreign (and, some would argue, domestic) political goals. It was not designed for the protection of individual rights and liberties. Rather, it functioned solely for the protection and maintenance of the military apparatus. The fusion of judicial and executive authority in the person of the Gerichtsherr in itself violates all liberal constitutional principles. However, the Nazis had not invented the Gerichtsherr. This military judicial institution was a time-tested Prussian tradition. Debating the system's constitutionality, trying to characterize it either as a perversion of justice or as the maintenance of constitutional standards, thus appears to be a futile endeavor.[38]

Dwelling myopically on the percentage of the draconian (and, conversely, mild) punishments imposed is the literature's second deficiency. Scholars may attempt to determine a prisoner's ultimate fate, but few scrutinize the evaluations and fitness reports assessing the men ensnared in the military judicial machinery. These documents, however, are crucial to any analysis. Only by following the complete paper trail from pretrial investigation to conviction, from incarceration to parole (if applicable), can one fully understand Wehrmachtjustiz.

Third, scholars fail to give the Wehrmacht's penal system the attention it deserves. The administration of justice did not stop with the imposition of a verdict. The verdict was only the beginning of the overall judicial process. The penal system, which was designed to achieve specific goals (both judicial and military), implemented the courts' decisions. An integral component of Wehrmachtjustiz, the penal system contributed significantly to its brutal nature. Put more simply, the means of executing punishments had a central role in transforming Wehrmachtjustiz into the draconian tool that it became. Many scholars, however, focus only on the high number of death sentences imposed during the war. Yet hundreds of thousands received simple prison sentences. After 1941, such punishments generally involved service in special parole units used for high-risk assignments or, after 1942, in penal units for hazardous work at the front.

Those not granted an early release still faced hazards in Wehrmacht prisons. Even short stays in a military prison could have lethal consequences because the Wehrmacht's penal system developed along the same lines as its civilian counterpart, where liberal theories of rehabilitation were replaced by Nazi concepts of atonement. The draconian nature of Wehrmachtjustiz, in other words, cannot be attributed simply to the high number of death and penal servitude sentences. The harsh living conditions, brutal discipline, and hazardous duty at the front that were associated with the prisons, penal units, and parole formations played no small part in the system's barbarization.

Both critics and apologists agree that the penal system, as it operated during the war, was quite brutal. The brutality was inflicted not by the jurists handing down the sentences but rather by the military agencies and officers that administered the prisons and penal formations.[39] For this reason, the apologists argue that the penal system's crimes cannot be blamed on the jurists. In their analyses they trivialize the system's role or ignore it altogether. Erich Schwinge, for example, considered the execution of punishments "a matter for military authority" (*Kommandogewalt*), and he therefore excluded it from his book.[40]

Critics, on the other hand, reject this interpretation and indeed consider the penal system to be part of the military administration of justice. These scholars demand that the jurists assume part of the responsibility for the penal system's crimes. The jurists, the critics assert, had the responsibility of monitoring prisoners after their introduction into the penal system and were well aware of what went on within the system.[41] The critics are correct in this assessment, but they generally proceed no further; doing so would undermine their attempt to place the entire blame for the military judiciary's crimes at the jurists' feet.

In order to support this accusation, they must downplay the Gerichtsherr's importance in, and indeed dominance of, the system. Yet the Gerichtsherr was the master of *both the judicial and penal systems*. He possessed the power to confirm or reject verdicts and the power to grant parole. He eventually received the power to decide whether a punishment would be served in a prison or penal formation. Once an individual entered the penal system, only the Gerichtsherr had the power to end an individual's detention, unless there was an intervention by the Oberkommando des Heeres (OKH, or Army High Command) or the Oberkommando der Wehrmacht (OKW, or Armed Forces High Command).[42]

The institution of the Gerichtsherr linked the judicial and penal systems, which were separate but symbiotic and complementary institutions. The Wehrmacht designed the prisons, penal units, and parole formations just as it designed the military judiciary, with specific military considerations in mind. The penal system's draconian nature is not being challenged here. Indeed, the Wehrmacht's perception of crime and appropriate atonement often reflected developments in the civilian sphere.[43] However, in order to appropriately represent the military judicial system, one must refer not to "the judicial system" or "the penal system" but rather to "the judicial-penal system," with the Gerichtsherr as the single unifying (and controlling) link between the two elements. Only by examining the system in this manner can one understand its true nature and function. Only by examining the system from this perspective can the centrality of military considerations in its function and the Gerichtsherr's power over the system be delineated exactly.

Unjustified generalizations based on the analysis of a single court's jurisprudence are the literature's fourth deficiency. Scholars untenably extend these generalizations to the defendants as well. In other words, depending on their agenda, scholars frequently depict these soldiers as a homogenous group, as either the victims of a perverted system of justice or as criminals who got what they deserved under harsh but necessary laws. It must be acknowledged here that men will commit crimes (often very heinous ones) that demand punishment even under a dictatorship and, conversely, that under a dictatorship many injustices will be perpetrated against innocent citizens. A distinction must be drawn between real crimes and imagined crimes, and between those individuals who deserved punishment regardless of the regime's nature and those who did not. Examining the prosecution and punishment of sex offenders more often than not makes these distinctions easier.[44]

Fifth, even though hundreds of Wehrmacht jurist personnel files survived the war, scholars have not investigated the jurists themselves. Many authors simply present commentaries and speeches by leading jurists and cite these as evidence of the ideological basis of Wehrmachtjustiz. However, they are unable to document any relationship between such commentary and the field courts' jurisprudence. In the same vein, historians readily embrace the oft-repeated theory of a military judiciary steered to conformity from above, yet the theory has not been proven by any broad-based examination of the actual case files.

Sixth, scholars have focused almost completely on political and military offenses, such as desertion, insubordination, and evasion of military service, the latter offense often prosecuted as subversion. Messerschmidt and Wüllner address postal theft in their account, but the political and military leadership considered this crime a military offense, one that hindered the war effort. Detrimental to unit cohesion and morale, postal theft allegedly hindered the material mobilization for war because individuals generally misappropriated scarce commodities. Jurists increasingly accepted the notion that, for soldiers and families, postal packages had "high objective values." The theft of these packages "disrupted the tie between home front and the frontlines," adversely affecting the nation's morale.[45] Other than this example, civilian crimes have been largely neglected.

Finally, as mentioned previously, scholars portray Wehrmachtjustiz as a uniform organization instead of as an organization composed of more than a thousand individual courts staffed by thousands of jurists. Scholars generally fail to take into account the fog, friction, and vagaries of war that changed according to location and time. In addition to the fog and friction of war, "there was such a flood of decrees, ordinances, provisions, directives, and implementation plans from the OKW and the three service branches that they nearly drowned each other out, contradicted each other in the details, or were already superseded by new ordinances."[46] For this reason, a commanding officer's outlook was generally the jurists' only point of orientation. With the pressure of war and the constantly changing and even contradictory guidelines under which the courts operated, it should be no surprise that courts-martial displayed wide variations in jurisprudence. In general, these variations can be attributed to the variation in the Gerichtsherren's perceptions of what was required to maintain discipline, order, unit cohesion, and military effectiveness. Indeed, the individual commanding officers' standards remained perhaps the only consistent yardstick for jurisprudence amidst a flurry of confusing and often contradictory ordinances flowing from above.

The perceived lessons of the First World War and their impact on Germany's military jurists are perhaps the most prevalent recurring theme in the secondary literature. Haunted by the accusation that lenient judges had been, in part, responsible for the revolutionary disturbances that rocked the armed forces in 1918—which, according to the "stab-in-the-back" legend, brought defeat in the Great War—Nazi Germany's military jurists had been determined to enforce discipline with all the means at their disposal. Although a few scholars give this theme the attention it deserves, most address only briefly the impact that 1918 had on Germany's military jurists. Instead, after a cursory discussion of the importance of the shock of defeat and the stab in the back, the critics quickly race ahead to count the number of party members on the bench, enumerate the number of "nazified" articles and commentaries in the professional law journals, and add up the number of death sentences. Conversely, the apologists count the number of judges involved in resistance activities and the number of soldiers granted a "merciful" parole.

If the stab-in-the-back legend was an important component in both National Socialist and national conservative ideology, regaining Germany's power position and obtaining continental hegemony was the shared foreign political goal. Is it surprising, then, that military jurists acted ruthlessly against soldiers who hindered the pursuit of that goal? Since the regime and the Wehrmacht agreed on the necessity of preventing another 1918 through an intensified military judicial process, is it productive to focus on punishments meted out to deserters and disobedient soldiers? What can be learned from an examination of the Wehrmacht's treatment of individuals who committed crimes hindering the regime's social goals? Why did military jurists heap scorn upon deserters and malingerers but not upon soldiers who were accused of raping German women or molesting young boys?[47] Why were deserters and "subversives," but not sex offenders, considered "evil parasites" that were to be purged from the Volksgemeinschaft?[48]

This book is not intended to be a comprehensive investigation into Wehrmachtjustiz. Rather, it is an attempt to restore balance to the historiography by examining a group of offenses that until now have been almost completely ignored. Although the draconian nature of Wehrmachtjustiz cannot be refuted, Wehrmachtjustiz must be analyzed one court at a time and case by case, because for every soldier who received a punishment that was completely disproportionate to the crime committed, one can find another soldier who simply received a judicial slap on the wrist. The time and location of the crime, the military situation in the court's sector, the war situation in general, and the personal outlook of the Gerichtsherr, the military commander responsible for the administration of justice in his unit, all affected the everyday reality of Wehrmachtjustiz. This is not an attempt at exoneration or condemnation. It is instead a challenge to the perception of Wehrmachtjustiz as a monolithic entity and a call to judge the commanders and jurists on a case-by-case basis.

The Wehrmacht's collaboration in Hitler's racial war of annihilation against the Soviet Union and the military leadership's agreement with the regime's foreign political goals are clear, as is the increasing influence of National Socialism in the Wehrmacht as the war progressed. It is equally clear that *völkisch* and Social Darwinist thought were prevalent in Germany since the early twentieth century.[49] It is equally clear that many fanatics sat on the bench, and the number most certainly rose as younger men who received their legal training during the Third Reich entered service during the war. However, Wehrmachtjustiz can be explained without recourse to the above litany of social phenomena because above all else it was a military institution. As such, it was designed for the pursuit of specific military goals and to meet practical military considerations, regardless of the regime's foreign policy objectives and the political outlook of the men sitting on the bench.

CHAPTER TWO

The Military Administration of Justice, 1933–39

During the revolutionary upheavals of 1848, German liberals criticized special military jurisdiction as a violation of the liberal constitutional principle of the equality of citizens. In the Imperial German era, socialists regarded the military administration of justice as a central feature of Prussian militarism—as a tool employed by reactionary forces for the maintenance of the traditional social and political structure.[1]

The Social Democrats took the lead in the battle against military jurisdiction after the November Revolution of 1918, and Article 106 of the Weimar Constitution abolished the military administration of justice, except on board ship and in time of war.[2] After the National Socialist seizure of power on January 30, 1933, however, the prerequisites for the reintroduction of military jurisdiction appeared to be at hand. Indeed, it was only a matter of time before the German Armed Forces (Reichswehr), once informed of Hitler's future military and foreign political plans, set about rebuilding the military administration of justice.[3] The Defense Ministry (Reichswehrministerium) began designing a new military penal code immediately after General Werner von Blomberg took office as Defense Minister on January 30, 1933.

On April 24, 1933, von Blomberg presented a draft to Hitler's cabinet. In support of his outline for the new military judicial system, he stated, "Since the political situation has changed, the time has come to reintroduce military jurisdiction in order to prevent the danger that would arise during war in this area, but also to guarantee the absolute requirements for the new, presumably changed, armed forces."[4] Von Blomberg referred in this passage to the perceived lessons Germany had taken from the First World War. In right-wing circles, the opinion had been widespread that it was not a superior opponent that had defeated the Imperial German Army in 1918. On the contrary, defeat had been caused, in part, by a weak military judiciary that allowed "thousands upon thousands of deserters, psychopaths, and malingerers to loaf around behind the front," traitors who "finally shoved a knife into the back of the fighting troops."[5] The war weariness and defeatism that spread through the ranks, the legend held, could be attributed not to the military leadership's poor strategic choices but instead to an ineffective military administration of justice eviscerated by weak penal codes and lenient judges.

Leniency would now be replaced by severity, and the penal codes intensified. "Wehrmacht jurists brought to expression their conception of . . . military law: harshness rather than mildness, freedom of form rather than 100 percent legal guarantees, speed rather than detailed thoroughness, and the priority of military interests rather than the interest of the individual."[6] The new military administration of justice would be the opposite of its predecessor.

Passed on May 12, 1933, the Law for the Reintroduction of Military Jurisdiction, one of the regime's earliest legislative measures, became effective on January 1, 1934.[7] Denied the opportunity to pursue their craft during the Weimar Republic, former military jurists, primarily right-wing nationalists, expressed overwhelming joy for this "gift from the Führer." Through modifications on November 23, 1934, and July 16, 1935, the German Armed Forces adapted the Imperial German Military Criminal Code of 1898 to fit the new requirements referred to by von Blomberg.[8] Most of the mitigation clauses that the Social Democrats had forced on Kaiser Wilhelm II during the First World War were expunged.[9] Despite much discussion and planning, however, the Defense Ministry never created a new National Socialist military criminal code.[10] To the military leadership and its new jurists, the Imperial German (that is, Prussian) codes, having been purged of all liberal elements, appeared quite sufficient for their purposes.[11]

From the beginning, Nazi Germany's military jurists had been driven to atone for what many on the right perceived as the military judiciary's failure during the First World War to maintain discipline. The military administration of justice, supposedly hampered by burdensome formalities and lenient sentencing provisions, allowed discipline to disintegrate after 1917, ultimately contributing to the November Revolution of 1918 and the mythical stab in the back.[12]

For militarists and right-wing nationalists, the numbers told the story. During the Great War, British courts-martial had imposed nearly 3,100 death sentences, with 346 executions carried out. French military courts handed down approximately two thousand death sentences, with one-third of these sentences purportedly completed. German courts-martial, by contrast, imposed just 150 death sentences, and only forty-eight were carried out.[13] Even the liberal Weimar Republic's legislative body, the Reichstag, accepted this assessment in 1928, blasting the military judiciary in a report submitted by a parliamentary board of inquiry, entitled *Soziale Heeresmißstände als Mitursache des deutschen Zusammenbruchs von 1918* (Social unrest in the military as a contributing factor to the German collapse of 1918).[14]

The National Socialist leadership shared this perceived lesson of history as well. "Hitler, among others, had bitterly criticized this sparring use of harsh punishment, claiming that a feeble military judiciary was a prime cause of the deterioration of the German army at the end of World War I."[15] In *Mein Kampf*, Hitler lamented, "During the war, the death sentence was practically eliminated; the articles of war were in reality nullified. . . . An army of deserters poured forth, especially in the year 1918, and assisted in forming those large organizations that we suddenly saw before us as the makers of Revolution after 7 November 1918."[16]

The political and military leadership, as well as the newly appointed military jurists, were determined that in any future conflict the military administration of justice would be swift, severe, and equal to the demands of total war. Germany's military chiefs and the Nazi leadership were united in the conviction that the appropriate lessons be drawn from the failures of the First World War:

> Today, it can certainly be assumed that during the World War the German legislature did not counter the forces of subversion and disintegration with the kind of energy and ruthlessness that was indicated by the seriousness of the hour. . . . Thus it was possible that the inclination to dereliction of duty and insubordination was able to creep into the German armed forces since the second half of the year 1917, with the consequence that the superb esprit de corps of the troops that had existed in the first half of the war was negatively affected and impaired. . . . If earlier an agitator and instigator who attempted to subvert the fighting power of the army could only be prosecuted on the basis of precisely

stipulated definitions of criminal activity and confronted with insufficient punishments, then such an individual now will be countered with laws without loopholes and the threat of the most severe punishment. . . . Signs of disintegration and subversion, which might threaten the esprit de corps and combat effectiveness of the German armed forces, can in this manner be crushed and nipped in the bud in the future.[17]

Thus, the military administration of justice under National Socialism was predicated on the fundamental determination that there could never be another November 1918.[18] In order to prevent a repetition of that month's events, the new military judiciary, as perceived by one leading military jurist in 1934, should be constituted for the protection of the "community of blood, sacrifice, and fate; . . . such that in an emergency it is a spiritual and potent weapon of the state, which maintains and increases the resistance power of the troops and population generally, free of all defects that can have unfavorable psychological effects."[19]

The military criminal code's "central object of protection" was *Manneszucht*, the "most valuable thing an army possessed." Manneszucht, a product of time-honored Prussian military traditions, may be translated as "discipline," but it has much deeper significance. According to Norbert Haase, Manneszucht "stood quasi-synonymously for discipline," the soldier's absolute "subordination to military order, and the unity of the troops for ensuring the skill and fighting power of the armed forces."[20] As the culmination of Prussia's militarist and authoritarian history, Manneszucht, as a concept and in practice, boiled down to nothing less than the soldier's complete subordination to the military and military order in every facet of his life. For the jurists, as the heirs of Prussian militarism and witnesses to 1918, Manneszucht became the guiding principle in the application of the law.[21] By maintaining Manneszucht at all costs and with every available legal (and illegal) weapon, the fatigue, war weariness, and demoralization that led to the dissolution of the armed forces in 1918 would be prevented. Aided by the regime's ruthless suppression of nonconformists and its psychological mobilization of the masses, Germany's military chiefs looked forward to building a *Wehrgemeinschaft*, a community of soldiers, for the next war.[22] Any disruptive elements that escaped the regime's instruments of repression and slipped into the armed forces would be identified and removed by the new military judiciary.

One did not have to be a Nazi in order to support this design. One did not have to agree with National Socialism or its domestic policies in order to implement it. One had only to have learned the lessons of the First World War that permeated German society during the Weimar Republic and post-1933 Germany.[23] In fact, one could argue that the military administration of justice after 1933 was the product of German nationalism as conceived by right-wing elites and allowed full expression under the new dictator, rather than the product of National Socialism. The military's conservative elites designed and implemented it willingly and enthusiastically.[24] If some other right-wing political group had attained power in 1933, the result would most likely have been the same. Hitler did not introduce the German right to stab-in-the-back legend, and the perceived lessons of World War I had been learned well before 1933.

Under the mantra of maintaining Manneszucht and discipline, Nazi Germany's military jurists blithely followed the directives and decrees that continuously intensified the military judicial process after 1939. The Wehrgemeinschaft had to be maintained; the events of 1918 avoided. Scholars frequently use the words "Volksgemeinschaft" and "Wehrgemeinschaft" interchangeably, but they were two distinct phenomena.[25] The Volksgemeinschaft, the racially pure Aryan nation whose "social harmony, unity, and political authority rested on the integration of people from all walks of life, thus transcending class conflict," remained the regime's ideal goal.[26]

The Wehrgemeinschaft, the brotherhood in arms—that cohesive community of soldiers unified and dedicated to one another through devotion to duty and fatherland—was the military's goal. Individuals willing to subordinate themselves completely to military order and the pursuit of the Wehrmacht's strategic tasks were welcomed into the Wehrgemeinschaft. An examination of sex offenders attests to this fact. It must again be emphasized that if some other right-wing political faction had attained power in 1933, the result would most likely have been the same. Indeed, Wehrmachtjustiz and the Prussian concept of Manneszucht were not "dominated by fascist goals (*Ordnungszielen*) such as the Volksgemeinschaft and racial political conceptions, but rather served the conduct of the war and were relatively independent of the accompanying fascist circumstances."[27]

On the other hand, the Wehrgemeinschaft that the military diligently erected and maintained fulfilled Hitler's requirements far better than a purified Volksgemeinschaft ever could. By including personnel that would have been purged from the Volksgemeinschaft, the military managed to mobilize many more men than would have been possible if the Wehrmacht had adhered to Nazi standards. Deserters, pacifists, and other individuals who demonstrated their unwillingness to fulfill their obligation to the Wehrgemeinschaft had to be purged, lest the events of 1918 repeat themselves. Rapists, child molesters, and, more often than not, homosexuals did not have to be excluded from the Wehrgemeinschaft if they were willing to carry a weapon in good faith. By maintaining the Wehrgemeinschaft rather than the Volksgemeinschaft, the military and its willing jurists ironically provided an instrument for the regime's foreign political plans that was far superior to the one desired by Nazi ideologues, despite Hitler's alleged dissatisfaction with Wehrmachtjustiz.

The military judiciary's blind pursuit of the Wehrgemeinschaft, however, cannot be explained solely within the context of Germany's perception of the causes of defeat in the First World War. The military's solution to total war, the Wehrgemeinschaft (and the desire to maintain it all costs) can be understood only if it is also viewed within the context of Germany's overall development and experiences since unification—that is, within the context of the evolution of the German concept of "war necessity" (*Kriegsnotwendigkeit*).

The roots of this phrase extend back to the Wilhelmine era, a time marked by "inner insecurity" and later by "pent up foreign political requirements." Never sharply defined, Kriegsnotwendigkeit can be understood as "that which benefits the war party, that is, the warring state" (Kriegsnotwendigkeit ist, was der Kriegspartei, d.h. dem kriegführenden Staat nütz).[28]

"War necessity" began to take shape in the minds of Imperial Germany's military leaders by the turn of the century, as indicated by the Great General Staff's 1902 treatise, Practices in Land Warfare. It placed the "attainment of war aims as far as possible above the . . . laws of war."[29] The political leadership's eventual acceptance of the concept had its consequences in the First World War. During that conflict, Germany employed reasons of state to justify the bloody reprisals and preventive measures against the Belgian resistance, actions that resulted in six thousand deaths. German violations of international law in the Great War must be considered in the light of the "decades-long devaluation" of liberal traditions in the name of "military realism" and war necessity.[30]

During the Third Reich, the concept of "total war" received its meaning only through the concept of "total enemy."[31] Under Hitler, the Wehrmacht combined Karl von Claueswitz's, Erich von Ludendorff's, and Ernst Jünger's theories on war and the state, producing the trinity of "total war—total state—total enemy."[32] But if the concept of war necessity facilitated the Wehrmacht's role in Hitler's total war against the Slavic masses in the east, it also facilitated the military judiciary's "reprisals and preventive measures" against the German people themselves. These were measures that the Wehrmacht considered as a war necessity—they were essential for maintaining the Wehrgemeinschaft. Like so many aspects of Hitler's Germany, the concept of war necessity was not invented by the Nazis: National Socialism just provided the environment for the concept's radicalization and its unfettered implementation by the Wehrmacht.[33]

Although the prewar judicial machinery and its peacetime activities have attracted little attention from scholars, its components (and the concepts upon which the components were based) were crucial to the operation and evolution of Wehrmachtjustiz during the Second World War. New ordinances and modified criminal codes after 1939 may have accelerated and intensified the military judicial process, but the system's basic components had been assembled prior to the war's outbreak. The machinery therefore required few additions in order to function smoothly, even when confronted by the demands of total war. Elements added after September 1939 were merely modifications of preexisting methods and doctrines.

The Jurists

Before 1939 the newly reconstituted military judiciary attracted little attention (even from Hitler) as it went about its business, keeping pace with the military's rapid expansion after 1935. The job of filling the positions created by the reintroduction of military jurisdiction after 1934 as well as those created by the armed forces' subsequent expansion was left to the German Armed Forces legal department and, after 1935, to the legal divisions within each of the Wehrmacht's three service branches.

Most scholars agree that neither Hitler nor the party interfered with the recruitment and appointment of military jurists and that party membership was not a prerequisite for admission to the military judiciary.[34] However, this does not mean that these new jurists were not members of the party or one of its organizations. The personnel records examined for this study reveal that party membership, or membership in a party organization such as the Sturmabteilung (SA) or the Schutzstaffel (SS), was not uncommon among the jurists.[35] In fact, among the jurists in the personnel file sample, approximately 44 percent who were recruited after 1934 belonged to such party organizations. Not one, however, belonged to a party organization before the seizure of power. On the other hand, membership cannot be regarded as a definitive indicator of an individual's affinity for National Socialism. Any number of factors, opportunism or coercion among them, could have prompted an individual to join the party or one of its organizations. This was especially true for those who joined the movement after January 30, 1933, the day of the Nazi *Machtergreifung* (seizure of power).[36]

Given a free hand in the selection of jurists, the legal divisions endeavored to recruit men from their own caste, from the circle of right-wing nationalist elites. The German bar had been a preserve of the right ever since Otto von Bismarck shifted his parliamentary base of support from the National Liberals to the conservatives. The legal profession subsequently developed into a closed, self-perpetuating circle of conservative nationalists.[37] Discrepancies in sentences handed down during the Weimar Republic clearly demonstrate the bar's monarchist right-wing character and its dissatisfaction with the Weimar "system."[38] From January 1919 to June 1922, 354 politically motivated murders by right-wing perpetrators led to just one death sentence and a combined ninety years' imprisonment. Twenty-two murders by left-wing perpetrators resulted in ten death sentences, three penal servitude sentences, and a combined 248 years in prison.[39]

Experience in the Great War initially proved to be an important criterion in the selection of jurists, as the Reichswehr legal divisions recruited First World War veterans with military judicial, general staff, or front-line experience.[40] In the personnel files, at least 50 percent of the jurists recruited after 1934 had served in the Great War. Even men receiving an appointment to Wehrmachtjustiz after 1939 very often had seen action during that conflict. Thus, even in the eleventh hour, Nazi Germany's military jurists were a highly homogenous group.[41]

Evaluations submitted for the jurists' conversion from military civil servants to officers in the Special Services (Truppensonderdienst) in 1944 indicate that, even at this late date, the majority of the jurists at the administrative and policymaking level, as well those presiding on the courts, had received their "university education and socialization" before 1933.[42] They had been "shaped by an outlook that was at least pre-democratic and often even antidemocratic." But to call them National Socialist jurists would be "greatly oversimplifying the question."[43] Michael Eberlein and Ludwig Hannemann arrive at similar conclusions. Eberlein's examination of the military court at Marburg indicates that the majority of jurists attached to this court had been born in the 1890s and had served in the First World War.[44] Hannemann's investigation reveals that out of 202 naval jurists in 1944, only 21 were younger than thirty-five years old, 148 were between the ages of thirty-five and forty-five, and 33 were over the age of forty-five.[45]

Although many of the younger jurists who were recruited after the beginning of World War II received their legal training under National Socialism, the jurists in place before September 1939—the men occupying the leading policymaking, administrative, and senior positions on the individual courts—were at their core conservative nationalists. Many of these men had witnessed firsthand the November Revolution of 1918 and most likely were steeped in the stab-in-the-back legend.

Finally, the primary yardstick for the Gerichtsherren, the judge advocates, and even the OKH (Army High Command) when evaluating jurists proved to be the jurists' comprehension of the role of courts-martial in maintaining discipline and protecting "military interests."

In the personnel files, performance evaluations focused on the jurists' understanding (or lack of understanding) of the "military administration of justice's role in the maintenance of Manneszucht."[46] On the other hand, the only reference to National Socialism found in the personnel files was the stock phrase (described in chapter 1) regarding jurists' adherence to, and support of, National Socialism.

Again, Wehrmacht jurists regarded the reintroduction of military jurisdiction as a "gift from the Führer." With the vast expansion of the armed forces after 1935, the Wehrmacht legal divisions recruited scores of First World War veterans, primarily conservative nationalists, to fill the growing number of positions. The potential for promotion and advancement in the fast-expanding Wehrmacht no doubt provided an incentive for jurists to abandon their civilian careers and enter the military judiciary. It may also be true, as many scholars have suggested, that the military judiciary was an attractive option to members of the legal profession who had run afoul of the party in their civilian practices.[47]

The desire to reverse the military judiciary's failure in the First World War and its alleged contribution to the mythical stab in the back may have been an additional incentive to enter Wehrmachtjustiz. Even if it was not a deciding factor, most of the jurists had witnessed the disturbances that rocked the armed forces in 1918. The vast majority of them were receptive to the ordinances, directives, and decrees after 1939 that facilitated their sacrosanct task of maintaining Manneszucht, discipline, and military order at all costs.

Whether the jurists understood at the time just how important their efforts would be in Hitler's racial war of annihilation may never be fully known. Their efforts nevertheless stabilized the regime until its final hours. How much of their work was the result of conscious ideological cooperation as opposed to the pursuit of shared foreign political goals also is difficult to answer.[48] Nevertheless, the military judiciary's central focus was to prevent another 1918.[49] That much can be agreed upon. On the other hand, whether the jurists were Nazis or not is beside the point because the military judiciary functioned in a "Nazi-like" fashion, and most scholars agree that no evidence suggests that Nazi judges imposed harsher punishments than non-Nazis.[50]

The Peacetime Courts

During peacetime, courts existed at the division and defense district (*Wehrkreis*) levels.[51] Normally, three qualified jurists and a plethora of support personnel staffed each court. Although the commanding officer as Gerichtsherr had the power to confirm verdicts during peacetime, an appeals system operated until the beginning of the war. The divisional courts (and naval and air units of similar size) functioned as the courts of first instance, with the army, fleet, and air wing courts functioning as the appellate courts.[52]

Created as the Wehrmacht's highest court in 1936, the Reich Supreme Military Court acted as the final court of appeals until the war, and its decisions became binding precedent for the lower courts. The court of first and last instance for treason (*Landesverrat*) and high treason (*Hochverrat*), the Supreme Military Court also had jurisdiction over cases against general officers and military civil servants of equivalent rank.[53] It also heard cases that the political leadership considered especially significant or crucial for the achievement of "unified jurisprudence by precedent." The important decisions were published in collected volumes.[54] Initially composed of two senates with five judges each, the court was expanded by two additional senates after the outbreak of the war.[55]

Scholars generally relegate the Reich Supreme Military Court to just a few lines or footnotes, and only a few studies of this important institution have been written. Norbert Haase has written the only book-length study of the court. According to Haase, "As the supervisory agency within Wehrmachtjustiz, the Reich Supreme Military Court was accountable to the chief of the OKW regarding the administration of justice (*Strafrechtspflege*) within the Wehrmacht. The immediate proximity to the political and military leadership enabled control and the exercise of influence on its practice. On the other hand, the Reich Supreme Military Court's basic decisions were binding law for other courts-martial."[56]

When the appeals process fell away under the wartime provisions, the Reich Supreme Military Court became competent only for cases of treason and espionage as well as for cases considered to be of special political significance.[57]

Although Haase admits the difficulty in placing the jurists of the

Reich Supreme Military Court in historical perspective, he contends that they seldom resisted the regime's prerogatives and, as a rule, "willingly fulfilled the expectations" of the National Socialist leadership and military command. The Reich Supreme Military Court's judgments, according to Haase, reflected the national spirit during the war; yet generally "there was no recourse" to Nazi language. The absence of such language more than likely contributed to the postwar legend of a politically neutral and benign military judiciary.[58]

During its lifetime, the court established a number of precedents that, at least theoretically, intensified the regular courts' jurisprudence. The most controversial decision proved to be the court's interpretation of "public" as defined under section 5, paragraph 1, of the Wartime Penal Code.[59] This provision allowed the death penalty for individuals who "publicly attempted to subvert or paralyze the will of the German or allied peoples to self-defense (*wehrhaften Selbstbehauptung*)." According to a ruling by the Second Senate of the Supreme Military Court on February 27, 1940, the normal interpretation of "public" did not meet the intent of section 5. On the contrary, information divulged privately could still endanger the nation's security, because even information imparted to intimates could reach beyond the private sphere, and this in fact might be the perpetrators' intent. This precedent literally turned idle gossip into a potential capital offense.[60]

To what extent the regular courts-martial applied the more nazified precedents passed by the Reich Supreme Military Court has not been fully explored. Although a few of the case files contain references to Supreme Military Court judgments, the category of offenses being investigated here did not fall under the court's wartime area of competency.

Building and Maintaining the Wehrgemeinschaft

When Germany again took a stab at world domination in 1939, "decisive measures" had already been undertaken to make a repeat of the revolutionary events of 1918 impossible.[61] The regime supplied the prerequisites for the Wehrgemeinschaft by suppressing dissent and destroying political opponents, which generally prevented disruptive elements from entering the armed forces. Through propaganda and organizations such as the Hitler Youth, Reich Labor Service, SA, and even the League of German Maidens, the regime also prepared the nation psychologically and physically for military service and war.[62] As the "school of the nation," the Wehrmacht would mold this human matériel into the Wehrgemeinschaft, the ultimate instrument of war.

In the Wehrgemeinschaft, Nazi Germany's military chiefs saw the solution to total war. By harnessing the power of a militarized and psychologically prepared society purged of all pacifist elements and nonconformists, Germany would avoid in the next war the revolutionary disturbances that allegedly brought defeat in the First World War, and Versailles would be reversed for all time.[63]

The Wehrmacht participated closely with the regime in identifying and isolating individuals who posed a threat to the Wehrgemeinschaft. The close cooperation between the Wehrmacht and police in these tasks attests to this fact.[64] And in the Wehrmacht, the military administration of justice became a valuable instrument in this effort. With Manneszucht at the center of its jurisprudence, it purged from the ranks the "disruptive elements" that had evaded the regime's filtering mechanisms and those who perhaps experienced a change of heart when the burdens of military service (and after 1939, the burdens of war) outweighed their devotion to duty and fatherland.[65]

One of the first measures for the prevention of a second stab in the back, section 13 of the National Defense Act of May 21, 1935, barred from military service habitual criminals and political opponents.[66] Section 13 contained the following provisions:

> Unworthy of service (*wehrunwürdig*) and therefore excluded from compulsory military service is whoever (a) is punished by penal servitude, (b) is not in possession of civil rights, (c) is subordinated to the measure for security and improvement according to section 42a of the Reich Penal Code, (d) has lost the worthiness to serve (*Wehrwürdigkeit*) through a military judicial judgment, (e) is judicially punished for subversive activity.[67]

Section 13 was not specifically a National Socialist measure. All military organizations employ similar precautions for the protection and morale of the troops. However, section 13 did expand the laws to encompass a much broader spectrum of people than were excluded from service during the Imperial German era. The provision, of course, ensured that the regime's most vociferous opponents would not be called up. But with the criterion stipulated under part (e), it excluded from military service even those punished for trivial subversive offenses.

Manpower demands, however, increased so rapidly after 1935 that the Wehrmacht was forced to make a change. Section 13 was modified, thus allowing the Wehrmacht to mobilize individuals convicted for "less serious" subversive activities. Henceforth, subversives were only classified as "unworthy of service" in conjunction with prison sentences of nine months or more.

Section 13 as initially promulgated and as subsequently modified illustrates three concepts that were central to building and maintaining the Wehrgemeinschaft. First, the provision provided a filtering mechanism that denied disruptive elements entrance. As modified, the provision expanded the pool of potentially usable "human matériel," while at the same time providing a deterrent.[68] In other words, the modified provision not only maximized manpower but also deterred malingerers from committing trivial political offenses as a means of avoiding service. These three concepts (filtration, maximum mobilization, and deterrence) would be refined, expanded, and intensified by the Wehrmacht during World War II.

Building and maintaining a frictionless military apparatus also required a method of identifying and isolating nonconformists who somehow managed to slip into the armed forces, despite section 13 of the National Defense Act and the regime's prior efforts at purging disruptive elements from society. The Wehrmacht was particularly concerned about individuals who might endanger the military apparatus by "recalcitrant, undisciplined, or otherwise unsoldierly behavior" as well as those refusing to conform even after "repeated disciplinary action." In other words, in maintaining the Wehrgemeinschaft, the military leadership became obsessed with soldiers who refused to conform but who nevertheless could not be pursued through military judicial action.[69]

Therefore, on May 25, 1936, the War Ministry ordered the creation of camp formations (*Lagerformationen*), later designated as disciplinary units (*Sonderabteilungen*), to handle conscripts who had civilian criminal records and thus posed a potential danger to discipline.[70]

Although these units had not been specifically a part of the military's penal system, the Wehrmacht would apply the same principles and methods for isolating (and later reclaiming) recalcitrant soldiers during the war on a much broader scale.

As per the War Ministry's order, the Wehrmacht began assembling seven disciplinary units at the defense district level on October 6, 1936.[71] The order specified exactly which individuals should be placed in the new "education units," as they were euphemistically called. First were conscripts whose behavior as civilians rendered them a threat to discipline in regular units—specifically, individuals sentenced by civilian courts to prison sentences of one year or more. Second were soldiers whose continued service with regular units was not desired; specifically, soldiers convicted by military courts for homosexual activity or repeated theft. Third was anyone convicted by a military court who simply appeared to be a danger to discipline.[72]

By the end of 1936 six disciplinary units had been assembled for the isolation of recalcitrant soldiers. In 1938 a seventh unit was established at Wahn. In that year the army's seven education units had a total complement of 1,357 intractable soldiers.[73] With flawless conduct, individuals could be transferred to a regular unit. Those who failed to subordinate themselves to military order despite "all educational measures" could be dismissed from service and turned over to the civilian authorities, which in practice meant incarceration in a concentration camp for the duration of the prisoner's stipulated term of military service.[74]

It must be emphasized that a military judicial conviction was not a prerequisite for placement in a disciplinary unit or transfer to a concentration camp. In addition, the Wehrmacht's cooperation with the civilian police agencies was strictly voluntary. In maintaining the Wehrgemeinschaft, the military leadership availed itself of the regime's assistance in removing nonconformists from the Wehrmacht's ranks. Approximately six thousand men passed through the disciplinary units before the war: at least 120 were ultimately dismissed from service and sent to Buchenwald, Dachau, or Sachsenhausen.[75]

Hans-Peter Klausch uses the disciplinary units as a vehicle to demonstrate the ideological agreement between the regime and Wehrmacht. He also sees the influence of both National Socialist racial-biological and Social Darwinist conceptions in the units' purposes and methods. According to Klausch, military psychiatrists since the First World War had defined the "agitator" in political terms, but the applicability of this point to the disciplinary units is questionable. The units clearly were not the intended repositories for political opponents. Their function was the "reeducation" of nonconformists. The goal was reorienting them toward service to the state and *Volk* and transforming them into "orderly, duty conscious, honor-loving, and fit soldiers."[76] Racial concepts and Social Darwinism had not been part of the equation.

In the disciplinary units, as in the Wehrmacht in general, the question simply became who would subordinate themselves to military order and who would not. Klausch, however, is absolutely correct in his contention that the deaths of those sent to concentration camps illustrate how "closely the Wehrmacht and National Socialist state were interwoven at an early stage." Indeed, the Wehrmacht proved "all too ready, before and at the beginning of the war, to hand over unusable conscripts to the terror of the concentration camps as so-called burdens and parasites (*Wehrmachtschädlinge*) in the general interest of military efficiency. . . . The Wehrmacht did so on its own initiative."[77] Its objective, however, was the Wehrgemeinschaft's preservation, not the Volksgemeinschaft's purification, and social conformity had little influence on the Wehrmacht's personnel decisions. The Wehrmacht merely served its own purposes by appropriating National Socialist terminology in its attempts to build and maintain the Wehrgemeinschaft.

With the attack on Poland in September 1939, all disciplinary unit detainees had to be transferred to a regular unit or turned over to the police for detention in a concentration camp for the war's duration; perhaps as many as 180 were sent to Sachsenhausen.[78] The reserve army commander nevertheless ordered the establishment of six new disciplinary units with the reserve army in order to unburden the troops of problem soldiers on January 3, 1940. However, with the special wartime provisions for the military administration of justice now in effect, courts-martial could make fast work of any soldiers running afoul of the expanded and intensified criminal codes, and the disciplinary units were reduced to only four by the spring of 1940. At least one disciplinary unit remained on the books until the spring of 1945.[79]

On February 1, 1940, field disciplinary units (*Feldsonderabteilungen*) were created as adjuncts to the reserve army's disciplinary units.[80] The OKW directed that every army group should also establish field disciplinary units for soldiers who remained unaffected by disciplinary measures, thus creating a danger to Manneszucht. Henceforth, recalcitrant soldiers would not be sent back to the reserve army as in the past because "there they formed in their accumulation a danger for the discipline of the younger classes of recruits (Jahrgänge)." Intended as a great dishonor, detention in a field disciplinary unit was expected to bring the prisoners to reason through hard work and poor rations. The various field disciplinary unit's disparate strengths and diverse modes of operation prompted the OKH in August 1941 to order their consolidation into the field disciplinary battalion (*Feldsonderbataillon*) "in order to achieve a uniform institution for the purpose of punishment." Sent to the eastern front in October 1941, the field disciplinary battalion performed heavy work within twenty-five kilometers of the front.[81]

According to Fritz Wüllner, as many as ten thousand servicemen passed through the field disciplinary battalion during the war.[82] Between 1938 and September 1944, when Heinrich Himmler assumed command of the reserves, perhaps one thousand soldiers, sailors, and airmen had been delivered to concentration camps: two-thirds from the disciplinary units or field disciplinary battalion.[83]

Not all the individuals delivered to the various disciplinary units had committed court-martial offenses. Many simply had been isolated for nonconformist behavior.[84] Wehrmachtjustiz, however, would adopt and refine the concept of isolating incorrigible soldiers during the war with the introduction of special penal formations, the field penal battalions (*Feldstrafgefangenenabteilungen*) and field penal camps (*Feldstraflager*).[85] These institutions had the additional function of mobilizing even the most recalcitrant soldiers for militarily useful purposes.[86] The detainees in these formations could conform or be turned over to the SS. Those who heeded the motivational endeavors of these special penal units, fully subordinating themselves to military order, were allowed to rejoin the Wehrgemeinschaft. Even those disliked by the regime could rejoin the regular troops if they were willing to carry a weapon in good faith.

CHAPTER THREE

Wehrmachtjustiz at War

The Wartime Provisions

While the prewar Wehrmacht possessed a strong weapon for the maintenance of Manneszucht—in the form of conservative jurists motivated to atone for 1918, criminal codes purged of liberal mitigation clauses, and special units for the isolation of recalcitrant soldiers—the wartime legal provisions enabled courts-martial to proceed against all crimes, real or imagined, with unprecedented speed and vigor. The few obstacles to arbitrary justice that remained after 1939 would be eliminated piecemeal during the war. The Wartime Penal Code and the Wartime Judicial Procedure Code, which were formulated in the general expectation of war during the Sudeten crisis and signed by Hitler on August 17, 1938, went into effect on August 26, 1939, just a few days before the German attack on Poland. The political leadership had not dictated these codes to the jurists. "Just as the Wehrmacht and its legal advisers had formulated . . . the decrees and orders for the racial war in the east, Wehrmacht jurists in 1938 designed . . . these new provisions."[1]

The Wartime Penal Code and the Wartime Judicial Procedure Code supplanted the Wehrmacht Penal Code, which had not been fully completed in 1939. "As it states euphemistically in the ordinances, they should close the gaps in the current laws. At the same time, they should draw on the experiences of the First World War. That is, to give total mobilization and the absolute priority of war necessity criminal-legal flanking protection."[2]

These two ordinances were the result of a collaborative effort between the Reich Ministry of Justice and the Armed Forces Legal Division (Wehrmachtrechtsabteilung) that stretched back as far as 1934, and the regime and military considered them the prerequisites for total war.[3] Both had been designed with Germany's perceived lessons of the First World War in mind.[4] "Just as food ration cards were prepared before the war to prevent a repetition of the dissatisfaction of the population because of food shortages in the First World War," just as the Wehrmacht's brothel system had been created to prevent the transmission of carnal flu, which sidelined so many soldiers during that conflict, so also was military criminal law prepared to avoid the military judiciary's alleged mistakes in the Great War.[5]

Conceived as the most important mobilization measure in the area of military criminal law, the Wartime Penal Code's goal was "preeminently the prosecution of any resistance to the war's conduct."[6] The code expanded a commander's disciplinary authority for the punishment of trivial criminal offenses. It also expanded the field of military criminal law, creating new categories of criminal offenses, and intensified punishments. In addition, by a modification on November 1, 1939, the code made it possible for courts to exceed any new or preexisting punishment parameters.[7]

Section 5 of the Wartime Penal Code established *Wehrkraftzersetzung* (subversion of fighting power) as a criminal offense. Acts such as refusing service, self-inflicted wounds, defeatist expressions, and any other behavior that even remotely appeared militarily obstructive could henceforth be prosecuted as a subversive act and punished with death under the catchall offense of Wehrkraftzersetzung. According to Messerschmidt and Wüllner, military courts convicted as many as thirty thousand servicemen for subversion during the war.[8] Section 5 contained the following clauses:

Subversion of Fighting Power

(1) For the subversion of fighting power is punished with death:

1. whoever openly promotes or incites the refusal of military service in the German or allied armed forces, *or otherwise* [emphasis mine] publicly attempts to subvert or cripple the will of the German or allied peoples for self-defense (*zur wehrhaften Selbstbehauptung*);

2. whoever attempts to suborn a soldier or reservist to commit insubordination, resistance, actions against a superior, desertion, or absences without leave, *or otherwise* [emphasis mine] attempts to undermine Manneszucht in the German or allied armed forces;

3. whoever attempts or abets the evasion of military service wholly, partially, or temporarily through self-inflicted wounds, through premeditated deception, *or other* [emphasis mine] similar means.

(2) In less serious cases penal servitude or prison sentences can be passed.

With competing laws subsumed under Wehrkraftzersetzung and the clause "or otherwise/other" incorporated into the provision, the Wartime Penal Code provided the jurists with "a broad and ambiguous legal tool" that allowed the severest punishments, including death, for nearly every form of opposition to the war or military service.[9]

The Comments on the Wartime Penal Code of August 17, 1938, explained precisely why these provisions had been drawn up: "The experiences of the First World War have taught that the united engagement of the entire nation, which stands behind the armed forces, can decide the outcome of a war."[10]

On November 1, 1939, the Armed Forces High Command (OKW) issued the First Ordinance for Supplementing the Wartime Penal Code. Among other changes, section 5a was inserted into the ordinance. Section 5a read as follows:

> Persons subject to the wartime process (*Kriegsverfahr*en) are to be punished by exceeding the regular parameters of punishment with penal servitude up to fifteen years, with lifetime penal servitude, or with death for punishable actions against Manneszucht or the precept of soldierly courage, *if the maintenance of Manneszucht or the security of the troops requires it* [emphasis mine].[11]

Additional guidelines provided further clarification, explaining that section 5a could be applied in cases such as cowardice, disobedience, insubordination, and mutiny as well as for nearly every crime: "It is also not excluded that Manneszucht can be damaged by grievous offenses against the general criminal law."[12] Indeed, under section 5a the courts could theoretically impose the death penalty for any offense.[13]

The Wartime Penal Code would be supplemented and amended six more times during the war, with section 5a specifically modified to further open room for the courts to maneuver in arriving at draconian penalties. The final change was made in October 1944.[14] The modifications made on March 31, 1943, swept aside every conceivable obstacle to arbitrary justice. As modified, section 5a read as follows:

(1) Persons subject to the wartime process are to be punished by exceeding the regular parameters of punishment with penal servitude up to fifteen years, with lifetime penal servitude, or with death for punishable actions against Manneszucht or the precept of soldierly courage, *if the maintenance of Manneszucht or the security of the troops requires it* [emphasis mine].

(2) The same is true for punishable actions through which the perpetrator has caused an especially severe disadvantage for the conduct of the war or the security of the troops, if the regular punishment parameters do not suffice for atonement *according to the people's healthy sense of morality* [emphasis mine].[15]

In practice, section 5a, by establishing "the people's healthy sense of morality" (*das gesunde Volksempfinden*) as a criterion for sentencing, released the courts henceforth from any adherence to the established criminal codes.[16] The normal sentencing parameters no longer had to be applied. Presiding judges only needed to invoke "the people's healthy sense of morality" in order to impose the death sentence for a crime that allegedly hindered the war effort. Very few, if any, offenses could not be so judged.[17] In May 1944 "the people's healthy sense of morality" as a punishment guideline was expressly extended in section 5a to cover "negligent criminal actions" that hindered the war's prosecution or threatened the security of the troops.[18] Negligence now could mean death for any soldier who was careless in the performance of his duty, if he came before a fanatic on the bench.[19]

The Wartime Judicial Procedure Code codified the procedural requirements for the military judicial process during the war. The front, rear areas, occupied territories, and home front were all subject to the code, and thus virtually everyone subordinated to Nazi rule was potentially subject to military jurisdiction.[20]

The Wartime Judicial Procedure Code introduced a greatly simplified and streamlined legal process that had a bare minimum of requirements. Only four criteria had to be met in order to convene courts-martial. First, cases had to be heard by a panel of three judges. The panel consisted of one military jurist acting as the presiding judge and two soldiers acting as lay judges (*Beisitzern*). One lay judge had to be an officer, the other from the same rank as that of the defendant.

Second, the defendant had to be informed of the specific charges and granted the last word. Third, convictions required a majority vote, and the court's verdict, along with its assessment of the evidence and relevant criminal codes, had to be submitted to the Gerichtsherr, the military commander possessing supreme legal authority over the court in question. Finally, the Gerichtsherr had to confirm the verdict in order for it to become legally binding.[21]

The procedure code also abolished the peacetime system of appeals. The Gerichtsherr's examination of a court's decision during the confirmation process was, with few exceptions, the only post-trial review of the verdict.[22] Defendants received counsel only if the death sentence was expected or if the Gerichtsherr considered representation appropriate. However, defendants could be denied counsel even in capital cases if the war situation made providing such representation problematic.[23] Again, the Gerichtsherr's post-trial review of the verdict was virtually the only protection the defendant had against a miscarriage of justice. A retrial could be granted if "new evidence or facts of considerable relevance came to light."[24] However, retrials seldom occurred because courts, soldiers, and witnesses were constantly on the move during the war. Once the Gerichtsherr had confirmed a verdict, the case was closed and the military judicial authorities seldom possessed the time or inclination to investigate the case again.[25]

The clemency petition was the only other option for a prisoner who considered himself unjustly convicted. Under the Wehrmacht Clemency Ordinance of July 1, 1938, soldiers could petition for parole, restoration of rank, sentence remission, and even expungement. Hitler and the commanders of each service branch (or a subordinate commander designated by them) possessed these clemency powers.

In February 1942 Hitler decreed that clemency petitions requesting rank restoration, sentence remission, or expungement would be judged henceforth on the basis of performance in the field. A prisoner could still request parole at the front, but all other petitioners had to have performed heroically as a parolee in order to have any chance of success.[26] According to Lothar Walmrath, the naval judicial authorities granted conversion, remission, and expungement requests very infrequently. Furthermore, sentence remission and expungement were evaluated separately "in order to conduct a two-stage model that maintained the motivation to fight."[27] Based on the case files, it appears that the army followed the two-stage model as well.

The Antisocial Parasite (*Volksschädlinge*) Ordinance of September 5, 1939, must also be characterized as one of the more iniquitous (if little known) tools that facilitated the imposition of draconian punishments. Section 4 of the ordinance empowered courts-martial to impose whatever punishment appeared appropriate, including death, if a perpetrator exploited wartime conditions in the commission of a punishable offense. "The people's healthy sense of morality" was the ambiguous yardstick for evaluating such crimes. Section 2 of the ordinance identified crimes committed during blackout conditions as one example of the exploitation of wartime conditions.[28]

Although many sexual assaults naturally took place under the cover of darkness, there is curiously little application (or even discussion) of the Antisocial Parasite Ordinance in the case files. While the courts very often applied the ordinance against soldiers convicted for plundering, they evidently felt that the normal punishment parameters provided for the sufficient punishment of sex offenders.

The Gerichtsherr

The Wartime Judicial Procedure Code abolished the peacetime appeals system and replaced the appellate process with a post-trial examination of the verdicts by the Gerichtsherr, the military commander exercising supreme legal authority over the court attached to his unit.[29] After reviewing a verdict (and if applicable, the sentence), the Gerichtsherr had to confirm the court's judgment before it became legally binding. With the outbreak of war, the Gerichtsherr became the military judicial (and penal) system's undisputed master. He controlled the criminal-legal process and bore immediate responsibility for its "effectiveness, necessary severity, and speed."[30]

Although the OKW possessed a legal department (the Armed Forces Legal Division), it was competent only for basic questions of military law. The legal divisions of the three service branches assumed actual control of day-to-day operations. Between these departments and the individual courts existed special administrative officials, the Supreme Judge Advocates (Oberstkriegsgerichtsrat) of the various supervisory regions (*Dienstaufsichtsbereich*). The Supreme Judge Advocates functioned, at least on paper, as the jurists' official and immediate disciplinary superior.[31]

The judge advocates may have exercised considerable control over daily administrative matters, but actual command and disciplinary authority over the jurists devolved to the Gerichtsherren. The personnel files reveal that the judge advocates assessed the jurists' performance on the basis of evaluations submitted by the Gerichtsherren. A jurist being reviewed for permanent appointment to Wehrmachtjustiz after the requisite ninety-day probation period had to have his Gerichtsherr's enthusiastic support to be confirmed in his position. Furthermore, individuals failing to adjudicate according to their Gerichtsherren's standards could be refused promotion or even exiled to an unpopular court. This was especially true for those jurists who did not meet the Gerichtsherren's expectations regarding punishments. Take, for example, the case of Judge Heinrich H., who was banished to a prisoner of war court. He had asserted his claim to judicial independence and consistently ignored his Gerichtsherr's demands for harsher sentences.[32]

The German system did not have an independent prosecuting agency equivalent to a civilian district attorney's office. In great contrast to the theory and purpose behind such independent civilian institutions, Wehrmacht jurists performed criminal investigations, arraignments, and prosecution duties. In short, the entire legal process was handled by the same office, which of course was subordinated directly to the Gerichtsherr. Jurists alternated as presiding judge, prosecutor, or lead investigator.[33] This arrangement led to regular contact between the jurists and their Gerichtsherren. According to the regulations, a jurist functioning as prosecutor had to follow the Gerichtsherr's instructions for the specific case. These instructions were given orally and included the charges to be lodged against a defendant and the sentence that should be requested upon conviction. This constant contact with the Gerichtsherren enabled jurists to quickly discern the Gerichtsherren's views on crime and punishment. In fact, jurists often grew to orient themselves completely around the views of their Gerichtsherren.[34]

Regulations expressly established a presiding judge's judicial independence, but close contact with the Gerichtsherr when the jurist was functioning as prosecutor led to a clear understanding of how he was expected to proceed when acting as the presiding judge.[35] He could rule accordingly or risk the Gerichtsherr's rejection of the verdict in favor of a retrial.[36] A presiding judge who consistently failed to meet his Gerichtsherr's expectations regarding punishments risked bad performance evaluations and the attendant consequences.

During the war, some courts with front-line units had only one judge attached to them. In these situations, the commanding officer appointed junior officers from each regiment to perform prosecutorial functions.[37] Even when such "court officers" fulfilled the prosecutorial role, the presiding judge nevertheless quickly became familiar with his Gerichtsherr's expectations and standards, even though he never received instructions on specific cases.[38] As the only person qualified for the bench, this lone judge would naturally preside over all courts-martial. Thus he adjudicated cases of every type and quickly learned which transgressions the commander deemed most deserving of severe punishments.

Germany's military chiefs believed that the revolutionary disturbances within the armed forces in 1918 were the product not only of eviscerated penal codes and lenient judges but also of insufficient severity on the part of the Gerichtsherren, the men ultimately responsible for the discipline and cohesion of their units. And the Gerichtsherr dominated the military judicial system under National Socialism. The defendant's fate literally rested in his hands. Scholars who downplay his importance in the process do so apparently from the desire to assign sole responsibility for the crimes committed in the name of justice at the military jurists' feet.[39]

In all truth, however, commanders functioning as Gerichtsherren exercised absolute control over the military administration of justice. They controlled investigations, and after reviewing the *Tatbericht*, an evidentiary summary of an alleged crime, they submitted indictments. They dismissed cases and they convened courts-martial. They selected the two soldiers who functioned as the lay judges.[40] If a suspect was exonerated during an investigation or acquitted at trial, the Gerichtsherr could still impose disciplinary punishment.

Upon reaching verdicts, the courts submitted their judgments to their Gerichtsherren along with their interpretations of the evidence and relevant criminal codes.[41] The Gerichtsherr had the power to confirm the judgment, which then became legally binding.

If as Gerichtsherr a division commander considered a verdict in error or a sentence inappropriate he sent his dissenting opinion to his military judicial superior, usually the commander of an army, who confirmed the judgment or ordered a retrial.[42] Division commanders also had the power to mitigate sentences upon confirmation and, by the second year of the war, the power to grant, at the time of sentence confirmation, an early release for front-parole.[43] The Gerichtsherr could also order the completion of a sentence in a disciplinary unit or Wehrmacht penal camp (*Straflager*),[44] regardless of the sentence's length, if he deemed this necessary for purposes of "education" or "security."[45]

Division commanders, however, did not possess the authority to confirm death sentences or prison and penal servitude (*Zuchthaus*) sentences of more than five years.[46] Confirmation power for the death sentence lay with the supreme commanders of the three service branches and, during the war, also with the reserve army commander. Hitler, as the Wehrmacht's supreme commander, reserved for himself the power to confirm death sentences imposed against officers. For prison and penal servitude sentences in excess of five years, the power of confirmation rested with the divisional commanders' immediate military judicial superiors, normally the commander of an army. Even in these cases, however, division commanders forwarded their opinions on the verdicts and their assessments of the defendants. These opinions should not be perceived as a mere formality. They were crucial to the defendants' fates.

Second opinions submitted by staff legal advisers were required before Gerichtsherren could confirm prison sentences of one year or longer.[47] Few of these "expert" second opinions (*Gutachten*) contained technical interpretations of the law and jurisprudence, at least in the cases of sex offenders. The majority of these opinions simply certified that the courts had satisfied the requirements established by the Wartime Judicial Procedure Code and comment on the punishment's suitability (or unsuitability). They very often also contained a recommendation for the appropriate means for execution of the sentence, such as detention in a special penal formation rather than in a prison.[48] When they found fault with a verdict or interpretation of the criminal codes, legal advisers frequently recommended the verdict's confirmation anyway if the punishment appeared appropriate, indicating that swift punishment rather than the letter of the law had been the primary issue.

If a staff legal adviser recommended that a verdict be rejected for technical legal reasons, the Gerichtsherr usually followed this advice. However, the Gerichtsherren were less concerned with the finer points of law than with securing a sentence that would maintain Manneszucht and military order.

If a Gerichtsherr often followed his adviser's counsel, it did not mean that the Gerichtsherr had no personal opinions about crime and punishment. As the man immediately and ultimately responsible for discipline, order, personnel matters, and the military effectiveness of his command, the Gerichtsherr took his judicial powers very seriously. In all truth, due to the Gerichtsherr's central role in the process, the "military judicial system" might be described more accurately as simply an extension of the commander's disciplinary authority. The military administration of justice, in essence, amounted to nothing less than a disciplinary process (rather than a legal one) that could result in imprisonment and even death.[49]

Beginning in November 1939 Gerichtsherren could also impose legal punishments without recourse to a trial. A proven time-saving device, the "punishment decree" (*Strafverfügung*) allowed commanders to sentence soldiers to a maximum of three months' imprisonment with the stroke of a pen. Naval commanders functioning as Gerichtsherren had this authority starting in 1926.[50] Bestowed upon army and air commanders during the Polish campaign, the authority to dispense justice with these single-paged decrees greatly eased the load on overburdened courts. The initial maximum of three months' imprisonment was raised to six months in 1942 in order to speed up the military judicial process even further.[51] The Gerichtsherr henceforth could also order a soldier directly to a penal camp, the most draconian form of punishment in the Wehrmacht's penal system. The Gerichtsherren and courts "helped themselves to this labor-saving device in increasing measure."[52] Indeed, soldiers could now be sent to penal camps and other special penal formations without a hearing of any kind.

According to Messerschmidt and Wüllner, perhaps 40 percent of convicted soldiers, nearly one-half million men, never had an oral hearing but received their punishment from the Gerichtsherr's "writing desk."[53] The authors neglect to mention, however, that every soldier had the right to contest a punishment decree. If a defendant raised an objection to a punishment decree, a court-martial would be convened. In the case files, however, soldiers rarely contested punishment decrees, which suggests that perhaps some form of plea bargaining took place in such cases.

Many scholars downplay the Gerichtsherr's importance in Wehrmachtjustiz and claim that the jurists and staff legal advisers decisively influenced the military judicial process and, hence, determined the nature of Wehrmachtjustiz. These scholars may base this conclusion on the dearth of commentary contained in the Gerichtsherren's confirmation orders.[54] However, if verdict confirmations included little elaboration, one need only examine the opinions contained in clemency petitions, which prisoners frequently submitted in hopes of winning front-parole, to find examples of the Gerichtsherren's views. These opinions demonstrate that commanding officers had very specific ideas about crime and punishment and that their overriding concerns were discipline, order, and Manneszucht.

The commentary found in clemency petitions also indicate that, even when faced with personnel shortages, commanders apparently did not perceive military effectiveness to be a matter of just sheer numbers. Even late in the war, commanders often refused to support a clemency request if they regarded the petitioner as a threat to Manneszucht.[55] Presiding judges and staff legal experts could cite legal codes and precedent, but the Gerichtsherr, the man personally responsible for his command's performance and fighting power, cited the maintenance of discipline as the most important criteria when meting out "justice."

Essentially, the institution of the Gerichtsherr combined both executive and judicial authority in a single individual, violating the liberal constitutional principle of the separation of powers.[56] Liberals in 1848 and socialists after 1871 bitterly opposed special military jurisdiction for exactly this reason. Although mitigating clauses and minor procedural adjustments were made in 1898 and during the First World War, the Prussian institution of the Gerichtsherr and his traditional power over the process survived intact. Even under the Weimar Constitution, military jurisdiction could be reconstituted in case of war, with the traditional power of the Gerichtsherr unsullied.

The combination of military command authority and criminal legal authority over servicemen in the person of the Gerichtsherr was a dominant feature of the military administration of justice during the Second World War, and underestimating the Gerichtsherr's power and influence on the judicial process prevents an accurate perspective on the military judiciary and its activities.[57] Wehrmachtjustiz was an instrument of war wielded by commanders for the achievement of specific objectives. The jurists, in many respects, merely assisted the commanders in its use.

The Wartime Courts

During peacetime, courts existed at the division and defense district levels.[58] With the onset of hostilities in 1939, courts were attached to every division and other formations of similar size, such as air and naval districts, as well as to the higher echelon units such as corps and armies. The courts carried the military unit's designation—for example, the Court of the Sixth Infantry Division for formations belonging to the field army, and the Court of Division Number 177 for formations belonging to the reserve army.[59] The basic difference between courts attached to an active division and those attached to a reserve formation was simply that reserve courts remained stationary while those with the field army moved with the moves of the division, whether from sector to sector or theater to theater.[60] Courts also were assigned to geographic commands, such as those in the rearward occupied areas (*rückwärtigen Besatzungsgebietes*) and the major cities of German-controlled Europe.[61]

During peacetime at least three judges staffed each court, but during wartime the courts had varying numbers of jurists qualified for the bench. The number naturally depended on the parent formation's size, function, and location. For example, courts assigned to geographic commands in the occupied areas and home front could have a large number of jurists at their disposal. The reserve courts were officially staffed with two, three, and in some cases even more military judges.[62] If the court represented a particularly large and important formation, such as the Court of the Wehrmacht Commander–Berlin, it too would be staffed with several jurists qualified for the bench.[63]

According to Franz Seidler, courts attached to frontline combat units officially had just one jurist on staff.[64] The case files and personnel records, however, indicate that jurists frequently rotated through the courts on a temporary basis, so that at any given time there could be at least two jurists qualified to preside over courts-martial with typical front-line formations.

Initially designated as armed forces civil servants (*Wehrmachtbeamten*), Wehrmacht jurists were transferred by Hitler into the Military Special Services (*Sondertruppendienst*) in 1944, which elevated them to a position similar to physicians in the medical corps.[65] Having passed the requisite state bar exams, the jurists were qualified for the bench as civilians. The courts also employed a variable number of lower-grade judicial officials who functioned as investigators, registrars, and clerks. As a whole, the jurists and supporting personnel formed Section III of the commander's staff.[66] As such, this legal team was directly subordinated to the Gerichtsherr. The jurists were bound to his instructions, although in theory the judge presiding over individual cases exercised judicial independence under section 7, paragraph 2, of the Wartime Judicial Procedure Code.[67]

The question of judicial independence appears frequently in the secondary literature. Although Erich Schwinge claims that judicial independence truly existed, most scholars contend that the judges had been steered in the their jurisprudence from above by a profusion of decrees and ordinances as well as frequent lectures and case reviews performed at the supervisory level by the judge advocates.[68] In addition, as Lothar Walmrath points out, "periodic reports on verdicts and punishments were submitted to the Gerichtsherr, the OKW legal division, the Reich Chancellery, and even the SD." According to Jürgen Thomas, this elaborate system of controls exposed the jurists to constantly increasing pressure from the military and political leadership.[69]

The personnel files suggest that the judge advocates monitored jurisprudence primarily during the requisite ninety-day probation period before confirmation to the bench. However, jurists not adjudicating according to their Gerichtsherren's standards often came under close scrutiny from above, including the legal authorities with the OKW.

The political leadership's attempts to steer the military judiciary may have been either superfluous or without effect because the jurists took their cue from the military leadership. "The military was their central point of orientation."[70] The naval administration of justice, which scholars generally regard as the most draconian of the three service branches, provides the best example. As early as 1938, Admiral Erich Raeder, the navy's commander-in-chief, made clear that military considerations had priority over justice. Although paying lip service to the jurists' independence, he emphasized his authority and responsibility for the maintenance of Manneszucht and stated:

> Independence of the courts signifies—correctly understood—that no binding instructions could be given [to the courts] for the decision of a specific case. However, the courts are also convened as *an institution and component of the Wehrmacht* [emphasis mine] to serve . . . the well being of the whole according to the directives of the responsible leadership. It alone can assess correctly whether and where dangers for the whole Wehrmacht threaten to arise and how they must be countered most effectively.[71]

Raeder's demand that the courts serve military interests would be followed during the war, as indicated by the fact that the naval commanders functioning as Gerichtsherren rejected only a small percentage of judgments as inappropriate.[72] When naval jurists deviated from their commanders' wishes, they opened themselves up to criticism not only from their commanders who served as Gerichtsherren but also from the Oberkommando der Marine (OKM, or Navy High Command). One court, after hearing a case for the third time still refused the Gerichtsherr's demand for a more severe punishment. The commander had rejected the first two judgments as too lenient. The OKM criticized this court during a Berlin seminar for naval judges in January 1942, stressing that the incident demonstrated "a complete misunderstanding of judicial independence. A presiding military court can deviate from the assessment of the military requirements by a high commander only if other facts are established or if it finds . . . other convincing reasons for a different judgment."[73]

If the political leadership throughout the war continued to demand ever more intense punishments and provided more and more statutes and provisions for arbitrary justice, it was generally unnecessary. The tools that had been placed at the jurists' disposal in the original Wartime Penal Code and Wartime Judicial Procedure Code were already sufficient for swiftly arriving at draconian punishments. In fact, based on the high number of death sentences imposed for desertion during the Polish campaign, Hitler himself intervened to restrain commanders with military judicial authority.[74] By a führer decree of April 14, 1940, Hitler established criteria for when the death sentence for desertion was "appropriate":

1. If the perpetrator acted out of fear of personal danger.

2. If the death sentence was necessary for the maintenance of Manneszucht.

3. If it was a matter of a joint or repeated case of desertion.

4. If the perpetrator attempted to flee abroad.

5. If the perpetrator had a considerable criminal record.

6. If the perpetrator committed crimes during the flight attempt.[75]

On the other hand, Hitler considered the death sentence inappropriate if "youthful indiscretion," "maltreatment" (*falsche dienstliche Behandlung*), serious domestic problems, or other reasons that were not dishonorable had prompted an individual to desert. In these cases, Hitler regarded penal servitude as sufficient punishment.[76] The führer's standards, however, ultimately proved to be optional as far as the military leadership was concerned. On April 27, 1943, Admiral Karl Dönitz, who replaced Raeder as the navy's commander-in-chief in January 1943, issued a directive on the handling of desertion, which stated, "Desertion is one of the most disgraceful crimes that a soldier can commit. It is a breach of loyalty towards the Führer, comrades, and nation. Whoever abandons the flag weakens Germany's battle strength and supports the enemy. . . . With justification, desertion is punished severely."[77]

Directly contradicting Hitler's earlier guidelines on how deserters should be punished, Dönitz further declared, "From the judgments presented to me, I have determined how slight the occasion for desertion often is, considering its grave consequences: homesickness, heartache, inability to conform (*mangelnde Einordnungsbereitschaft*), maltreatment, fear of a disciplinary or legal punishment. None of these or similar reasons justify abandoning the troops."

Dönitz ordered all commanding officers to explain the significance and consequences of desertion to their troops on a quarterly basis, and stressed that every individual must realize that "desertion will cost you your head." "Whoever nevertheless commits desertion," his directive demanded, "must be punished remorselessly hard. I expect the courts-martial to measure the failure of such perfidious weaklings only to the loyal willingness of all the decent soldiers to fight to the death."

In the final analysis, however, the individual commanders who functioned as Gerichtsherren were the decisive figures at the level of the individual case, and military order was their central concern. The presiding judges were well aware of their commanders' views on justice and ruled accordingly, although of course there were exceptions. Scholars have documented many cases in which commanders refused to confirm lenient sentences, only to have a second and even a third court refuse to impose harsher punishments.[78] If sufficiently stubborn and determined, however, a commander could refuse confirmation and order retrials until he obtained the desired result.

Despite the directives and decrees handed down from on high, at the time of confirmation the Gerichtsherr's opinion (or that of his immediate superior) was decisive. The commanders with military judicial authority perceived justice in terms of Manneszucht and military effectiveness. Despite the flurry of decrees, commentaries, and even the theories of party ideologues, it was the commander on the scene who played the primary role in deciding who posed a danger to the Wehrgemeinschaft and its mission.[79]

The Confirmation of Verdicts

The verdicts of courts-martial did not become legally binding until confirmed by the competent Gerichtsherren. In the case files, a high degree of consensus prevailed between the courts and the commanders regarding punishments. Gerichtsherren confirmed more than 90 percent of the verdicts after the first trial. The case files also reveal that Gerichtsherren confirmed a high percentage of verdicts even if the court-imposed sentence was at variance with the punishment requested by the prosecutor, who of course represented the Gerichtsherren's interests at trial. In these situations, the court-imposed punishments were as a rule lower than the punishment demanded by the prosecutor (and by extension, the Gerichtsherr). In fact, in those instances in which Gerichtsherren confirmed sentences that did not match their own expectations, the ratio of lighter punishments to more severe punishments exceeded 2:1.[80] What does this tell us?

First, it suggests that if the jurists did not have complete judicial independence at the level of the individual case, they could deviate to some extent from their Gerichtsherren's standards. Take, for example, the case of Judge Walter H. His Gerichtsherr sharply criticized him in a performance evaluation for not ruling in certain cases according to his (i.e., the Gerichtsherr's) standards, which were "in the interest of the troops." However, the Gerichtsherr acknowledged Judge H.'s understanding of the importance of maintaining "military interests," which indicates that some commanders could accept certain differences of opinion with their jurists, as long as the court-imposed sentences fell in the ballpark of the commanders' standards.[81]

Second, it suggests that if the political leadership successfully steered the jurists toward ever harsher punishments, the sentences the jurists handed down were still generally milder than those demanded by the Gerichtsherren. This would suggest that the commanders on the ground wanted to proceed even more ruthlessly against crime than the political leadership, the legal policymakers, and the Reich Supreme Military Court.[82] Considering the high confirmation rate, a third scenario is also likely: The jurists ruled in fairly close accordance with the views of their Gerichtsherren, regardless of how closely the punishments coincided with the expectations of policymakers.

Lothar Walmrath suggests commanders' criticisms of judgments that deviated from their sentencing guidelines "demonstrates the tense relationship between military and judicial standards." He too, however, documents a high level of agreement between Gerichtsherren and jurists in his assessment of a broad range of offenses.[83] According to his analysis of seven hundred naval courts-martial, the Gerichtsherren confirmed verdicts after the first trial 86.5 percent of the time, while refusing confirmation at a rate of only 13.5 percent. Of those verdicts not confirmed after a first trial, the Gerichtsherren rejected 85 percent because they considered the punishment too light and only 6.5 percent because they considered the punishment too harsh.[84] This strongly suggests that the commanding officers on the spot led the way in demanding harsh and even draconian punishments. The jurists did not lead them down that path, as many scholars claim. Walmrath may see tension in the few cases of disagreement, but the overall picture indicates that the commanders and their jurists were on the same page for the most part.[85]

The case files also reveal that Gerichtsherren, at the time of verdict confirmation, arranged for a high percentage of prisoners to be paroled after serving just a fraction of their judicially imposed sentences. Such parole orders were issued *even if the court-imposed punishment was milder than that demanded by the Gerichtsherr*. In other words, commanders, at the very same time that they were demanding higher punishments than the courts were imposing, often were planning for the early release of the perpetrators. It appears then that punishments frequently were not meant to be fully atoned and that the sentence was merely symbolic, intended to send a forceful message. The message to the soldier was that henceforth he must conduct himself flawlessly and battle for the final victory or face the harsh conditions of the penal system. It was, as Fritz Wüllner recognizes, a sword of Damocles.

The military judicial system, as it operated on the ground, aimed not at imposing ideal punishments, nor at serving the needs of the Volksgemeinschaft. Instead, the system's purpose was to channel men back to the front with the motivation to perform to their best ability, while simultaneously identifying those no longer willing to fulfill their service obligation. This purpose is different than "purification," even though the military judicial authorities labeled many of those relegated to Wehrmacht penal camps as "asocial" or "inferior."

In addition to "filtering" soldiers for the purpose of military effectiveness, the system fulfilled a secondary mission of "deterring others from committing similar infractions." This phrase appears frequently in the court transcripts of sex offenders, especially in cases of homosexuality and rape. The documents also reveal that deterrence served as a primary justification for harsh sentences. Indeed, the concept of deterrence also became more important as the war got longer. Nazi slurs and ideological rhetoric appear infrequently in cases of sex offenders, but deterrence for the preservation of Manneszucht was a universal language spoken by both commanders and jurists. This they absolutely agreed upon.

The overall agreement, up and down the military judicial chain of command, on what constituted an acceptable punishment, at least as far as sex offenders were concerned, is incredibly striking. Courts passed judgments that, in the vast majority of cases, the Gerichtsherren confirmed. The Gerichtsherren infrequently rejected the opinions of their staff legal advisers who in turn seldom contradicted the court. When advisers did find fault with judgments, they more often objected over technical legal questions than over the punishment. And when a commander refused to confirm a sentence? He more often than not based his decision on the punishment's purported inability to maintain order and discipline. In such cases, his military judicial superior usually concurred, further suggesting the centrality of military considerations.

It cannot be denied, however, that punishments were frequently draconian, especially with regard to militarily obstructive acts (desertion, absence without leave, and insubordination, for example). The unprecedented number of death sentences speaks clearly to this point, and scholars generally agree that as the war progressed, the frequency of severe punishments increased.

With sex offenders, however, the average punishment did not automatically become more severe during the war. For example, despite Heinrich Himmler's demand for increasing harshness against homosexuals, the average sentence for homosexual offenses did not change appreciably from 1939 to 1945. Between 1939 and 1940, the courts in the sample imposed an average prison sentence of approximately twelve months, while the averages for 1941–42 and 1943–45 hovered just above and below that number. The real indicator of the everyday reality for homosexual offenders, however, is the time spent in detention before parole. This number decreased considerably during the war, which can be explained by the Wehrmacht's attempts to rectify an increasingly perilous manpower problem. The average time spent in detention before a sentence's deferment for front-parole averaged approximately six months for 1939–40, five months for 1941–42, and slightly less than three months for 1943–45.[86]

On the other hand, the punishments for rape crimes fluctuated greatly during the war, with average sentences varying widely from one year to the next. Again, however, the real story is found in the average incarceration period before the deferment of a sentence for parole. In 1939–40 convicted rapists spent on average nearly eight months behind bars before reintegration. The average incarceration period decreased to 3.5 months in 1941–42 and 2.5 months in 1943–45.[87]

Although the Wehrmacht executed deserters at an ever-faster pace as the war lengthened, it reintegrated sex offenders back into the troops more and more quickly, indicating that an individual's willingness to carry a weapon in good faith was the ultimate criterion for inclusion in the Wehrgemeinschaft.

Limitations on Military Jurisdiction

Hitler imposed successive jurisdictional limitations on the military administration of justice during the war. The führer's piecemeal proscription of the military courts' sphere of competence has become a tendentious topic of debate and disagreement among scholars. The establishment of independent jurisdiction for the ss in 1939, the Barbarossa Jurisdiction Decree of 1941, the termination of jurisdiction for political offenses committed by servicemen after Stalingrad, and the creation of summary courts in the war's final weeks are the four most conspicuous examples of this phenomenon.[88] The Barbarossa Jurisdiction Decree is most pertinent to the prosecution of sex offenders, and it is discussed here together with the associated Commissar Order.

Unfortunately, the debate regarding the origins of these successive jurisdictional limitations often degenerates into polemics over Hitler's attitude toward Wehrmachtjustiz. According to the apologists, Hitler was dissatisfied with the jurists, seeing insufficient severity in their jurisprudence. This, the apologists claim, proves that the military administration of justice was benign.[89] Those critical of Wehrmachtjustiz, of course, argue the opposite, and the result is a meaningless war of words over the wrong issue. If the debate is taken out of this context and placed within the context of the regime's nature and the character and course of the war, the jurisdictional limitations are explained readily, without recourse to histrionics over Hitler's perception of Wehrmachtjustiz, even if the ultimate consequences of the limitations remain disputed.

Barbarossa Jurisdiction Decree and Commissar Order

Hitler imposed the second major limitation on military jurisdiction in 1941 as part of the preparations for Germany's assault on the Soviet Union, Operation Barbarossa. Upon Hitler's instructions, the OKW, the OKH, and the appropriate legal departments within the Wehrmacht worked together closely to prepare the Decree on the Exercise of Military Jurisdiction in the Barbarossa Area and Special Measures by the Troops, commonly referred to as the Barbarossa Jurisdiction Decree. Field Marshal Keitel issued it as a führer order on Hitler's behalf on May 13, 1941.

Section I of the decree, Treatment of Criminal Offenses by Enemy Civilians, stipulated that crimes committed by enemy civilians in the Barbarossa theater of operations would not be tried by courts-martial but instead would be handled immediately by the troops.[90] Under the provisions, the troops received the mandate to liquidate all partisans on the spot without recourse to legal proceedings. "Guerrillas were to be ruthlessly finished off in combat or while trying to escape. All other attacks against the Wehrmacht by the civilian population were to be likewise 'instantly crushed with the utmost means, up to . . . the annihilation of the attacker.'" Individuals suspected of partisan activities were also denied due process under the decree. These individuals would not be turned over to the military judicial authorities but instead would be brought before an officer who would decide on execution. If no culprits could be found, the decree authorized collective reprisals.[91]

Section II, Treatment of Criminal Offenses by Members of the German Armed Forces and its Retinue against Local Inhabitants, abolished the obligatory prosecution and punishment of German servicemen for crimes against enemy civilians in the Barbarossa area of operations, even if the crimes represented felonious military offenses.[92]

Again at Hitler's behest, the OKW created in cooperation with leading military jurists the infamous Directive for the Handling of Political Commissars, more commonly referred to as the Commissar Order.[93] Issued on June 6, 1941, the directive denied Soviet political officers belligerent status and the customary legal protection afforded to uniformed soldiers under international law. In other words, as "political functionaries" and not soldiers, Red Army commissars were refused combat status. According to the Commissar Order, all political officers with Soviet military units were to be separated on the battlefield from other prisoners and "shot on the spot by the fighting forces themselves." The provisions also required the troops to hand over all civilian commissars and other party functionaries to the Special Task Forces (Einsatzgruppen) of the security police or the ss Security Service (Sicherheitsdienst, or sD).[94]

The army's commander-in-chief, Field Marshal Walther von Brauchitsch, distributed both directives to his field commanders with several supplementary guidelines attached.[95] The supplements attached to Section I of the Jurisdiction Decree instructed the troops to undertake direct action against Soviet civilians only in overt cases of rebellion or uprising. Von Brauchitsch emphasized that the "army's primary task . . . was to fight the Red Army. 'Search and destroy' operations should therefore 'on the whole' be ruled out." Section II, as modified by von Brauchitsch, authorized military judicial action against German soldiers for crimes perpetrated against enemy civilians, if such actions were required for the maintenance of discipline or the preservation of military order in the ranks. Von Brauchitsch's supplement further obligated superior officers "to prevent, under all circumstances, arbitrary excesses by individual members of the army."[96]

As for the Commissar Order, von Brauchitsch's supplementary guidelines stipulated that Soviet political officers should be executed only if they placed themselves in flagrant opposition to the Wehrmacht by "a specific identifiable action or attitude."[97] Furthermore, the liquidation of Red Army commissars had to take place outside the combat zone proper, inconspicuously, on the order of an officer.

Hitler's Barbarossa Jurisdiction Decree and Commissar Order were crucial to his racial war of annihilation against the Soviet Union, and the origin, meaning, and application of von Brauchitsch's supplementary guidelines have sparked heated arguments. At issue is the Wehrmacht's role in Nazi atrocities in the east; thus the stakes in this debate are quite high.[98] Just what prompted von Brauchitsch to issue his supplementary instructions? Were they an honest attempt to mitigate the impact of Hitler's criminal orders? Or were they simply a cynical attempt to ensure discipline among the troops but nevertheless implement Hitler's planned racial war of annihilation?

The Institute for Military Historical Research's multivolume account, *Germany and the Second World War*, offers conflicting interpretations of von Brauchitsch's guidelines, indicating the complexity of the issue. In volume 4, Ernst Klink states, "To demote Brauchitsch's ordinance to the status of a noncommittal formula or to view it solely as a measure for the preservation of discipline—even though that is of overriding importance in any army in the world, if only in the interest of orderly combat—does not seem fair." In other words, according to Klink, von Brauchitsch had the sincere desire to conduct the war in the east according to international law, at least as far as possible considering Hitler's intention to implicate the Wehrmacht in his racial war of annihilation. "What divergences occurred in practice and under what conditions they were ordered, tolerated, or punished," according to Klink, "is another question."[99]

On the other hand, Jürgen Förster, in the very same volume, states that the Jurisdiction Decree, "despite the army commander-in-chief's supplements, marked the formal beginning of a new road. With it, the Armed Forces and the Army High Command largely accepted Hitler's intentions."[100] According to Förster:

> The Army High Command . . . must surely have realized that by the jurisdiction decree the methods of warfare in the east became dependent on the attitude and ideology of the individual officer. If it had really wished to prevent an undermining of the troops' sense of justice as a result of the ideological precepts of the supreme leadership, then it at least should not have made a contribution of its own towards the bending of international law and should have more vigorously resisted the limitation of its jurisdiction. Brauchitsch's supplements by no means rescinded the Führer decree.[101]

As for the Commissar Order, Förster states that von Brauchitsch's supplemental order "cannot be regarded as a genuine restriction of the okw's guidelines."[102] He further states that "the shooting of troop commissars and . . . the summary execution of Jews, communists, and Russians by army units for unsolved acts of resistance" remained part of the daily order.[103]

The case files do not provide a definitive answer to these questions. They nevertheless indicate that some German soldiers were court-martialed for crimes against Soviet civilians. However, they also suggest that Jürgen Förster may be closest to the truth with his assertion that "methods" in the east became "dependent on the attitude and ideology of the individual commander." Indeed, the case files suggest that, in the eastern occupied areas, the military penal code rarely determined which actions were criminal. The Jurisdiction Decree had essentially nullified it, and von Brauchitsch's supplementary guidelines placed the burden of distinguishing between crime and policy upon the commanders in the field. Violence against civilians in the eastern territories, in other words, was only considered a crime if perpetrated outside the chain of command. Reprisals and requisitioning became murder and plundering only if carried out on one's own initiative, rather than on the order of an officer. The line between crime and official occupation policy became very fine indeed.[104] The Jurisdiction Decree, as modified by the army's commander-in-chief, must have caused much confusion among the troops.

German soldiers, however, did appear before courts-martial for perpetrating crimes against civilians in the east. Approximately 20 percent of the case files contained in the Federal Archive's Eastern Collection represent military judicial action against soldiers accused of committing crimes against eastern inhabitants.[105] A significant number of these cases involved charges of rape or attempted rape. The prevalence of such crimes in the Eastern Collection perhaps should not be a surprise. In June 1941 a member of von Brauchitsch's staff explained to two separate groups of officers and jurists that "court proceedings should be instituted in all cases where discipline was threatened and there was a risk of chaos in the ranks, *especially in the case of sexual offenses*' [emphasis mine]."[106] It also should be noted that the documents in the Eastern Collection case file sample contained only one specific reference to the Jurisdiction Decree.[107]

On the other hand, the official Wehrmacht Criminal Statistics reveal that convictions for sexual assault reached their peak in the third quarter of 1940 (immediately after the conclusion of the French campaign) but declined after the beginning of Barbarossa.[108] Considering that the majority of German soldiers were employed in the east, the statistics might indicate restraint in the prosecution of such crimes on the eastern front.[109] However, the decline may also be attributed to the reluctance of victims to report such crimes.[110] Considering the brutal nature of the war and occupation in the east, this supposition should not be dismissed quickly.[111]

According to Christoph Rass, the Jurisdiction Decree completely changed the relationship between German soldiers and civilians that had existed in France before the assault on the Soviet Union. In his social history of the 253rd Infantry Division, Rass contends that the decree allowed soldiers wide latitude in their treatment of the Soviet population, especially with regard to plundering and sexual assault. The division's military judicial authorities, for example, did not prosecute plundering after August 1941, even if the perpetrator brutalized a civilian in the process, as long as the misappropriated items served the division's material war effort. Only when a soldier intended to enrich himself personally did the authorities prosecute him.[112]

Sexual assaults, according to Rass, also clearly demonstrate the room to maneuver that the Jurisdiction Decree allowed soldiers in their treatment of eastern inhabitants. During the war, the Court of the 253rd Infantry Division heard sixteen rape cases. Nine of these took place in the twenty-two months between September 1939 and the beginning of Operation Barbarossa in June 1941. Only seven rape cases came before the court in the next three and one-half years, which may indicate this particular division's restraint in prosecuting sexual assaults against Soviet citizens. The maintenance of Manneszucht was cited as the primary reason that these seven cases came before the court.[113]

Rass concludes that, in general, "merely existential interests of the Wehrmacht," such as the misuse of material resources and the maintenance of discipline, limited German soldiers' mistreatment of Soviet civilians. According to Rass, "Among the soldiers developed under these conditions . . . a consciousness of total power with regard to persons who were not tied into the institutional structures of the German military and occupation apparatus, because no agency existed that could offer this segment of the population sufficient protection."[114]

The case files support Rass's contention that the Wehrmacht's "existential interests" were, more often than not, the military judicial authorities' primary consideration when prosecuting and punishing servicemen for sexual crimes perpetrated against Soviet civilians. The courts regularly cited the maintenance of discipline, the orderly prosecution of occupation policy, and the adverse impact that sexual assaults had on the partisan movement as reasons for severe punishments.

The Wehrmacht's complicity in Nazi crimes is not being challenged here. However, an objective appraisal of the Wehrmacht's handling of sex offenders indicates that commanding officers frequently placed the maintenance of discipline ahead of the unqualified implementation of Hitler's racial war of annihilation. Put more simply, certain crimes, even those committed against Slavic "subhumans" (*Untermenschen*), had to be prosecuted in the interest of military order and discipline within the ranks.[115] Without military order, the Wehrmacht's strategic goals and occupation tasks would be at risk.

Unfortunately, the case files do not answer the question of the overall frequency of prosecution. Humanitarian concerns for eastern inhabitants, however, were not part of the military judicial equation when cases were prosecuted. Even if one places the most favorable spin on von Brauchitsch's supplementary guidelines, the military judicial authorities punished German soldiers for crimes against Soviet civilians not for reasons of compassion but rather for the orderly prosecution of the war and occupation policy. This required the cooperation of the local inhabitants. Of course, the importance of local cooperation was recognized by the Wehrmacht only after its initial attempts to achieve its occupation goals through extreme brutality failed.

Finally, the often repeated claim that the jurisdictional limitations prove that Wehrmachtjustiz was not a "secure instrument" for Hitler's plans is unsubstantiated.[116] The jurists did not have to be coerced in order for them to deal harshly with recalcitrant soldiers, and the reasons for the restrictions imposed on Wehrmachtjustiz lay much deeper than Hitler's alleged dissatisfaction with the military jurists.

The reasons can easily be found in the regime's overall nature, its conduct of the war, and the consequences of that conduct. On the other hand, the leading jurists' acceptance of Hitler's perception of the war in the east does not change the designed function of Wehrmachtjustiz. It was designed to prevent the kind of disturbances that shook the German armed forces in 1918 and to channel usable human matériel back to the front.

CHAPTER FOUR

The Wehrmacht's Penal and Parole System

The Wehrmacht developed a parole system and adapted its penal institutions to meet practical military considerations during the Second World War. These institutions and their practices also found justification in National Socialist ideology. The practice of paroling soldiers to the front and the use of prisoners for militarily useful purposes fulfilled the wishes of both the political and military leadership and party fanatics and Nazi ideologues, causing disagreement among scholars about what actually drove the developments.

The penal and parole system developed by the Wehrmacht after 1939 provided a filtering mechanism that channeled "usable" soldiers back to the front in one capacity or another. Conversely, it channeled recalcitrant or "incorrigible" soldiers, those who resisted the (usually draconian) motivational endeavors of the prisons, penal units, and parole battalions, in the opposite direction, to concentration camps for "destruction through work."[1] The system fulfilled practical military requirements but could be justified ideologically at the same time. The justification, however, like much under National Socialism, proved to be mere window dressing.

The system of parole, which required service at the front for the duration of the war, and the creation of penal units satisfied fanatics' demands that the "bad" should not be conserved in prisons while the best youths risked their lives at the front. In essence, Nazi ideologues feared that a kind of Darwinian "counter-selection" would occur if the "inferior" and "asocial" spent the war in the safety and relative comfort of prisons behind the lines. Preventing counter-selection would have been academic if the war were lost, however, and in fact the penal and parole system evolved in response to successive military crises, not in response to pressure from ideologues and fanatics in the party or Wehrmacht.[2]

The parole and penal system evolved during the war to meet pressing manpower needs, while nevertheless preserving Manneszucht, discipline, and military effectiveness. If the Wehrmacht's early war-

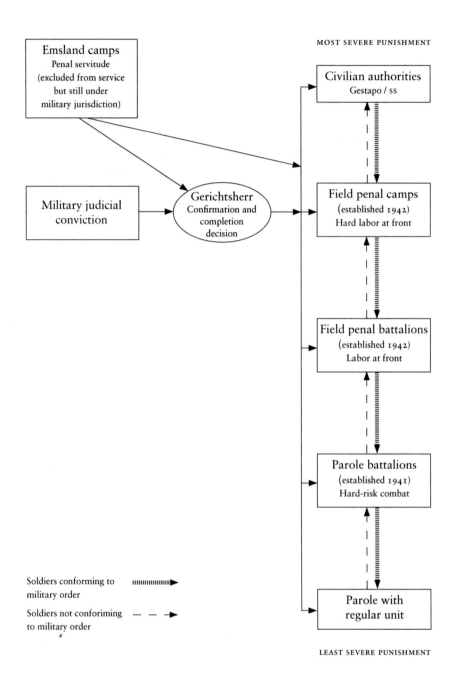

MOST SEVERE PUNISHMENT

Emsland camps
Penal servitude
(excluded from service
but still under
military jurisdiction)

Military judicial
conviction

Gerichtsherr
Confirmation and
completion
decision

Civilian authorities
Gestapo / SS

Field penal camps
(established 1942)
Hard labor at front

Field penal battalions
(established 1942)
Labor at front

Parole battalions
(established 1941)
Hard-risk combat

Parole with
regular unit

Soldiers conforming to
military order

Soldiers not conforiming
to military order

LEAST SEVERE PUNISHMENT

Wehrmacht Penal and Parole System

time successes had continued, it is doubtful that the various methods of employing prisoners for militarily useful purposes would have evolved as they did, regardless of fanatics' concerns about counter-selection.

Under National Socialism, bearing arms for the führer and Volk might have been the greatest honor, and before the war, Nazi ideologues such as Erich Schwinge rejected the use of individuals court-martialed for "dishonorable" crimes for military purposes. The Wehrmacht, for example, automatically branded individuals sentenced to penal servitude as "unworthy of service" (*wehrunwürdig*), dismissed them from service and turned them over to the Reich Administration of Justice for the punishment's execution. In a 1939 commentary in the *Journal for Military Law*, Schwinge stated that the use of these dishonorably discharged individuals in special formations was out of the question.[3]

During the war, however, fanatics (both in and out of the military) deemed it unacceptable to allow convicted soldiers to spend the war safely incarcerated behind the lines, while the best and brightest perished in combat. Penal formations and the system of paroling soldiers to the front thus not only prevented counter-selection but also contributed to positive selection by using "inferior" lawbreakers for hazardous assignments in operational areas. The military, however, designed the penal and parole system to identify those who would not (or could not) subordinate themselves to military order. Soldiers ensnared in the military judicial machinery and introduced into the Wehrmacht penal system had a simple choice: they could conform to military order and make their contribution to the war effort or risk winding up in the hands of the ss for destruction through work.

This "filtration" process could be justified ideologically, but it served the interests of the Wehrmacht, interests that were purely military, not ideological. Indeed, it would have been absurd for the Wehrmacht to put weapons in the hands of criminals or put prisoners in a position to go over to the enemy if there had not been a practical reason to do so.[4] The regime had other instruments for the purification of the Volksgemeinschaft and the prevention of counter-selection that did not entail these risks, including employment with the Organization Todt, which also performed militarily useful work.

In 1942, Hitler stated, "Every war leads to negative selection," and for this reason, he characterized jurists as the "bearers of racial self-preservation." The führer further warned, "If I decimate the good while conserving the bad in prisons, then the same thing will happen that occurred in 1918, when five or six hundred vagrants (*Strolche*) raped an entire nation."[5] Although Hitler refers to counter-selection in this discourse, his conclusion indicates that he considered the prevention of revolutionary uprisings to be a primary function of the military administration of justice. The prevention of negative selection and the achievement of his foreign policy goals may have been mutually reinforcing, but the latter appears to be the dominant theme in this discourse.

Despite the Wehrmacht's escalating need for replacements after the blitzkrieg's failure, some individuals simply could not be reintegrated into the troops. Judging by the case files, commanding officers preferred insufficient personnel to receiving replacements who refused to conform. It must be emphasized that some individuals would not (for example, conscientious objectors and antifascists) and others could not (for example, those with mental disorders) subordinate themselves to military order. In maintaining the Wehrgemeischaft, the Wehrmacht regarded the reason for an individual's inability to conform as immaterial. These individuals had to be sent somewhere. If that ultimately turned out to be a concentration camp, many commanders probably viewed that solution as preferable to having such individuals in their unit. This should not be interpreted as justification for a penal system that used destruction through work as the ultimate solution to the problem of recalcitrant soldiers. The important point here is that Nazi ideology provided a solution to a military problem, a solution that the military gladly and willingly seized upon. Yet for the Wehrmacht, the problem of recalcitrant soldiers still boiled down to issues of personnel management, military effectiveness, and the Wehrgemeischaft.

The filtering mechanism, which delivered usable human matériel to the front and channeled nonconformists to concentration camps, probably was viewed by military commanders as an eminently sensible approach to personnel management. Their willingness to feed the regime's machinery of destruction can be explained not only by the Wehrmacht's partial identity of aims with the political leadership, but also by the concept of "war necessity" as it had developed in the German military after the turn of the century.

In essence, the penal and parole system was personnel management of the most callous and calculated kind. The Wehrmacht's reduction of men to war matériel, expendable according to the necessities of war and discarded when no longer useful, is just as reprehensible as fanatics' demands for the Volksgemeinschaft's purification through the destruction of those they considered "asocial" and "inferior."[6] Nevertheless, practical military considerations were the driving force behind the system's development.

The Deferment of Prison Sentences for Front-Parole

The perceived lessons of the First World War, just as they influenced the strengthening of the military criminal codes, also affected the regulations for the completion of prison sentences at the beginning of the Second World War. According to section 104 of the Wartime Judicial Procedure Code, prison sentences, as a rule, were deferred until after the war unless the Gerichtsherren ordered their completion.[7] Convicted soldiers, according to the initial guidelines, were to remain with their units if they posed no obvious threat to discipline. Section 104 contained the following provisions:

Suspension of the Execution of Punishment with Imprisonment

(1) The completion of prison sentences imposed on members of the Wehrmacht and German civilians liable for conscription is suspended until after the end of the war circumstances.

(2) The Gerichtsherr can at any time, however, order the punishment's immediate completion if immediate atonement of the sentence is required for important reasons.[8]

Section 104's purpose was twofold: first, to ensure that the troops were not deprived of personnel, and second, to prevent soldiers from avoiding combat by committing criminal acts.[9] The deferment of prison sentences was contraindicated, however, if the prisoner's unit was not engaged in combat operations. Deterrence proved to be one of Wehrmachtjustiz's primary functions, and releasing soldiers to a quiet sector would hardly have had a deterring effect on either the parolees or their comrades.[10]

Scholars have frequently misinterpreted section 104, asserting that, under the provision, prison sentences would not be calculated while the war was in progress.[11] In other words, although incarcerated, the time an individual spent in detention during the war would not be credited as time served. Only when the war was concluded would the actual punishment be atoned.[12] This, in fact, was true *for individuals sentenced to penal servitude* (Zuchthaus) and those detained in Wehrmacht penal camps.[13] However, for simple prison sentences, which accounted for the vast majority of punishments handed down, the military judicial authorities did indeed calculate the time spent in detention during the war as time served, and this time was credited to the soldier's account.[14] Scholars who have investigated the case files closely, rather than concentrating on decrees and penal codes, know this.[15]

The confusion most likely stems from the provision's use of the verb *aussetzen*, which translates as "to suspend," rather than the more precise verb *aufschieben*, which translates as "to defer." The latter more accurately describes the actual process. Section 107 of the Wartime Judicial Procedure Code, however, clearly outlines the proper procedure for calculating prison sentences during the war.[16]

Section 104 aimed at providing Gerichtsherren with the utmost flexibility in personnel management. On a case-by-case basis, when confirming a sentence, commanders could scrutinize an individual's service record, his potential for future offenses, the unit's immediate personnel requirements, and the war situation itself.[17] For example, the case files indicate that, during operational periods, the Sixth Infantry Division's commanding officer immediately paroled to the front those soldiers who were convicted for violations of paragraph 175, the criminal code against homosexuality. Conversely, three individuals convicted for the same offense during quiet phases were ordered to serve their sentences.[18]

Based on experience during the Polish campaign, the Wehrmacht considered the practice of deferring sentences for front-parole to be a great success.[19] Section 104, however, required some adjustments in order to serve as a more flexible and effective instrument for managing the Wehrmacht's human matériel. The OKW therefore issued a directive on September 30, 1939, that authorized military commanders functioning as Gerichtsherren to subsequently change their initial order on how the punishment would be executed (commonly referred to as the "completion decision"). Henceforth, the Gerichtsherr could parole an inmate after the partial completion of the sentence or order a prisoner transferred to a Wehrmacht penal camp (Straflager) if the prisoner had behaved unacceptably during detention. The Gerichtsherr also received the power to parole penal camp inmates or transfer them to a military prison for the orderly completion of their sentence.[20]

Although Fritz Wüllner protests strongly about the dissonance between the military judiciary's use of the word "parole" and their deferment of judicially imposed punishments for the sole purpose of sending prisoners directly into combat, this dissonance can be easily (and from the Wehrmacht's perspective, rationally) explained.[21] The provision was not based on mere malice, as Wüllner suggests, but rather on the perceived lessons of the First World War. In that conflict, war-weary troops and malingerers purportedly avoided combat in a number of ways, including committing criminal offenses.[22]

Wüllner's efforts at exposing the fabrications in leading apologist Erich Schwinge's analyses are laudable, but his polemics are often counterproductive. Wüllner effectively refutes Schwinge's claim that granting parole was an act of mercy, but he proceeds no further. An OKW clarification on the parole system, dated January 13, 1940, stated that parole should be used "so as not to give the dishonorable and cowards incentive to avoid service at the front" by committing a punishable offense.[23] Wüllner, by calling the reader's attention to this clarification, successfully rebuts Schwinge's assertion that parole was a humanitarian act by compassionate jurists. However, by limiting himself to polemics, Wüllner fails to carry the analysis to its logical conclusion. One may see any number of human rights violations in the Wehrmacht's wartime parole requirements, and even ridicule them as Wüllner justly does, but the requirements were not specific to National Socialism, nor were they grounded in Darwinian principles of selection. Indeed, one need only to have perceived the lessons of the First World War in order to support paragraph 104 and the system of front-parole as it operated after 1939.

Making absolutely clear to the field commanders that they had maximum latitude in their personnel management decisions, the Seventh Implementation Ordinance for the Wartime Judicial Procedure Code, of May 18, 1940, which was promulgated one week into the French campaign, outlined the following alternatives available to the Gerichtsherr when confirming a sentence: partial or complete suspension of the sentence for front-parole; immediate and full completion of the sentence; or, for reasons of security, maintenance in a Wehrmacht penal camp.[24] For the French campaign, the Wehrmacht paroled a large number of men for combat. The military judicial authorities released 2,762 prisoners from detention for the Western Offensive. Of that number, 93.6 percent remained free after proving themselves in combat, while only 6.4 percent (or 177) soldiers had their paroles revoked.[25] The Wehrmacht regarded these statistics as further vindication of the parole system.[26]

The Parole Battalions

With the conclusion of the French campaign, the possibility of front-parole fell away, and except for the most trivial offenses, conviction was indeed followed by incarceration after the armistice with the Vichy regime in June 1940. The commandant of the Wehrmacht prison system subsequently complained that hundreds of soldiers were sitting in cells—prisoners "who have the honorable wish to make amends for their one-time blunders by special bravery, but who have, however, no opportunity for that."[27] With military prisons filling up, and influenced by the statistics cited above, the Wehrmacht examined new possibilities for parole.

Rudolph Lehmann, the chief of the Armed Forces Legal Division, in a memorandum dated September 18, 1940, discussed the problem at length. Despite the führer's insistence that the strongest means be employed in war to maintain Manneszucht, Lehmann advocated a more balanced approach based on the lessons of the First World War and the experiences of the current conflict. According to Lehmann, it was crucial not to destroy the lives of the many men "who had blundered once" but were otherwise "orderly" and thereby "usable" soldiers. The system of front-parole accomplished this. But, Lehmann asserted, the possibility of parole should exist even for soldiers whose units were not engaged at the front. "The Wehrmacht," he noted, "has been forced in the war to use unusual means for securing Manneszucht. It is its duty to find balance for this harshness, that is, through new and difficult ways." As a solution, Lehmann proposed the creation of special parole units.[28]

After consultations between the OKW and the OKH regarding the appropriate size of the proposed parole units,[29] the OKW legal division approached Hitler with the plan for paroling to convicted soldiers whose units were not engaged at the front, especially those who might simply have committed a "one-time blunder."[30] On December 21, 1940, Hitler ordered the establishment of special parole formations.[31] The führer's directive, Suspension of the Execution of Punishments for the Purpose of Parole, emphasized that the "strongest measures are necessary . . . to maintain Manneszucht in the troops, to suppress cowardice, and to give members of the Wehrmacht who had blundered one time the opportunity for parole."[32]

Promulgated on April 5, 1941, the OKW's initial provisions stipulated that soldiers meeting certain criteria could be released for service in the new parole battalions (*Bewährungstruppe*) after partial atonement of their sentence. The remainder of the sentence would be deferred until after the war.[33] The seven criteria initially laid down were:

1. The convicted must have conducted himself flawlessly (*einwandfrei*) until the time of the crime for which he was condemned and he could be legally punished previously only very insignificantly.

2. The crime must represent a one-time blunder (*einmalige Entgleisung*) and could not have its cause in a deficiency of character.

3. The convicted must have the sincere intention to prove himself against the enemy (*vor dem Feind*) and must express this intention in a formal petition for parole.

4. The convicted must be a member of the armed forces or liable for military service (*Wehrpflichtiger sein*) or fit for employment as a soldier.

5. The convicted must be fit for employment in an infantry battalion.

6. The remainder of the punishment must amount to at least six months.

7. Prisoners serving punishments in a civilian penal institution and prisoners in penal battalions of the Wehrmacht must pass a one-month fitness examination at a Wehrmacht prison.[34]

According to Hitler's initial instructions, service in the new formations would be regarded as "honored service" (*Ehrendienst*), just as it was in any other military unit: "It should in no way have the character of a penal formation." The OKW demanded stern but correct treatment of parolees, emphasizing that battalion members were to be handled with "judicious rigor" (*wohlabgewogener Strenge*) but also with "absolute fairness" (*unbedingter Gerechtigkeit*). In addition, battalion commanders were to refrain from revealing any "degrading information" about a parolee's punishment, "especially before the collective unit (*Mannschaft*)." Promoting and strengthening the sense of honor in the battalion members was part of the program.[35]

A subsequent OKH directive of February 17, 1941, required the Gerichtsherr, upon the confirmation of a verdict, to decide whether a soldier would be eligible for parole after the partial completion of the sentence, and if so, whether the prisoner should be released to a regular unit or to a parole battalion. Those receiving simple prison sentences could be sent directly to a parole battalion. Soldiers serving penal servitude punishments and Wehrmacht penal camp inmates had to pass a one-month "fitness" examination at the infamous Torgau prison complex near Berlin before they could be released to a parole battalion.[36]

Hans-Peter Klausch offers an interesting analysis of the parole battalion fitness exam. According to Klausch, the month-long examination essentially boiled down to drill, hard work, and physical endurance. "One gets the impression from reading the evaluations," states Klausch, "that a certain mental or character deficiency could be compensated for by strength and daring recklessness," while the opposite was seldom true. Klausch's observation points to a penal system dedicated to mobilizing hardened fighters, individuals suitable for integration into the Wehrgemeischaft, not the theoretical cream of the Volksgemeinschaft's crop.[37]

Klausch also provides insight into the harsh regimen's purpose. According to his interpretation, it went beyond simply instilling in the prisoners utterly slavish obedience (*Kadavergehorsam*). Above all, based on the experiences of the First World War and its perception of the current conflict, the Wehrmacht desired soldiers with a feeling of invincibility, self-confidence, and superiority over their opponent. Yet after weeks of dehumanizing drill and harsh treatment, the men, who up to this point had been treated no better than "well-dressed animals," suddenly found themselves treated humanely once they had passed the test. The entire process, according to one contemporary account, proved to be very effective in motivating the men, instilling in them a fresh sense of "courage and new hope."[38]

Approximately 24 percent of the prisoners tested at Torgau in 1941 failed the exam and were returned to the appropriate penal facility, which usually meant Emsland, the concentration camp that housed soldiers sentenced to penal servitude. The need for manpower after the great losses in the winter of 1941–42 immediately affected the selection process, and the failure rate on the fitness exam dropped quickly to about 10 percent. The failure rate most likely continued to drop as the war progressed. The success rate obviously never reached 100 percent, however, due to the incapacitating effects of the Emsland complex, which remained the primary source of candidates for the exam process.[39]

Finally, Klausch concludes that the ratio of common criminals who received transfers from Emsland to the parole formations was much higher than the ratio found in the overall Emsland population. In other words, the Wehrmacht demonstrated a greater readiness to re-activate soldiers punished for common criminal offenses than soldiers who had violated discipline and Manneszucht. The military judicial authorities apparently considered cowardice and desertion to be more heinous crimes than murder, rape, and theft.[40] Inclusion in the Wehr-gemeischaft required only the will and capacity to fight, and trans-gressions that did not specifically hinder the war's conduct could be forgiven, while those that did hinder the war could not.

After months of preparation during the winter of 1940–41, the first parole unit, designated Infantry Battalion 500, was established on April 1 at Meiningen with instructions to be ready for operations on June 1, 1941 (three weeks before the beginning of Barbarossa).[41] Si-multaneously, work commenced on combined Reserve Infantry Company (Infanterie-Ersatz-Kompanie) 500, the reserve formation that assembled and supported the parole battalion. In the fall of 1941, the reserve formation continued to handle arriving replacements for Battalion 500. It also prepared four additional parole units, Infantry Battalions 540, 550, 560, and 561. Infantry Battalion 540 began operations with Army Group North in November 1941. Ready for operations in March 1942, Infantry Battalion 550 was assigned to Army Group Middle. Infantry Battalions 560 and 561 were ready for combat and sent east in August 1942 and April 1943 respectively.[42]

Eventually, the parole battalions matched the capabilities of a strengthened rifle battalion with three rifle companies, one pursuit platoon (*Jägerzug*), one antitank platoon (*Pakzug*), and one engineering platoon (*Pionierzug*).[43] Accommodating men from all three service braches and retinue, their effective strength reached nine hundred men in 1943 and nearly one thousand by 1944.[44] In many platoons, 80 percent of the parolees had been officers and noncommissioned officers (NCOs) who had been demoted to the lowest conscripted level upon their convictions.[45]

Although no special provisions existed for sentence remission as a reward for service in the parole battalions, individuals could earn a transfer to a regular unit with flawless behavior and outstanding performance in combat.[46] A point system based on bravery, conduct, and operational readiness was the primary yardstick. Volunteering for especially dangerous assignments, such as reconnaissance patrols, could earn parolees a large number of points. Those volunteering for such hazardous duties had a good chance for an early transfer, if they were not killed or captured first.[47]

The internal evaluation system promoted the desired image of a parole battalion soldier: the constantly "prepared and relentless daredevil warrior (*Kämpfer*)." Submitted by the battalion staff on April 3, 1945, an evaluation of parolee G., a former naval officer with Infantry Battalion 500, declared:

> G. proved himself to be extremely brave in the most difficult military
> engagement. During the Russian counterattack on December 9, 1944,
> he remained with his detachment despite his wound and did not allow
> the connection to the companies to be severed in spite of a furious bom-

bardment. Also, in a subsequent fighting retreat through East Slovakia, G. was always engaged with the enemy and through his relentless action was a constant example to his comrades. And even when the enemy's tanks broke through during a huge armored assault, G. did not retreat but participated in the defensive battle with rifles and hand grenades.[48]

On the other hand, the competent Gerichtsherr could order parolees who failed to conduct themselves flawlessly returned to the appropriate penal institution for the execution of their sentence. With "exceptional failure," the parolees could be transferred to a Wehrmacht penal camp, the military's most draconian form of punishment. A formal warning, however, had to precede any such transfer.[49]

Other than relieving overburdened prisons, no immediate requirements existed when Hitler promulgated the order for the parole battalions in December 1940. Practical military considerations, however, were central in the creation of the battalions. The parole formations' establishment must be viewed within the context of the Wehrmacht's plans for Operation Barbarossa, the assault on the Soviet Union. Hitler ordered its preparation three days prior to issuing his parole battalion directive.[50] "Despite the illusions that the Wehrmacht had about the strength of the Red Army, it was still cognizant of the fact that this war against the Soviets would place far higher demands on the discipline of the troops than the previous campaigns."[51]

> As a quasi-prophylactic measure, the creation of the battalions represented on one hand a considerable expansion . . . of the existing instruments for deterrence that were necessary for the "maintenance of Manneszucht" and, on the other hand, a proven means to reintegrate [severely punished, yet still usable soldiers] back into the troops. Thus, it is no accident that the first parole battalion was declared "fit for operations (*Feldverwendungsbereitschaft*)" just as the German divisions were taking-up their positions for the assault on the USSR.[52]

Indeed, with the war's expansion to the south (i.e., the Balkan campaign) and east, Hitler and the Wehrmacht recognized the need for reserves of every type. This was the authoritative reason that the OKW made preparations for the parole battalions in February and March 1941.[53]

The Wehrmacht's initially stringent selection criteria for service with the parole battalions were gradually relaxed as the war progressed, constantly expanding "the circle of prisoners deemed worthy of parole . . . corresponding to the increasing need for soldiers capable of combat."[54] As early as the winter of 1942, the OKW stated that the only criterion for selection should be whether a soldier would be "useful to the troops." He had only to be "physically and mentally fit for service with the infantry" and "to display during his detention that he had the honorable will to atone for his crime through model performance and good conduct with the troops."[55] In 1944 the prerequisite that prisoners had to have at least six months remaining in their sentence in order to be considered for the battalions was rescinded, thus opening the formations to virtually any soldier running afoul of the law.[56] By the end of the war, "fitness for combat" remained the only criterion, and at times even this was ignored. Heavily armed, the parole battalions had increased in size to nearly one thousand parolees each by 1944.[57]

Many scholars characterize service in the parole battalions as a virtual death sentence. Stressing that the formations were used for dangerous operations on the eastern front, they portray the parolees as nothing more than cannon fodder.[58] Hans-Peter Klausch, the expert on the parole battalions, arrives at a more balanced appraisal. According to Klausch, the parole battalions initially possessed an almost elite quality due to the stringent selection criteria and the fundamental requirement that parolees conduct themselves exceptionally and "prove themselves before the enemy."[59] Although the formations were indeed employed constantly in the east, it would be inaccurate to label them as suicide squads. Considering their exceptional capabilities, it would have been absurd to squander these units in suicide operations.

The political leadership had not consciously planned and calculated the parolees' deaths, as many contend. On the other hand, the parole battalions did receive important high-risk assignments that produced extremely high casualty rates. The formations' initial elite qualities decreased rapidly after September 1944 as manpower shortages resulted in the drastic relaxation of the selection criteria. By the end of the war, the parole battalions had lost much of their effectiveness and may have been militarily counterproductive as their ranks swelled with true criminals and individuals unfit for combat.[60]

Few relevant documents survived the war, preventing an accurate estimation of the total number of men employed in the parole battalions. High casualties produced such an excessive turnover rate that estimates based on the battalions' average effective strength should be regarded as meaningless.[61] Employed constantly at the front for high-risk assignments, such as advance parties, shock troops, and partisan operations, the parole formations suffered "enormous attrition," and constant replacements were necessary. The courts, according to one scholar, had the "quasi-function of a reserve factory."[62] Franz Seidler estimates that eighty-two thousand men served at one time or another in the parole battalions. Hans-Peter Klausch's well-documented study places the number at only twenty-seven thousand.[63]

The number killed during service in the parole formations cannot be determined either, although Franz Seidler suggests that the death rate reached as high as 50 percent.[64] Three of the parole battalions disappeared without any trace in the final weeks of the war, with documents simply listing them as "destroyed in battle."[65] This was not a unique phenomenon on the eastern front, however, with scores of regular units suffering the same fate.

Regardless of the numbers, the parole battalions played an important role in the Wehrmacht's attempt to mobilize manpower and maintain the Wehrgemeischaft through deterrence.[66] The parole battalions' origin and development must be considered with regard to the "tension in which the military leadership found itself in Hitler's Germany." The Wehrmacht wanted all subversive elements excluded from the troops, yet the military's plans demanded recourse to the highest possible reserves of "human matériel." This was especially true after the blitzkrieg's failure before Moscow in 1941-42 when the war became a conflict of long duration.[67]

The Wehrmacht's Special Penal Formations

The Wehrmacht's system of parole in regular units had been based on the German military's perceived lessons of the First World War. Then, based on the Wehrmacht's experiences in Poland and France, the parole system was refined by the introduction of the parole battalions. Deferring sentences for employment at the front in regular units and service in the parole battalions was intended to deter those hoping to avoid the danger of combat by committing crimes and to ensure that the troops were not deprived of necessary personnel.

The political and military leadership, however, considered the system insufficient for the task facing the Wehrmacht after the blitzkrieg failed in Russia at the end of 1941. High losses in the east and the war's continuation into 1942 prompted the military to make dramatic changes in the execution of punishments. The Wehrmacht took the doctrine of deterrence to the next level and found new methods of mobilizing prisoners for militarily useful purposes.

The Blitzkrieg's Failure and the Wehrmacht's Response

After the blitzkrieg's failure, Hitler demanded that more possibilities for parole be made available. To obtain replacements for the eastern front, he ordered that individuals convicted for crimes "that had their cause in negligence or youthful indiscretion" were to be immediately paroled.[68] In addition, the disciplinary units, which hitherto had served as a means of punishment, now received the educational mandate of turning inferior soldiers into usable instruments of war.[69] It soon became obvious, however, that these steps would be insufficient.[70]

In April 1942, Hitler determined that the continuing conflict against the Soviet Union required the mobilization of every available soldier.[71] Losses on the eastern front surpassed three hundred thousand by November 1941. After the Soviet Union's successful counterattack in December of that year, the Wehrmacht required six hundred twenty-five thousand replacements.[72]

The Army High Command had expected and planned for high losses at the beginning of Barbarossa. However, not only did actual losses far exceed expectations, but the high casualty rates continued into the spring of 1942. Combing out the rear services and enlisting female auxiliaries could not compensate for the unexpected casualties, forcing the Wehrmacht to call up the entire class of 1923 nearly a year earlier than planned.[73] A diary entry made at the end of 1941 by the army's chief of the General Staff, General Franz Halder, reflected the seriousness of the reserve situation:

> Conversation with [General] Bock: Guderian reports that the condition of the troops is so critical that he does not know how he is supposed to

fend off an enemy attack. A crisis of trust (*Vertrauenskrise*) of a serious nature in the troops. Declining battle strength of the infantry! In the rear, all available forces (*Kräfte*) were assembled. . . . The Army Group needs people![74]

An OKW Command Staff study written in the spring of 1942 laconically stated, "Without resort to the class of 1923 and without resort to key defense industry personnel, no reserves are available." Faced with this crisis the Wehrmacht made "decisive changes" in how legally imposed punishments would be executed.[75] In a directive signed on April 2, 1942, Hitler declared the following:

The execution of sentences during the war must be adapted as soon as possible to the changing requirements of the military situation. Measures cannot be adhered to that proved effective under other circumstances. The possibilities for parole on the eastern front must be used much more than hitherto. . . . Many convicted soldiers will not be able to be employed with the fighting troops immediately and some not at all. Unstable elements that count on this must be denied any incentive, through the intensification and gradation of punishments, to evade operations at the front because they are atoning a prison sentence. For this purpose, field penal battalions must be established immediately and mobilized for the hardest labor under dangerous circumstances as close as possible to the fighting troops.[76]

The resulting order from the OKW, the New Ordinance for the Execution of Punishments of April 14, 1942, translated Hitler's demands into action. Parole at the front and the intensification of punishments now had top priority.[77] To fulfill the latter requirement, the OKW decreed the establishment of the first three field penal battalions.[78] Intended as a punishment more severe than imprisonment, the penal battalions were designed to also serve manpower needs. Employed for militarily useful work at the front, the formations (in theory) freed up a corresponding number of active soldiers for combat.

The intensification of punishments did not end there. In order to provide commanders with a graduated system of punishment alternatives, the OKW, on the day before the New Ordinance for the Execution of Punishments was promulgated, ordered the Wehrmacht's existing penal camps (Straflager) converted into field penal camps (Feldstraflager). Destined for the eastern front, the field penal camps, like the field penal battalions, would be employed for dangerous work in operational areas. Intended as an even harsher form of punishment than the field penal battalions, the camps sat at the apex of the Wehrmacht's new graduated penal system.

These new penal formations reconciled a fundamental conflict between section 104 of the Wartime Judicial Procedure Code and field officers' desire to maintain discipline, morale, and their unit's military effectiveness. Section 104 was intended as a deterrent against the commission of crimes as a means of avoiding combat. Many commanders, however, had been skeptical about accepting legally punished and therefore "bad" soldiers into their units. Commanding officers certainly had an interest in a steady flow of reserve personnel, but numbers alone did not guarantee combat effectiveness. By mobilizing manpower for use in the field, but in separate self-contained penal formations, section 104 of the Wartime Judicial Procedure Code and the commanders' concerns about maintaining discipline had been reconciled.[79]

With the new penal formations, commanders now had at their disposal graduated punishment alternatives that enabled them to use even the most recalcitrant soldiers for militarily useful purposes. Once introduced into the penal system, a soldier could conform and move down the penal chain with the attendant reduction in harshness of punishment. If he refused to conform, he would be channeled in the opposite direction, which meant increasingly harsh treatment as he moved up the chain, with the field penal camps providing the most intense form of punishment. Failure here meant being dismissed from service and placed in the custody of the SS or Gestapo.[80]

From this point forward, the field penal camps and field penal battalions replaced Wehrmacht prisons as the primary destination for convicted soldiers. According to the provisions, the Gerichtsherr should order prisoners to atone their punishments in prisons only in exceptional cases. In a subsequent implementation order, the OKW directed all commanding officers functioning as Gerichtsherren to "conduct themselves according to the spirit of the new ordinance."[81]

They apparently did not need to be coerced. In the case files, nearly 40 percent of those soldiers convicted to simple prison sentences after April 1942 were ordered directly to a field penal battalion upon the commander's confirmation of the sentence. Less than 2 percent, however, were ordered immediately to a field penal camp, which strongly suggests that the Wehrmacht normally reserved the penal camps for those who refused to conform after their introduction into the penal system.[82]

Again, the creation of the field penal battalions and the conversion of the penal camps into field formations was a reaction to unexpected personnel shortages during the winter of 1941-42. Hitler's order for the establishment of the penal battalions very clearly focuses on military considerations and the "war situation," not the purification of the Volksgemeinschaft, the prevention of counter-selection, or the attainment of some other Nazi racial goal. The field penal battalions as well as the field penal camps were intended as a deterrent, one that also served manpower requirements.[83]

Although subsequent statements by party ideologues and fanatics inside and outside the military contained Social Darwinist arguments to justify the existence of the formations, the formations nevertheless were designed to fulfill the military's immediate personnel needs.[84] Many Nazi proponents undoubtedly obtained satisfaction from the fact that criminals would no longer be "conserved" in prisons while the nation's best youths risked their lives at the front.[85] This, however, does not alter the fact that the establishment of the new penal formations was a response to the Wehrmacht's critical manpower shortages in the war's third year.

If Wehrmachtjustiz in general and the penal system in particular was dedicated to the Volksgemeinschaft's purification or the prevention of counter-selection, why did this work only begin in earnest in the war's third year? The field penal camps and penal battalions had been designed to channel manpower for militarily useful purposes, while at the same time assisting in the original military judicial task of identifying those who would not subordinate themselves to military order. Although fanatics may have correctly perceived a dovetailing of purposes between their ideological goals and the Wehrmacht's strategic goals in creating the formations, this does not change the reality of their origin or purpose. On the other hand, the reality of their origin and purpose does not lessen the system's brutal methods and often lethal consequences. Nor does this reality change the fact that Nazi ideology justified the brutality or that Nazism provided an environment in which brutality would escalate.

The Field Penal Camps

The field penal camps generally served the same purpose that the disciplinary units had served before the war. Although one disciplinary unit operated until the war's last months, the Wehrmacht generally placed its most recalcitrant soldiers in field penal camps beginning in April 1942.[86]

The field penal camps were the direct descendants of the Wehrmacht penal camps, which were established at various military prisons according to OKW and OKH directives shortly after the war's beginning.[87] The intended repositories for soldiers convicted by military courts before the war, the penal camps received prisoners whose reintegration into the troops might pose "a danger to Manneszucht" and whose isolation was deemed necessary for "security" or "education." Directly subordinated to the prison commandant, the penal camp represented the harshest form of punishment that a soldier could receive without being dismissed from service and turned over to the ss.[88]

With the April 1942 changes in the execution of punishments, the OKW ordered the existing Wehrmacht penal camps converted into field penal camps and their detainees transferred to the new formations, regardless of their fitness rating.[89] Field Penal Camp I, established by Defense District IV (Dresden) at Torgau, accommodated six hundred inmates selected from Wehrmacht Prisons Torgau–Ft. Zinna and Anklam. Field Penal Camp II, also established at Torgau by Defense District XI (Kassel), received six hundred inmates from Wehrmacht Prisons Torgau-Brückenkopf, Graudenz, Bruchsal, and Freiburg and from the military penal camp at Donau. Employed initially in Norway and Finish Lapland, these two penal formations were eventually sent to the eastern front where they remained for the rest of their existence. Regular army officers, NCOs, and enlisted personnel commanded and supervised the field penal camps, which consisted of four companies each.[90]

Field Penal Camp III followed in August of 1942.[91] It too was employed on the eastern front. By 1943 every army group on the eastern front had a field penal camp at its disposal.[92]

Recalcitrant soldiers sentenced to prison or penal servitude could be sent to the field penal camps. Just as in the former penal camps, time served in the field penal camps during the war was not credited to the prisoner's account. Also like the penal camps, the field penal camps required inmates to perform heavy work, but in operational areas. Constantly employed under "especially dangerous circumstances" and without weapons, the inmates cleared mines, retrieved corpses, and worked on field emplacements and fortifications.[93]

In addition to doing this hazardous work, the inmates received formal military drill and training. If the regularly scheduled working hours could not be fully utilized, the time was filled with additional drill. Franz Seidler writes, "It consisted as a rule of formal military training (*Formalausbildung*) and battle simulations (*kriegsnahen Übungen*), and differed in no way from the barracks square exercises of basic training."[94] It seems unlikely that this emphasis on drill and training exercises was incorporated into the daily routine as part of the inmates' punishment. No doubt it was intended to hone the individual's martial skills as part of the system's priority of reclaiming usable soldiers. A review of the records of twenty-two sailors in Field Penal Camp I indicates that it was not necessarily a serious criminal past that lead to detention in the field penal camp, but rather the "militarily determined estimation of the potential for education."[95]

The normal workday lasted twelve to fourteen hours and at least four hours on Sundays and holidays.[96] The punishing routine and reduced rations quickly led to hunger, exhaustion, and the gradual deterioration of the inmates' physical and mental health. Suicide was allegedly a daily event in the Wehrmacht's version of the civilian concentration camp.[97]

The guards treated the inmates as "cowards, weaklings, and parasites (*Schädlingen*)." According to one contemporary account, the guards' behavior "bordered on sadism."[98] In Field Penal Camp II, which was sent to Finnish Lapland shortly after it was established, the guards made extensive use of their weapons. According to Hans-Peter Klausch, the guards shot inmates who were collapsing from sickness or exhaustion during the trip north from Torgau, accusing them of insubordination if they could not comply with the order to get up. The number executed on the trip for such "insubordination" may have been as high as fifty.[99]

Under the initial provisions for the field penal camps, the regimen resulted in high death rates; it amounted to nothing less than destruction through work as practiced by the SS in civilian concentration camps.[100] Mortality rates allegedly exceeded those in the civilian camps operated by the Reich Administration of Justice.[101] After a few months, however, the Wehrmacht determined that the death rate had become militarily counterproductive and implemented changes by the end of 1942. First, the detainees received higher rations. Second, reversing the initial guidelines that provided for detention in the camps for the war's duration, the Wehrmacht imposed limits on detention. Henceforth, a stay should last between six and nine months.[102] However, with exceptional conduct inmates could be paroled after only three months.[103] To be certain that the field penal camps continued to serve manpower needs, front-parole became a priority. The differentiation shifted from "incorrigible and uneducable" to "completely incorrigible and uneducable." If not classified as completely incorrigible, an inmate could be transferred to a field penal battalion and then, with continued good conduct, to a regular unit.[104]

Only the competent Gerichtsherr had the power to end an inmate's stay in a field penal camp. If the inmate exhibited good conduct, the Gerichtsherr could decree the orderly completion of the sentence, which meant transfer to a field penal battalion (or occasionally to a parole battalion) where time in detention was calculated as time served. Of course, those deemed completely incapable of education and those who had to be disciplined repeatedly had to be dismissed from service after nine months. These unfortunates were turned over to the civilian police agencies for internment in a concentration camp.[105] The Thirty-second Infantry Division's commanding officer, for example, ordered a soldier dismissed from service on September 21, 1943, after detention in a field penal camp failed to produce the intended results. "He possesses neither the capacity nor the will to be a soldier of good quality," the commander declared. "He is a danger to the other inmates who are still capable of education. He is worthless as a soldier."[106]

The most draconian instrument of punishment available to the Gerichtsherr, the field penal camps sat at the top of the military's new graduated system of punishment. Failure to conform here meant an inmate's almost certain destruction through work at the hands of the ss. The camps were liquidated in early 1945 when the war was fought exclusively on German soil, and they either sent their charges to the field penal battalions or turned them over to the ss.[107]

According to the original okh implementation order, the field penal camps were designed to "exercise a lasting deterrent on the unstable (*unsicheren*) elements in the troops and to counteract decisively the incentive to avoid one's duty by incurring a prison sentence." For this reason, "the chances of survival" for penal camp inmates were intended to be no better than the chances for "the regular troops."[108] If the field penal camps prevented counter-selection, this was merely icing on the cake for Nazi fanatics. The timing of the creation of the camps, prompted by Hitler's decision to adapt the execution of punishments to the war situation, indicates that they were created to fulfill specific military needs: solving the Wehrmacht's manpower problems at the front, while also providing an irresistible deterrent.

The Field Penal Battalions

Translating Hitler's decision to adapt punishments to the (deteriorating) war situation into action, the okw's April 1942 New Ordinance for the Execution of Punishments provided for the creation of the field penal battalions. The ordinance directed Wehrmacht prisons at Glatz, Gemersheim, and Anklam to establish the first three battalions. Initially, each had two hundred inmates selected from various Wehrmacht prisons according to a predetermined ratio.[109] Although the penal battalion inmates may have been combed from these prisons initially, the case files reveal that the formations subsequently received prisoners from almost every prison and penal facility operated by the Wehrmacht.

The ordinance of April 14, 1942, included the following specifications for the battalions in section 1, paragraph 3:

> For the execution of punishment in the field penal battalions comes into consideration . . .: Wehrmacht prisoners, so far as they are k.v., g.v.F.,

and g.v.H., except those who will be dismissed from detention in the near future because of visible improvement (with the remainder of the punishment perhaps up to six months)—specifically—: cowards (for example, those convicted of desertion, serious cases of absence without leave, and subversion of fighting power), and those repeatedly and strikingly punished, as well as those punished for other intentionally dishonorable offenses.[110]

Quickly amended in June, the specifications encompassed nearly every soldier facing at least three months of continued incarceration, as long as they had the above-mentioned fitness ratings and parole did not appear realistic for the foreseeable future. Front-parole with a regular unit or service with the parole battalions, as per Hitler's instructions of April 2, 1942, continued to have the highest priority.[111] According to an OKW directive, considering the personnel "bottleneck," prisoners should no longer sit out their sentence; rather, they should serve. Even those deemed unworthy of wearing the honored field gray uniform before the war—that is, individuals who had been convicted for dishonorable crimes and discharged as "unworthy of service"—could be granted temporary "worthiness" and sent to field penal battalions.[112]

The first three field penal battalions began operating in May 1942. Nine more were established by the end of that year. By the end of 1943 a total of twenty had been created. In 1945 the Wehrmacht mobilized two more battalions: Field Penal Battalions 21 and 22.[113] Commanded by a regular army officer and supervised by seventeen NCOs and thirty-three enlisted men, the battalions initially had four, then five, and sometimes even six companies with 166 prisoners apiece.[114] Including convicted soldiers with limited fitness ratings in the circle of prisoners eligible for employment in the field penal battalions facilitated the Wehrmacht's mobilization of a large number of men, indicating the Wehrmacht's desire to alleviate the pressing manpower shortage. The field penal battalions had the distinction of being the Wehrmacht's largest penal organization in the field, with a capacity twice that of the parole battalions.[115] Performing necessary work at the front, the battalions also freed up (in theory) an approximately equal number of soldiers for combat.

Maintenance in the field penal battalions normally lasted three to nine months, and in contrast to the field penal camps, the time spent in detention was calculated as time served.[116] With good conduct, inmates could earn parole to a regular unit or receive a transfer to a parole battalion. Those refusing to conform to military order or classified as "incapable of education" (*unerziehbarkeit*) were transferred after nine months (earlier with especially bad conduct) to a field penal camp.[117] The military judicial authorities regarded the reasons for failure as immaterial. Prisoner assessments tell the tale. For example, one commander wrote that "the prisoner can only be returned to the troops after further soldierly education" because otherwise he would have "no military use." With this sort of assessment, officers had few scruples about subjecting individuals to the harshest punishments.[118]

The regulations regarding work, rations, and discipline in the field penal battalions differed only slightly from those for the field penal camps. As a rule, however, conditions were more tolerable in the battalions, fulfilling the Wehrmacht's desire to provide commanders with graduated instruments of punishment.[119] Also contributing to the better treatment may have been that the Wehrmacht considered the penal battalions to be military units. The battalion inmates, unlike those in the field penal camps, were not stigmatized as cowards and parasites.[120]

The inmates performed dangerous work at the front, more often than not as construction troops. For this reason, the penal battalions were subordinated to a divisional engineering battalion. The provisions established a ten-hour workday as the minimum. Although normally unarmed, in certain cases trusted inmates could be issued weapons and employed as "attack companies" against partisans or as reinforcements for critically weak segments of the front.[121] Just as in the field penal camps, reduced rations in the battalions led to perpetual hunger. According to Hans-Peter Klausch, "It is a matter of record that great hunger prevailed in nearly all the field penal battalions, that there was a multitude of escape attempts and insubordination, as well as an extraordinarily high number of death sentences imposed and carried out there. It is obvious there is a connection between the three."[122]

Klausch, however, warns against assuming that conditions in the individual penal battalions were equally bad. He found humane treatment in Field Penal Battalion 14, which he attributes primarily to the attitude of the commander and his staff, and has identified other penal battalions in which detention had been bearable. He cannot, however, determine whether humanitarianism on the part of command staffs or practical military considerations explains the better conditions.[123]

Little doubt exists, however, about the harsh conditions in the field penal battalions. After all, they were designed with deterrence in mind and one of their functions was to impress upon the inmates the difference between punishment and service with the regular troops.[124] Contemporary accounts are graphic in detail and clear about the draconian nature of the field penal battalions and penal camps.[125]

But just as the memoirs of Hitler's generals must be taken with (at least!) a grain of salt, so too must the prisoners' accounts be assumed to have biases and agendas.[126] The high percentage of penal battalion and penal camp inmates eventually reintegrated into the regular troops indicates that their health was not irreparably damaged, even after several months with the formations. This indeed leads one to wonder just how badly the inmates were treated. In the case files, more than 70 percent of the individuals sent to either a field penal battalion or penal camp ultimately rejoined regular units or were transferred to parole battalions. Considering the fragmentary nature of many of the case files, this percentage might actually have been as high as 85 to 90 percent.

Fritz Wüllner contends that penal formation inmates seldom descended the penal chain, with very few obtaining a transfer to a parole battalion or regular unit. Indeed, he maintains that the vast majority of prisoners went in the other direction, from the parole and field penal battalions to field penal camps and ultimately to civilian concentration camps. This channeling of prisoners toward concentration camps, according to Wüllner, proved to be the rule rather than the exception. Hans-Peter Klausch submits, however, that the exact opposite was the normal scenario, with inmates moving down the graduated penal chain in the direction of parole with a regular unit or parole battalion. In other words, Klausch says, the system operated as designed, channeling men back to the front as armed combatants, or at least in that direction.[127] The case files overwhelmingly support Klausch's conclusion.

Klausch's observation should not be regarded as an apology or justification for the penal formations' existence and methods. Again, the military judicial authorities considered the reason for an individual's failure to conform immaterial. For example, the Wehrmacht showed no mercy to those with psychological disorders.[128] The military judicial system identified, isolated, and channeled this unusable human matériel through the penal system, eventually dismissing nonconformists from service. Dismissal, of course, meant incarceration in a civilian concentration camp. Alternatively, the Wehrmacht often did the dirty work itself, executing recalcitrant soldiers after they committed an offense threatened by death. This action may have "purified the Volksgemeinschaft," but the individuals who were purged were those who could not or would not subordinate themselves to military order, not those disliked by the regime. Communists, pacifists, and "asocials" could remain in the Wehrgemeischaft if they conformed to military order.[129]

The ruthless system of "personnel management" stands as one more indictment of the Wehrmacht. It demonstrates just how far Germany's military chiefs would go to assist the regime in achieving its foreign political goals. The Wehrmacht's readiness to turn soldiers over to the ss is a clear illustration of its seamless (and voluntary) integration into the apparatus of state.

Nevertheless, these were issues of personnel management. An OKH memo nicely summarizes the purpose of the field penal camps and penal battalions in the following text of a circular published in the fall of 1942. It clearly explains the objectives of the Wehrmacht's newest penal institutions:

Atonement and Deterrent Doctrine (*Abschreckungsgedanke*)

Through the severity of the punishment . . . it must be brought strikingly and clearly to the consciousness of prisoners or the penal camp inmates respectively that they have transgressed severely, and for this, they have brought upon themselves and must feel palpably punishment in the form of the deprivation of freedom of the most varied type. The knowledge of this severity must deter others from committing similar crimes. Only if this knowledge actually comes to the consciousness of wider circles will the punishment fulfill its purpose.

Improvement and Educational Doctrine

It must be clear to prisoners and penal camp inmates (*Verwahrten*) that they can "ascend" with good conduct; that is, they can earn alleviation and privileges . . . which promotes them so far that they can be proposed for parole with the regular troops, or transfer from a penal camp for the orderly execution of the punishment. But they must first of all feel the full severity of the punishment. . . . Every alleviation of suffering presumes an especial merit of the prisoners or penal camp inmates through flawless conduct and good performance.

Work Doctrine

The work is not the punishment; much more the circumstances and burdens under which it must be carried out should deter the prisoners or penal camp inmates respectively and all the people (*Allgemeinheit*) in general. A different interpretation would degrade the work of the front fighters, which in part is just as hard and difficult. For this work, which the prisoners carry out in the interest of the whole as important to the war effort and which supplies a criterion for his performance evaluation, the inmates must be kept physically and mentally fresh and fit for work through suitable measures.[130]

The circular clearly establishes deterrence as a primary objective of the two penal institutions, with the idea that the inmates ultimately should be reclaimed if they fully subordinated themselves to military order. In fact, it was almost never too late to conform. The field penal camps were liquidated in early 1945, and their most recalcitrant inmates were sent to concentration camps. The provisions, however, still allowed for reintegration into the troops if, after arriving in a concentration camp, an inmate demonstrated that he might become a usable soldier.[131]

Reclamation, not societal purification, remained the Wehrmacht's objective. Regardless of the crime that led to an individual's incarceration in a penal unit, the Wehrmacht's special penal formations had been geared toward reclaiming those who had temporarily forgotten their duty or committed a one-time blunder, recycling this manpower, and sending these soldiers back into the field sufficiently motivated to contribute to the *Endsieg* (the final victory). The Wehrmacht, following Hitler's wish to adapt punishments to the war situation after the blitzkrieg's failure, diligently provided the führer with a graduated system of punishment.

In short, the Wehrmacht created a machine for the recycling of its usable human matériel through the most brutal methods. The machine also aided in the destruction of any unusable human matériel in seamless cooperation with the ss, regardless of the reason for the inmates' failure. The men at the machine's controls—the staff officers who designed the formations, the Gerichtsherren exercising ultimate authority over the inmates, and the formations' command and supervisory staffs—had not been members of the ss but regular army officers, NCOs, and enlisted personnel.

Tempo über alles

Based on the Wehrmacht's predictions about total war, Wehrmacht-justiz was devised with speed in mind. As the war unfolded, Germany's military chiefs concluded that the Wehrmacht's management of convicted soldiers also required streamlining. The Wehrmacht's processing of parolees and prisoners, it was decided, needed to be accelerated in order to meet the demands of the total war that Germany had unleashed.

The OKW's Directive for the Execution of Punishments in War and Special Operations of September 30, 1939, was the first step in tweaking the Wehrmacht's management of convicted soldiers. When confirming verdicts, Gerichtsherren simultaneously submitted specific instructions on how the court-imposed punishment should be executed. Commonly referred to as the "completion decision," these instructions were very specific. The OKW's September 30, 1939, directive stipulated that henceforth a Gerichtsherr could change his completion decision if necessary. The intent, of course, was to provide commanders with greater flexibility in the management of prisoners. According to section 5 of the directive, Gerichtsherren could:

> a. suspend the remainder of the sentence after partial atonement of the punishment and give the convicted an opportunity for parole, or order the prisoner transferred to a Wehrmacht penal camp;

b. in cases in which he has already given the convicted an opportunity for parole, order the execution of the punishment or a transfer to a Wehrmacht penal camp;

c. interrupt maintenance in a penal camp of the Wehrmacht and give the convicted an opportunity for parole or order the completion of the punishment.[132]

These guidelines allowed the Gerichtsherr to transfer prisoners at any time from prison to parole and back again, depending on the inmate's or parolee's conduct as well as the division's immediate personnel requirements.

In addition, when revoking a parole the Gerichtsherr had two options. The first option was to transfer a parolee to a penal institution where time in detention was calculated as time served, such as a Wehrmacht prison. Conversely, the second option was to transfer a parolee to an institution in which time in detention *was not* calculated as time served, such as a penal camp. The difference between the two options, of course, was no small matter for a prisoner. If a soldier received a one-year prison sentence but was incarcerated in a penal camp, he could in theory (and occasionally in reality) spend more than twelve months in custody, yet his judicially imposed sentence would still not be considered as atoned.

The provisions in the OKW's directive of September 30, 1939, it has been alleged, had a sinister purpose: ensuring that no soldier convicted of a crime could ever escape the clutches of the military judicial system. Allowing commanders to freely transfer men in and out of penal institutions where time was not calculated as time served, according to the legend, meant that no prisoner could ever hope to actually serve out his full sentence and return to the troops as a free soldier. In essence, the provision turned prisoners into *Freiwild*, persons without rights who could be sacrificed at anytime. The penal provisions were intentionally designed to keep convicted soldiers forever under Damocles' sword.[133]

Documentation supporting these allegations, however, has not been produced. On the contrary, the case files indicate that prisoners/parolees were sent to such penal institutions exclusively for failure to conform, not for the purpose of preventing the full atonement of a sentence. Perhaps just as important, the documents reveal that commanders often paroled large groups of prisoners simultaneously for major operations, indicating that the penal system functioned as a reserve pool, not as a Freiwild trap. If soldiers remained under Damocles' sword for long periods of time, this can be explained by the fact that parole had been intended to last for the duration, which the optimistic military leadership did not expect would be past 1941.[134]

When the Wehrmacht turned west in 1940, it encountered problems in the parole process. According to the regulations, the officer who initially issued a completion order was the only one who could subsequently change it. In other words, the original Gerichtsherr continued to have jurisdiction over a soldier after a verdict's confirmation. This applied regardless of where a soldier had been imprisoned or paroled in the interim, and regardless of the location of his original unit.[135] As a result, conduct reports and case files had to be shuttled between the original court and the institution or unit in possession of the prisoner or parolee in order to grant or revoke a parole. From a personnel management perspective, this caused unacceptable delays.

Therefore, on May 18, 1940, eight days into the French campaign, the Seventh Ordinance for the Implementation and Supplementing of the Wartime Judicial Procedure Code changed section 104 of the penal code. Henceforth, the provision stipulated that "the commander who has confirmed the verdict, *or a Gerichtsherr empowered by him* [emphasis mine], can change the completion decision for important reasons."[136]

Many commanders apparently failed to expressly empower subsequent Gerichtsherren, because section 104 underwent further modification after the attack on the Soviet Union. Communication problems in the east led to intolerable delays, especially when commanders did not empower Gerichtsherren to make changes.[137] Therefore, on April 7, 1942, the Eighth Ordinance for the Implementation and Supplementing of the Wartime Judicial Procedure Code modified two sections of the Wartime Judicial Procedure Code. Section 102, paragraph 2, now read as follows: "The first decision over the execution of punishment is made by the commander who confirms the sentence; moreover, he can for important reasons reserve to himself the right to make any changes to it. If he . . . does not reserve the right to change the decision to himself, then the Gerichtsherr is competent for this decision under whom the convicted is subordinated; he instead makes all decisions that are necessary during the execution of the sentence."[138]

Section 104, paragraph 2, now simply read: "The completion decision can be changed for important reasons."[139]

Before these modifications, the original Gerichtsherr had to expressly empower subsequent commanders to make changes. Now, however, all succeeding Gerichtsherren could alter a completion decision, unless the original Gerichtsherr reserved that authority for himself. In other words, if the commander did not specifically claim this authority, he automatically relinquished control over a prisoner or parolee as soon as the soldier left his commander's jurisdiction to be delivered to a prison, penal formation, or parole unit. Whatever the prisoner's or parolee's destination or location, he automatically fell under the authority of the commander whose jurisdiction he entered. The new Gerichtsherr could make changes in his status as a prisoner or parolee on the spot—no red tape, no delay.

On January 25, 1945, in a last attempt to forestall the inevitable, Field Marshal Keitel declared that the situation required the mobilization of "every German that can carry a weapon." He thus ordered that "all prisoners still useable, physically capable, and worthy of parole" be sent immediately to the parole battalion reserve formation at Brünn. According to Keitel's order, the Gerichtsherr did not have to be consulted; he just had to be informed that a prison inmate had been paroled and that, henceforth, the decision devolved to the prison commandants. Seeking the Gerichtsherren's permission with the Allies closing in would have taken far too much time.[140]

One additional arrangement to reduce delay in managing convicted soldiers came with the introduction of the penal platoon (*Strafvollstreckungszug*). Implemented at the army and division levels, these penal formations allowed lightly punished individuals to serve their sentence at the front, eliminating costly travel time. This not only accelerated the atonement and parole process, it also alleviated manpower problems. By ordering a prisoner to serve his sentence in a divisional penal platoon, the Gerichtsherr never relinquished jurisdiction over his human matériel.

Unfortunately, little has been written about the penal platoons. Norbert Haase, for example, simply notes that the penal platoons were established for the further acceleration of the atonement process.[141] According to Franz Seidler, the Wehrmacht introduced the penal platoons in 1944, but no central regulations existed for their operating procedures and methods.[142] However, the case files suggest that the penal platoons might have been introduced as early as late 1942.[143] The case files also indicate that the commander of the 253rd Infantry Division made extensive use of his unit's penal platoon. *Tempo über alles.*

PART TWO

Sex under the Swastika

THE REGIME, THE WEHRMACHT, AND THE CASE FILES

CHAPTER FIVE

Method and Selection of Case Files

The Federal Archives Central Documentation Agency in Aachen-Kornelimünster houses all surviving military judicial case files from the Nazi era in Germany's possession. The collection includes approximately one hundred and ten thousand case files that fell into the Western Allies' hands at the conclusion of the Second World War. These files subsequently were returned to the Federal Republic of Germany. The agency also possesses fifty-five thousand case files that fell into Soviet hands in 1945.[1] The files were initially stored in the German Democratic Republic's Potsdam military archive but were moved to the Aachen-Kornelimünster facility after reunification. They are now designated the Eastern Collection (Bestand Ost).[2]

While archivists in the former Federal Republic chose to catalogue and store the case files by unit, East German archivists chose to catalogue the case files by offense. With sex offenses representing only 1 to 2 percent of all cases that came before courts-martial during the war, the East German cataloguing method has proved fortuitous for this study. Retrieving a significant sample of sex offense case files from the (former) West German collection would have required the examination of hundreds of punishment lists or thousands of individual case files in order to obtain a sufficient number of relevant cases. (The punishment lists allow the identification of courts-martial, but that does not guarantee that the specific case file survived the war. In fact, only about 10 percent of the case files survived, rendering the use of punishment lists for the selection of case files quite laborious.)[3] However, with the Eastern Collection's case files already catalogued and stored by offense, its 418 sex offense case files could be retrieved and exploited easily. At least four dozen different courts are represented in the Eastern Collection's sex offense subgroup, providing an excellent basis for delineating commonalities and variations in jurisprudence.

In contrast to previous scholarly efforts, this study concentrates primarily on what the military judicial authorities (including but not limited to the courts, officers functioning as Gerichtsherren, their staff legal advisers, and the commanders of the penal and parole institutions) reported and wrote about individuals ensnared in the military judicial machinery, rather than simply presenting statistics on how many soldiers received (or did not receive) draconian punishments.[4] Although statistics are addressed, this investigation's main objectives are to discover how the authorities evaluated those falling afoul of the law, to identify the factors that the authorities considered when reintegrating convicted sex offenders, to gain a better picture of the military judicial process, and to assess to what degree Nazi ideology permeated this process.

More than 40 percent of the Eastern Collection's 418 sex offense case files represent legal processes for violations of paragraph 175, the criminal code against homosexuality. Finding sufficient material for this offense therefore did not present a problem, and only those case files for proceedings against violations of paragraph 175 undertaken by *army* courts-martial have been included in the study.[5] In order to obtain a substantial sample of case files for sex offenses that came before courts infrequently, such as child molestation and incest, it was necessary to include judicial proceedings against air force personnel.

Many case files contained in the Eastern Collection are nearly empty, containing only a few pretrial or post-trial documents. Because this study's primary objective is to discover how the military judicial authorities evaluated sex offenders and not the documentation of unassailable statistics, case files that are extremely fragmentary have been excluded from the sample.[6]

In addition to the documents contained in the Eastern Collection, the surviving sex offense case files from two typical front-line formations, the Sixth and 253rd Infantry Divisions, were identified and retrieved from the former Federal Republic's case file collection.[7] Unfortunately, the surviving case files for these two divisions contained only a handful of processes against sex offenders, primarily for violations of paragraph 175, rendering any in-depth analysis of other categories of sex offenses impossible.[8] Also, surviving sex offense case files from the Court of the Wehrmacht Commander–Berlin were included in the case file sample in order to gauge any differences in jurisprudence between this large and important garrison's court, which was situated in proximity to Nazi Germany's political and military center of power, and the active and reserve field courts scattered across German-oc-cupied Europe.[9]

Whether this selection method has produced a case file sample that is representative of the everyday reality of Wehrmachtjustiz is difficult to assess. According to Messerschmidt and Wüllner, death sentences imposed by army courts-martial and ultimately carried out would not be present in the Central Documentation Agency's collection because these case files did not survive the war.[10] This fact, however, does not pose insurmountable problems for this investigation. According to the Wehrmacht Criminal Statistics, only one soldier received the death sentence for violating paragraph 175 between January 1940 and the end of 1942. Considering that nearly 4,600 individuals came before military courts during this three-year period for homosexual offenses, it seems safe to assume that the case file sample selected for this investigation, which yielded one death sentence for violations of paragraph 175, is fairly representative of Wehrmachtjustiz.[11]

Although the official statistics catalogue rape, child molestation, and incest together with other (non-homosexual) sexual offenses, a few assumptions nevertheless can be made about the frequency of the death penalty in rape cases. An assessment of the death sentence card-file index at the Central Documentation Agency reveals that courts imposed the death penalty for rape crimes very infrequently. When courts did impose the death sentence, the perpetrator usually had committed other serious crimes in conjunction with rape.[12] Ludwig Hannemann reports that none of the 256 sailors receiving the death sentence in his sample had been convicted for rape.[13] If one considers that scholars generally regard the naval administration of justice as the most draconian among the three services, one can safely assume a low percentage of death sentences for rape crimes for the entire Wehrmacht, most likely less than 1 percent. In the case file sample for this study, eighty individuals were convicted for rape crimes. With the sample yielding one death sentence, it appears fairly representative.

More than four hundred case files for legal processes conducted by military courts were examined for this study. If one assumes, based on the death sentence rates for homosexual offenses and rape esti-mated above, that sex offenses in general brought the death sentence at an overall rate of less than 1 percent, less than four death sentences would be expected in the four hundred case file sample, which indeed proved to be the case (one death sentence for rape and one for a homosexual offense). Thus it seems safe to assume that the case files held in the Federal Archives Central Documentation Agency are fairly representative of the military judicial *Alltag* with regard to sex offenders. Again, however neither unassailable statistics nor the enumeration of every single draconian (or disproportionately light) punishment handed down for sex offenses is the objective of this study. The primary goal here is to ascertain what factors the military judicial authorities deemed most important in the prosecution and punishment of sex offenders and what issues the authorities considered before reintegrating convicted sex offenders into the troops.

One final important point must be made. No method exists for determining whether the testimony and evidence as recapitulated in the documents correspond to the actual events. Although Wehrmachtjustiz did not conduct show trials, verifying the validity of the courts' conclusions and interpretations is impossible, nor can it be determined if confessions or testimony were extracted by force, which of course, would be no surprise. In the cases presented then, the information contained in the court transcripts, even if not the whole truth and nothing but the truth, will be accepted as the courts' honest interpretation of the evidence, even if that evidence was extracted by forceful means.

CHAPTER SIX

Homosexuality and Violations of Paragraph 175

Perhaps more than any other offense, the Wehrmacht's handling of servicemen convicted for violating paragraph 175, the criminal code against homosexuality, demonstrates its concern for the recycling of usable human matériel and the maintenance of the Wehrgemeinschaft. Homosexual cases also illustrate the great variations in jurisprudence and sentencing practices that characterized the everyday reality of Wehrmachtjustiz. Close scrutiny of the case files also reveals the dominance of the Gerichtsherren in the military judicial process.

Paragraph 175
After the Weimar Republic's (relatively) liberal treatment of homosexuals, the Third Reich established new criteria for the prosecution of homosexuals.[1] With the *Röhm Putsch* in 1934, homosexuals became public enemies, and Nazi leaders proclaimed the extermination of these "genetic contagions" (*Volksseuche*) a national priority.[2] Hitler and Himmler classified gays along with criminals, "asocials," and Jews as "deviant subhumans." The führer and *Reichsführer-ss* vowed to eradicate these "cosmic lice."[3]

Upon unification, Imperial Germany had incorporated the Prussian penal code against homosexuality as paragraph 175 into the Reich Criminal Code of 1871.[4] From 1871 to 1935, the provision threatened punishment only for sodomy (*widernatürliche Unzucht*). In practice, the courts interpreted the law narrowly and considered as punishable only those acts that simulated heterosexual intercourse.[5]

Proving such activity in court proved to be exasperatingly difficult as far as Himmler and other fanatics were concerned. Therefore, on the heels of the Röhm Putsch, the regime modified the provisions in 1935 to both facilitate and broaden the scope of prosecution. Struck from paragraph 175, "sodomy" was replaced simply with the word "indecency" (*Unzucht*).[6] Henceforth, all "indecent activities" (*unzüchtige Treiben*), not just coitus, became punishable.[7] The modified and amended penal code "encompassed any form of 'criminal indecency' between men," as well as any personal conduct that offended "public morality" or aroused "sexual desires in oneself or strangers."[8] Henceforth, even enticing glances between men could lead to prosecution under paragraph 175.[9] In fact, according to precedent established in 1935, any act violating the "people's healthy sense of morality" could be punished, effectively nullifying the long established principle of "no law, no crime."[10]

Paragraphs 175 and 175a contained the following provisions:

Paragraph 175

1. A male who indulges in criminally indecent activity with another male or who allows himself to participate in such activity will be punished with imprisonment.

2. If one of the participants is under the age of twenty-one and if the offense has not been grave, the court may dispense with the sentence of imprisonment.

Paragraph 175a

A term of penal servitude up to ten years, or if mitigating circumstances can be established, a term of imprisonment of no less than three months will be imposed upon:

1. Any male who by force or threat of violence to life and limb compels another man to indulge in criminally indecent activities or allows himself to be used for such activities;

2. Any male who forces another male to indulge with him in criminally indecent activities by using the subordinate position of the other man, whether it be at work or elsewhere, or who allows himself to participate in such activities;

3. Any male over twenty-one years who seduces a male person under twenty-one years to participate in criminally indecent activities or anyone under twenty-one who allows himself to be used for such activities.

4. Any male who indulges professionally and for profit in criminally indecent activities with other males or allows himself to be used for such activities or who offers himself for the same.[11]

Heinrich Himmler, the driving force behind the persecution of homosexuals, pursued what he considered to be deviant sexuality to the point of obsession, and his antipathy toward homosexuals went far beyond traditional homophobia. Demonstrating the link that he perceived between homosexuality, genetic health, and population policy, Himmler established in 1936 the Reich Central Security Office for Combating Homosexuality and Abortion.[12] Although Burkhard Jellonnek has effectively destroyed the legend of a Reich-wide uniform homosexual holocaust, Himmler and other fanatics indeed had been determined to eradicate homosexual practices, if not the entire homosexual population itself.[13] The Reichsführer-SS, more than any other Nazi leader, "articulated the sexual policies and fears of the Third Reich. If Hitler clothed himself in respectability mainly to win popular support, Himmler seemed obsessed with the danger of deviant sexuality to the Third Reich."[14] Although indeed particularly virulent, Nazi homophobia can be characterized as little more than a confused mix of traditional stereotypes, clichés, and pseudoscientific racial theories. It contained four basic elements.

First, homosexuality endangered the German nation. By renouncing their duty to procreate, homosexuals deprived Germany of valuable offspring, putting the Aryan race's future at risk. Second, the true homosexual endeavored to seduce every youth with whom he came into contact. Himmler and other theorists believed that youths seduced by homosexuals developed "degenerate personalities." They, in turn, became seducers themselves, spreading homosexuality like a virulent contagion.

According to Maiwald and Mischler, the Nazis appropriated Kraepelin and Bonhoeffer's infectious disease theory (*Seuchentheorie*) of homosexuality. The theory attributed homosexuality to the seduction of youths by older men. Through this seduction, homosexuals infected "the entire body of the Volk with the disease of homosexuality."[15] In 1937, *Das Schwarz Korps*, for example, asserted that only 2 percent of all homosexuality was congenital. Nevertheless, this 2 percent could be expected to "corrupt two million German men."[16] Himmler, however, thought that most homosexuals could be reeducated through hard work. On the other hand, he also believed that "seducers" were incurable. As traitors, they had to be eradicated.[17]

Third, Nazi homophobes assumed that the ties between homosexuals were tighter than their ties to the state. Therefore, all homosexuals represented potential enemies of the state. Extending this assumption further, Nazi homophobes feared that homosexuals, because of their close ties, would form cliques in government, first dominating whole departments and then entire areas of government. Finally, Himmler and other homophobes believed that homosexuals, as "deviants," were criminally inclined.[18]

This confused brew of clichés and Nazi pseudoscience drove Himmler on his crusade to stamp out the "contagion." The crusade reached its peak between 1937 and 1939 when the regime convicted twenty-five thousand German men and adolescents for violations (real or imagined) of paragraph 175 and 175a, approximately half of all those convicted for homosexuality during the Third Reich. The intensity of this period suggests that the "radicalizing impact of the war" was not what fueled the regime's "persecutory drives." Before the modifications to the criminal code in 1935, the number of convictions amounted to only several hundred annually.[19]

If the Wehrmacht had perceived homosexuality through the Nazi lens, it undoubtedly would have considered homosexuality to be particularly dangerous to the armed forces. No special provisions, however, had been incorporated into the military criminal code. The military administration of justice prosecuted homosexual acts by servicemen during the Third Reich according to the civil codes. Military courts after 1935 also followed their civilian counterparts, prosecuting soldiers, sailors, and airmen for any "indecent" activity, not just coitus-like (*beischlafähnlich*) acts. However, in contrast to the civilian sphere, where a mere glance could land an individual in the "protective" custody of the Gestapo,[20] in the Wehrmacht, specific homosexual activity had to occur before charges were leveled, and the minimum requirement usually was contact (or attempted contact) with an individual's genitals.[21]

The fact that the Wehrmacht took an exacting approach is not necessarily an indication that it looked favorably upon homosexuals or intimate contact between men. In the Prussian tradition, punishments could indeed be severe.[22] But while the civilian authorities after 1940 automatically transferred individuals violating paragraph 175 to concentration camps after they had atoned their judicially imposed punishments, the Wehrmacht reintegrated the majority of offenders back into the troops.[23]

The courts represented in the case files demonstrate great diversity in jurisprudence and sentencing practices when prosecuting individuals committing homosexual offenses. Court reactions range from indifference to traditional homophobia and stereotyping and, in a few cases, to obvious outrage.[24] However, simple cases of same-sex intimacy seldom provoked more than mild reproaches from the bench, with each count for first-time offenders normally bringing a prison sentence of three to six months. More importantly, the majority of these sentences were partially or fully suspended in favor of parole at the front. It should also be noted that the type of sexual contact seldom proved to be the courts' decisive yardstick when allocating punishments: manual contact with the genitals could bring punishments equal to, and even longer than, punishments for oral and anal sex. As a rule, the courts characterized sexual acts between men as offensive to the "people's healthy sense of morality," according to the 1935 precedent.

When allocating punishments, however, the courts most frequently cited the maintenance of Manneszucht as a central factor in their decisions, consistently stressing the danger that homosexual activity (allegedly) poses to morale and discipline within the ranks. This was especially true after the winter of 1941–42 as the war continued with no end in sight. After the blitzkrieg's failure, the courts frequently justified aggravating circumstances (and hence more severe punishments) by citing the "increasing duration of the war, which increases the danger of these types of offenses" and "the difficulty in preventing such offenses as the war gets longer," or words to this effect.

For servicemen, one provision introduced during the war was of special significance. Most likely under pressure from Himmler, Hitler declared that the military had been "too lenient in its treatment of deviants," and in May 1943 the Wehrmacht introduced a "habitual offender" (*Hangtäter*) review process that classified offenders into three categories: (1) incorrigible homosexuals; (2) men who committed one or two infractions, possibly after being seduced; and (3) those whose inclination was dubious. All personnel convicted for a homosexual offense after the May 1943 implementation date were subject to this review process. Commanders at the army level or higher reviewed each case and determined the offender's status according to the new classification system. According to the guidelines, individuals falling into category 2 should be punished severely but "rehabilitated." Individuals falling into category 3 should be sent to a penal unit and returned to the troops if they could be rehabilitated. Individuals falling into category 1, as "incorrigible" homosexuals, had to be dismissed from service and turned over to the Gestapo. As a rule, being turned over to the Gestapo meant incarceration in a concentration camp.[25]

The review process also included an evaluation of individuals who had been court-martialed for homosexuality but who nevertheless had returned to duty before the review process's implementation. Divisional commanders submitted opinions to the reserve army commander, who made the ultimate decision. Those who had rejoined the ranks after a homosexual offense could be dismissed from service if the military judicial authorities determined that they possessed a true homosexual inclination, even if they had not committed a subsequent violation of paragraph 175 since returning to duty. According to the provisions, however, only those reintegrated into the regular troops before the review process was implemented should undergo the habitual offender review.[26] Those still detained in penal units and prisons *were not subject to review*.

The origin and intent of this provision need to be investigated. As mentioned above, the habitual offender review most likely was implemented at Himmler's behest. The OKH may have insisted on the provision's inclusion in the guidelines in order to protect its human matériel as follows. If an individual returned to the troops after a conviction for homosexual activity, presumably the military judicial authorities would have viewed him as a low risk for a future violation. This individual therefore would more than likely survive the habitual offender review process and remain in the military. Conversely, an individual deemed an unacceptable risk and therefore not reintegrated also would remain under the military's auspices because, according to the provision under discussion, he would not be subject to the review process. He would remain available to the Wehrmacht for service in special penal units.

This provision should not be interpreted as an indication that the Wehrmacht was acting out of compassion for homosexuals or intentionally protected them from the regime. It merely suggests that the

Wehrmacht desired to husband its human materiel. However, further investigation of the provision's origin and intent is needed.

Richard Plant contends that, because of manpower considerations, the Wehrmacht did not implement the review process for homosexual offenders demanded by Himmler (nor subsequent stricter policies).[27] However, the case files reveal that the Wehrmacht did indeed dismiss convicted soldiers from service and turn them over to the civilian authorities. However, it happened much less frequently than one would expect, given the increasing persecution of homosexuals in the civilian sphere. Of the 203 individuals in the case files who were convicted for violations of paragraph 175 and 175a, only thirteen, or 6.4 percent, were dismissed from service as habitual homosexual offenders.

The case files also indicate that the military judicial authorities required insurmountable evidence of an individual's same-sex orientation before sacrificing the Wehrmacht's human matériel.[28] On the other hand, the Wehrmacht had few reservations about cooperating with the Gestapo to rid the military of individuals who could not control their homosexual desires. To the military mind, such individuals presented a serious threat to the martial apparatus.

Unlike individuals dismissed as habitual offenders, individuals sentenced to penal servitude and discharged from the armed forces as "unworthy of military service" remained under the military's jurisdiction. The Wehrmacht turned these individuals over to the Reich Administration of Justice for incarceration in the Emsland camps. These prisoners, however, could be paroled to a regular unit or mobilized for service in a penal formation at any time. An individual discharged as a homosexual habitual offender was permanently excluded from service. Once that individual was placed in police custody, the Wehrmacht relinquished all control over him.

According to myth, the courts prosecuted homosexual offenders for "subversion" under Wartime Penal Code section 5a in order to impose lengthy penal servitude sentences. Erich Schwinge effectively refutes this legend, yet his conclusion that penal servitude sentences for homosexual violations represented a "seldom exception" is inaccurate.[29] Punishments in the Prussian tradition could indeed be severe. Approximately 8 percent of the homosexual offenders encountered in the case file sample received penal servitude sentences.

Unfortunately, as reproduced in the secondary literature, the Wehrmacht Criminal Statistics do not provide percentages for homosexual offenders receiving prison and penal servitude sentences, so it is impossible to assess whether the case file sample can be considered truly representative. The statistics, however, do reveal that between the war's outbreak and the end of 1942, the courts imposed the death sentence for a homosexual offense in only one case out of thousands.[30] In the case files, only one of the more than two hundred individuals convicted for violations of paragraph 175 received the death penalty. Therefore, based on the average implied in the criminal statistics, one could say that the death penalty is actually overrepresented in this study.[31]

Repeat Offenders and Reintegration

Himmler and other fanatics demonstrated great concern about Germany's "sexual balance sheet" when it came to homosexuals.[32] The military judicial authorities, however, were far more concerned with the maintenance of Manneszucht and manpower, and they carefully weighed an offender's potential for successful reintegration back into the Wehrgemeinschaft after a conviction for violations of paragraph 175.[33]

The Wehrmacht, however, did not automatically brand individuals convicted for same-sex intimacy as homosexuals. In fact, it called up known homosexuals, including those who had been convicted and incarcerated as civilians for violations of paragraph 175. In the case file sample, at least thirty-one of the individuals court-martialed for homosexual conduct as soldiers also had civilian convictions for homosexual activity.[34] Two of these had even worn the pink triangle, the patch that identified prisoners as homosexuals, spending part of their incarceration period in concentration camps.[35] Indeed, the Wehrmacht gave even repeat offenders the opportunity to rejoin the Wehrgemeinschaft after civilian or military judicial convictions for violations of paragraph 175. Those ultimately willing to practice abstinence and submit fully to military order could remain in uniform.[36]

With repeat offenders, the courts frequently cited alcohol use or enforced abstinence as justifications for relatively lenient punishments.

Conversely, they exploited previous convictions to justify harsh sentences. However, as in most sex offense cases, the judicially imposed sentence was largely symbolic. Courts weighed the mitigating or aggravating factors against the established sentencing parameters to arrive at a "just" punishment, but the commanding officers who functioned as Gerichtsherren ultimately determined how long prisoners remained incarcerated. Not only masters of the courts, the Gerichtsherren were also masters of atonement.

Take, for example, the case of grenadier Ernst E. With a civilian conviction for violating paragraph 175, he was convicted on similar charges in 1942 by the Court of the 346th Infantry Division. His sentence was six months' imprisonment.[37] The Gerichtsherr confirmed the verdict but ordered the sentence served as six weeks of intensified arrest.[38] Ernst E. rejoined his unit after serving the abbreviated punishment. Staff Lance Corporal Johann H., another repeat offender, also benefited from his commander's power as Gerichtsherr and the Wehrmacht's desire to husband its human matériel. Johann H. received six months' imprisonment in 1942 for a repeat 175 offense.[39] As in Ernst E.'s case, the Gerichtsherr ordered Johann H. to serve only six weeks of the judicially imposed punishment, and the twice-convicted homosexual offender indeed returned to his unit after six weeks.

The 1940 case of Corporal Karl W. also demonstrates the Wehrmacht's willingness to reintegrate repeat offenders, even those receiving the most draconian of punishments. Sentenced to a lengthy term of penal servitude, Karl W. languished in the Emsland concentration camp complex for twenty months, yet he ultimately returned to duty. Despite civilian and military judicial convictions for violations that indicated he was more than likely a homosexual and quite possibly a pedophile, he received parole in 1942 and rejoined the regular troops.[40]

Reintegration rates, in fact, remained high even after the introduction of the habitual offender review process in May 1943. The case files from the war's second half indicate that, despite the radicalizing impact of the war and increasing pressure from ideologues, the Wehrmacht still required considerable evidence of an individual's same-sex orientation before refusing to consider reintegration. Sergeant Erwin B.'s case provides such an example. Known to the

police as a homosexual since 1932, he ran afoul of the civilian authorities in 1936, receiving a ten-month prison sentence for violating paragraph 175. The Court of the Ninety-fifth Infantry Division
sentenced him to eight months' imprisonment for a new violation
in 1943. With an otherwise impeccable service record and characterized in his fitness report as a diligent soldier "proven before the
enemy," Erwin B.'s entire sentence was suspended in favor of an
immediate parole by the Gerichtsherr. The two-time homosexual
offender and long-time object of police scrutiny thus remained a
member of the Wehrgemeinschaft. The case files contain many such
examples.[41]

Commanding officers functioning as Gerichtsherren dominated the
military judicial process. They, not the jurists, confirmed verdicts, determined where and how long prisoners atoned their punishments,
and without question controlled the reintegration process. An offender's willingness to carry a weapon in good faith, his martial qualities,
and the military's manpower requirements, not tolerance for homosexuals on the part of the Wehrmacht, were the primary factors in
the Gerichtsherren's decisions. The following case, reviewed in detail,
is representative of the military judicial Alltag and reflects the previously outlined trends.

Paul H.

The Court of the Fifty-second Infantry Division sentenced Private Paul
H. to eighteen months imprisonment in October 1940 for four violations of paragraph 175.[42] With a previous civilian conviction for homosexual activity, the defendant in this case had participated in anal
and oral sex before and after his induction. The court, referring to his
confession and good conduct, granted mitigating circumstances and
imposed five months' imprisonment for each infraction.[43] (According
to the penal codes, the sentences did not run consecutively. Instead,
multiple punishments were combined and calculated according to a
predetermined formula, which in this case totaled eighteen months.)
The Gerichtsherr confirmed the verdict and ordered the punishment
completed.[44]

Paul H. was incarcerated and assigned to a mobile prison unit
(*Wehrmachtgefangenenabteilung*). The OKW and OKH issued decrees

on March 25, 1941, mandating a review of prisoners suitable for parole. In response, the prison unit commander proposed that Paul H. be paroled to a regular formation. He emphasized that Paul H. could "again be a useable soldier" and lauded the prisoner's efforts to "make up for his failure."[45] In May, the commanding officer and Gerichtsherr of the Fifty-second Infantry Division, noting the absence of operations, rejected the parole petition. When units are at rest, he asserted, homosexuals form an "extraordinary danger." He also contended that Paul H. was not even a good candidate for the parole battalions because he was "considerably pre-punished," referring to Paul H.'s two convictions for violations of paragraph 175.

After the Barbarossa campaign began, the prison unit commander submitted a second favorable report in July, and the Gerichtsherr and commander of Fortresses Upper-Rhein, who now had jurisdiction over Paul H., paroled the twice-convicted homosexual offender to a regular unit.[46]

This case illustrates the Wehrmacht's willingness to reintegrate repeat homosexual offenders, especially those with good service records and a demonstrated willingness to carry a weapon in good faith. It also suggests the influence of manpower considerations on the reintegration process. The commander of the Fifty-second Infantry Division rejected the first parole proposal, explaining in his decision that "homosexuals present an extraordinary danger [to the troops] at rest." On the basis of Paul H.'s record, he assumed that Paul H. possessed a same-sex orientation and clearly documented this position. The Gerichtsherr who subsequently received jurisdiction for this case presumably discounted fears about the "danger" posed by Paul H.'s inclination when the Barbarossa campaign demanded manpower. Thus, Paul H., who admitted during his court-martial to homosexual activity that stretched over several years and included at least four partners, rejoined the Wehrgemeinschaft.

The examples discussed here are not presented to suggest that the military administration of justice under Hitler was benign. Incarceration in every Wehrmacht penal institution subjected detainees to the harshest treatment, and parole placed very high physical and emotional demands on parolees. On the other hand, the military judicial authorities required considerable evidence of an individual's same-sex orientation before dispensing draconian punishments with no chance for eventual reintegration into the Wehrgemeinschaft.

With repeat offenders being reintegrated at high rates, it should come as no surprise that first-time offenders also experienced high reintegration rates. Many soldiers with clean records committed violations of paragraph 175. For homosexuals and heterosexuals alike, the war experience creates conditions that can facilitate a homosexual encounter. The courts characterized such incidents as "one-time blunders" (*einmalige Entgleisung*). In fact, this was the courts' most frequent justification for granting mitigating circumstances, imposing (relatively) mild punishments, and facilitating rapid reintegration. By classifying a homosexual encounter as a one-time occurrence, the courts avoided stigmatizing the individual as a homosexual.

In order to characterize a violation of paragraph 175 as a one-time blunder, the courts often cited alcohol consumption, long periods of abstinence, and even the enforced closeness of military life. It is not clear whether the one-time blunder had its origin in a Reich Supreme Military Court decision or whether it was an invention of the lower courts. The courts represented in the case files generously characterized many infractions as one-time blunders, even with repeat offenders.[47]

Paragraph 175a

If the preceding examples suggest relative tolerance on the part of the military judicial authorities, it should not be assumed that the military administration of justice was benign or that homosexuals received compassionate understanding. Punishments could indeed be severe, especially for violations of paragraph 175a. Paragraph 175a provided for more severe punishment if one of the participants in a homosexual encounter was under twenty-one (175a, number 3) or if a superior abused his authority in order to coerce subordinates to engage in same-sex intimacy (175a, number 2).

Although the courts, as a rule, dealt ruthlessly with superiors who abused their authority to facilitate intimate contact with subordinates, their treatment of older men engaging in sexual activity with young partners (under twenty-one) covered the spectrum of intensity. In many cases, the courts went to great lengths to shield defendants

from the more severe punishments by expressly (or implicitly) rejecting the application of paragraph 175a in favor of paragraph 175. The
Court of the 299th Infantry Division, for example, refused in 1942
to invoke paragraph 175a, number 3, during the trial of corporal
Heinz S., who had intimate contact with two unit members under the
age of twenty-one. Instead, the court applied paragraph 175 and its
milder punishment parameters. The court's reasoning? "Soldiers in
the field," it observed, "are considered adults without respect to their
age."[48] This justification for not invoking paragraph 175a finds no
mention in the criminal codes, nor is it likely to have been a Reich Supreme Military Court precedent. The Gerichtsherr suspended Heinz
S.'s prison sentence entirely and granted an immediate parole.

Another example of creative jurisprudence is found in the case
of Sergeant Ernst F. He was arrested in May 1944 and sentenced to
eight months' imprisonment for attempted sexual contact with four
soldiers, two of whom were under the age of twenty-one. Ernst F.,
however, was convicted for violating paragraph 175 rather than 175a
because, in the court's words, the defendant had not been "conscious
of their ages."[49] This qualification also finds no expression in paragraph 175a. The Gerichtsherr nevertheless confirmed the verdict and
ordered the punishment served as four weeks of intensified arrest, followed by front-parole. The remainder of the sentence, of course, was
deferred until after the war, as was the case in all instances of parole.

Curiously, the court in this case characterized four separate incidents
as a one-time blunder. In cases such as these, one gets the impression
that the courts and commanders accepted occasional intimate contact
between soldiers as an accident or by-product of war, and therefore
consciously avoided doing excessive damage to the individual—damage that could adversely affect the individual and, perhaps more importantly, reduce manpower and hinder the war effort. In this case, the
Gerichtsherr apparently considered Ernst F.'s infractions as not so serious that he should be kept from his duties for more than four weeks.[50]

Many courts, however, dealt ruthlessly with men carrying out
homosexual relations with men under the age of twenty-one. Such
discrepancies in jurisprudence undermine the thesis of a military judiciary steered to conformity. The case files do not reveal whether
some commanders and the jurists who were subordinated to them

believed the Nazi theory that seduced youngsters became seducers themselves.

Regardless of their beliefs, however, the courts very often imposed severe punishments for violations of 175a, number 3. Organization Todt administrator Fritz E. is a case in point. In 1942 the Court of the 319th Infantry Division sentenced this repeat homosexual offender to three years of penal servitude for his involvement with a teenage sailor. In great contrast to most homosexual offenders, Fritz E., who had already been convicted four times from 1927 to 1938 for violations of paragraph 175, did not rejoin the Wehrgemeinschaft. Five convictions for violations of paragraph 175 evidently convinced the military judicial authorities of Fritz E.'s same-sex orientation. His repeated appearances before the bench fulfilled the burden of proof not only about his sexual orientation but also about his inability to restrain his behavior.[51] As valuable human matériel, however, his services were not lost to the Wehrmacht, which ultimately mobilized him for militarily useful purposes, assigning him to a penal construction unit in 1944.[52]

Although the courts demonstrated inconsistency in their jurisprudence for contact between older and younger men, they consistently demonstrated outrage toward the "predatory" behavior of men in positions of authority. Violations of paragraph 175a, number 2, as a rule, brought extremely draconian punishments. Officers and NCOs who abused their authority in order to coerce subordinates to engage in homosexual activity received the courts' wrath in addition to harsh sentences. The frequency of severe punishments for such infractions indicates that commanding officers and the courts subordinated to them considered the abuse of command authority as a serious threat to the Wehrgemeinschaft's integrity, functioning, and authoritarian structure. Put more simply, the Wehrmacht considered such abuses of authority a grave threat to Manneszucht—grave enough, in fact, to merit the death penalty. In the case files, the lone death sentence for a homosexual offense was indeed imposed for violations of 175a, number 2, as detailed below.

Friedrich A.

On July 14, 1943, the Court of the 159th Reserve Division sentenced Technical Sergeant Friedrich A. to death for coercing two young recruits (ages eighteen and twenty) to engage in anal sex after he first plied them with alcohol.[53] Blasting Friedrich A. for his "unscrupulous behavior," the court characterized him as a "typical homosexual" who "methodically" stalked "his victims," selecting recently enrolled youths with little understanding of the mechanisms for their protection.[54]

Friedrich A. committed suicide shortly after the verdict, preventing its confirmation as per regulations. The post-trial paper trail is nevertheless instructive. The division commander supported the death sentence and wrote this in the requisite opinion that he submitted to the reserve army commander, who possessed the power of confirmation in this case.[55] The reserve commander's staff legal adviser, however, criticized the death sentence as excessive. Friedrich A., he emphasized, had proven himself in combat, had been wounded, was judged well by his superior, and had no previous punishments. Based on this assessment, it remains uncertain whether Friedrich A. would have been executed. On the other hand, even if the reserve army commander had rejected the verdict in favor of a retrial (or granted clemency after he confirmed the verdict), Friedrich A. most likely would have faced several years of penal servitude.

In a contemptuous diatribe, the court in this case lashed out at the defendant. In addition to its homophobic declaration that homosexuals "stalk their victims," the court characterized the defendant as a "beast in human form" and his offense as "pernicious." These insults, however, do not necessarily indicate a nazified court bent on the Volksgemeinschaft's purification. The court, in fact, delivers its harangue during its discussions of the dangers that the defendant's behavior posed to Manneszucht. The language rings of National Socialism, but ideology does not appear to be at work here. The court's anger is directed primarily at Friedrich A.'s abuse of command authority, and its overriding concern clearly is the protection of young recruits. In short, the court's outrage is fueled by the alleged effect of the crime on the Wehrgemeinschaft and those within it, rather than by ideology. This does not absolve either the court or the military commanders involved, but serves only to draw a distinction between ideologically based jurisprudence and jurisprudence aimed at maintaining command authority at all costs.[56]

Cases involving indigenous personnel from the eastern occupied territories, though rare, provide valuable insight into the nature of Wehrmachtjustiz. These cases conform to the previously identified trends
of high reintegration rates, disparate jurisprudence, and Manneszucht
as the military judicial authorities' central point of orientation. In addition, the courts and commanders demonstrate great concern about
the impact that criminal behavior by German troops might have on
occupation policy and pacification efforts. Perhaps surprisingly, the
military judicial authorities displayed little overt prejudice toward the
local indigenous personnel involved. In general, their testimony was
taken and evaluated without extreme prejudice and only occasional
qualification or reference to their non-Aryan descent.[57]

The case of Sergeant Walter B. is representative of such cases.[58] In
September 1943 the Court of the Third Panzer Army sentenced him
to eighteen months imprisonment for four violations of paragraph
175 and paragraph 175a, number 2. The defendant had engaged in
mutual masturbation with four Russian members of an indigenous
military police service (*Ordnungsdienst*). His behavior, according to
the court, had "grievously violated his duty as a superior" and was
"suitable to undermine indigenous units' trust in their German superiors and the German armed forces." It also stressed the crime's
potential impact on occupation policy. Such crimes, the court noted,
endangered pacification efforts in the east because "the civilian population also must hear about such incidents." The Gerichtsherr confirmed the sentence and ordered the punishment completed. Walter
B., however, was paroled to a regular unit five months later.

The case file does not reveal whether or not the military judicial
authorities subsequently prosecuted Walter B.'s Russian partners for
participating in "criminal indecency" as stipulated in the criminal
codes. More than likely, no charges were lodged. Himmler had decided at an early date that foreigners in the occupied lands should not
be punished for homosexual activity because it led to "racial degeneration."[59] Whether the military judicial authorities strictly followed
this guideline could not be determined from the documentation in
the case files. However, considering the war's nature in the east, the

possibility that the Russians were liquidated after the trial should not be completely discounted. On the other hand, if Christoph Rass is correct, the Russian policemen, as members of the German Occupation Authority's institutional structures, may have received a certain degree of protection from such arbitrary treatment.[60]

Given the racial nature of Hitler's war of annihilation in the east, one might expect uniform jurisprudence when Slavic partners were involved, yet the case files suggest otherwise. In four cases involving Slavic teens tried between November 1942 and April 1944, four different courts arrived at three different rulings on the applicability of paragraph 175a, number 3. Two courts invoked the code with its more severe punishment parameters.[61] One court refused to invoke it on the basis of citizenship, ruling that it was intended only "for the protection of German youths."[62] And finally, one court refused to apply the code for reasons other than nationality.[63] These decisions, when compared to one another, appear completely arbitrary.[64] The courts ruled either according to their own personal interpretations of the law or, perhaps more likely, according to the wishes of their Gerichtsherren. Less uniform jurisprudence, however, does not seem possible. If the higher political, military, and judicial authorities attempted to steer jurisprudence, they appear to have failed miserably. These divergences support the argument for judging Wehrmachtjustiz one court at a time and on a case-by-case basis.

Entrapment

Cases of entrapment also demonstrate great divergence in jurisprudence. Unit members often took matters into their own hands, exposing suspected homosexual comrades through various means of entrapment. The discrepancies can best be seen in the courts' application of paragraph 175a, numbers 2 and 3. In such cases, the courts were confronted with the following questions: Can a defendant who has been entrapped be charged with abuse of authority? Can a suspect who has been entrapped be convicted for the attempted seduction of someone under age twenty-one? In other words, can the "victim" setting the trap ever be seduced or abused? The courts ruled both ways, and, surprisingly, it was not just a matter of different courts disagreeing on these points. The discrepancy occurred even on the same court.

The Court of the Wehrmacht Commander–Berlin, in fact, rendered conflicting interpretations on the ramifications of entrapment in cases against homosexual offenders in late 1941 and early 1943.[65]

Although the trials were separated by twenty months with different judges presiding, the different rulings on entrapment are startling. After all, entrapment and homosexuality were not new phenomena to German courts (civilian or martial) during World War II. Two such different opinions are especially intriguing when one considers the Berlin court's proximity to the center of political, military, and judicial power. If such differences in jurisprudence occurred in Berlin, it should be no surprise if they also occurred on the field courts at the front.

In the following two cases, the perpetrators were taken into custody after being entrapped. In addition to illustrating the discrepancies in jurisprudence, these cases provide insight into the priorities of Wehrmachtjustiz. Although both were convicted for violations of paragraph 175, these two confessed homosexuals experienced two very different fates. These cases also clearly demonstrate that for gay men, subordinating oneself completely to military order (and practicing abstinence) could mean the difference between service with the regular troops and being turned over to the civilian authorities. This, of course, meant being placed in the hands of the ss.

Adolf H.

On February 17, 1943, the Court of the Seventh Panzer Division sentenced Corporal Adolf H. to two years and three months' imprisonment for multiple violations of paragraph 175 and 175a, number 3. The defendant initiated intimate contact with as many as six members of his unit. Once Adolf H.'s apparent sexual orientation became known, a unit member, under a sergeant's order, entrapped him. The court ruled that the defendant's conduct during the entrapment scheme likewise violated paragraph 175a, number 3, because he intended to seduce his prospective partner, who was indeed under twenty-one; not knowing he was being set up, according to the court, was irrelevant. The Gerichtsherr confirmed the verdict and ordered the punishment served in a field penal battalion.[66] The penal battalions, of course, were created in response to manpower shortages after the failure of the blitzkrieg in late 1941. These special formations ensured that prisoners served out, rather than sat out, their punishments.

In October 1943 the Seventh Panzer Division's commanding officer, based on Adolf H.'s admission in court that he had acted from a "same-sex inclination," classified Adolf H. as a habitual offender. He instructed Field Penal Battalion 12 to initiate proceedings for the prisoner's dismissal from service per the homosexual habitual offender provisions. In his response the penal battalion commander stated that Adolf H. "had been a model" for the other prisoners and had even been employed with weapons. In this case, the battalion commander reported, a "relapse" seemed unlikely. Characterizing Adolf H. as a "usable soldier," the commander recommended paroling the prisoner to a regular unit, rather than discharging him as an incorrigible homosexual.[67] After the appropriate authorities reviewed the case, the reserve army commander decided against dismissal. On November 1, 1943, Adolf H. was paroled and sent to a regular unit with the Sixth Army.

In the second entrapment case, the defendant likewise admitted his homosexual orientation at trial. The prisoner's fate, however, was vastly different than that of Adolf H.

Franz G.

The Court of the 253rd Infantry Division on October 5, 1942, sentenced medical corpsman Franz G. to three years' imprisonment for two violations of paragraph 175. On watch, in a discussion with Lance Corporal E., the defendant revealed his aversion to women. The corporal, suspecting that Franz G. might be gay (*warmen Bruder*), turned to Sergeant B. for advice. With the assistance of another NCO, Technical Sergeant Bu., they devised a scheme to entrap the defendant. On the next watch, the defendant attempted to grab Lance Corporal E.'s genitals as he relieved himself. The corporal strung the defendant along, explaining that such activity on watch would be neglect of duty. He offered, however, to meet the defendant at a later time. They made a date to meet in Lance Corporal E.'s quarters. There, as soon as the defendant opened the corporal's pants, Technical Sergeant Bu. emerged from his hidden observation point and took the defendant into custody. The Gerichtsherr confirmed the verdict and ordered one year served in a field penal battalion, followed by front-parole. He stipulated, however, that Franz G. be reviewed for parole at an earlier date.[68]

The court convicted Franz G. on two separate counts, ignoring the fact that the two incidents on the night in question had been part of the same scheme to entrap him. The case file contains no document criticizing this ruling or the entrapment itself.

On the basis of Franz G.'s admission that he had engaged in homosexual practices in the past, the court imposed a severe punishment for such minor infractions. His behavior before the bench most likely contributed to this outcome. Franz G. not only failed to express remorse for his actions, he also demanded "in an indecorous manner understanding for his pathological feelings (*Empfinden*)," which outraged the court. It therefore considered him an especially grave danger to the troops. "With [Franz G.]," the court concluded, "the danger exists that he will exploit every opportunity for homosexual activity."

On March 1, 1944, nearly eighteen months after Franz G.'s conviction, Field Penal Battalion 2 reported that, according to a medical expert's opinion, the serviceman had to be classified as a homosexual. The reserve army commander subsequently ordered him dismissed from service as a habitual offender. The civilian authorities incarcerated Franz G. in the District Court Prison (Landgerichtgefängnis)– Landau on June 18, 1944. Whether he subsequently entered a concentration camp cannot be determined based on the case file.

The fates of Franz G. and Adolf H. are indeed instructive. In each case a suspected homosexual was entrapped. Both defendants admitted to same-sex orientations during their courts-martial. However, the reserve army commander dismissed only one of the men from service as an incorrigible homosexual. Their respective conduct during their punishments in the field penal battalions most likely explains their different fortunes.

Adolf H. proved to be a model prisoner, receiving high praise from the battalion commander. He apparently not only had the ability to restrain his inclination, but perhaps more importantly, he had the ability to fully subordinate himself to military order. He rejoined the regular troops. In the second case, the penal battalion authorities punished Franz G. on numerous occasions for deficient performance, lying, and dishonorable conduct toward a superior. Evidently, in addition to being a homosexual, Franz G. either would not or could not conform. The military judicial authorities therefore excluded him from the Wehrgemeinschaft. He was not a usable instrument of war.

A prisoner's "usability" as a soldier, his ability to function as an instrument of war, was perhaps the most important question the military judicial authorities considered when evaluating sex offenders. Gerichtsherren judged prisoners and parolees on the basis of their usefulness as combatants, not their value to the Volksgemeinschaft. And it was always a military officer who had the final say. The jurists merely assisted the Gerichtsherren in this task. Whether basing their decisions on unit fitness reports or assessments generated by officers within the penal system, the Gerichtsherren, as masters of the military judicial process, determined which sex offenders were expendable and which could still potentially serve the war effort.

Court of the Wehrmacht Commander–Berlin versus the Field and Reserve Courts

The case files reveal that similar violations of paragraph 175 under similar circumstances often resulted in vastly different punishments. In some cases these differences may be attributed to the fact that different judges were presiding, but primarily they are explained by differences in the attitudes of the commanding officers exercising authority over the various courts, the timing of the offense vis-à-vis the war, manpower requirements, and the individual offenders' service records.

Differences in sentencing practices also existed between the field and reserve courts and the Court of the Wehrmacht Commander–Berlin. The Berlin court has been selected for this study for two reasons. First, a large number of its case files survived the war.[69] Second, as an important formation close to the center of power, the Berlin garrison's court provides an intriguing basis for comparison with the reserve and field courts.[70]

Two courts from typical front-line units not represented in the Eastern Collection also have been selected for a comparison with the Berlin court: the Court of the Sixth Infantry Division and the Court of the 253rd Infantry Division. Although a relatively high number of case files from these two courts survived the war, the number of case files representing homosexual offenses proved to be quite small compared to the Berlin court. Only eight cases involving eight defendants survived from the Sixth Infantry Division, while only six case files involving seven defendants survived from the 253rd.

The Court of the Wehrmacht Commander–Berlin's jurisprudence and sentencing practices have been compared to all other courts involved in this investigation. The Berlin court sentenced a much higher percentage of soldiers to penal servitude than the overall average in the sample investigated, imposing penal servitude for violations of paragraph 175 or 175a at a rate of approximately 15 percent, compared to an average of 6.4 percent for all other courts.[71] The Berlin court also applied paragraph 175a with its intensified punishments at a rate of 29 percent, while all other courts applied paragraph 175a at a rate of just 21 percent. The Berlin court's average prison sentence for violations of paragraph 175 amounted to approximately 13.4 months, compared to an average of 10.5 months for all other courts.

For violations of 175a the Berlin court imposed, on average, 16.4 months' imprisonment and 34 months of penal servitude. For all other courts the average was 13.2 months' imprisonment and, interestingly, 42 months of penal servitude. The field and reserve courts' higher average penal servitude sentence most likely is explained by field officers' desire to maintain command authority, one of the most frequent justifications for severe punishments for violations of paragraph 175a, number 2. In other words, commanding officers in the field considered the abuse of command authority a serious threat to the Wehrgemeinschaft's authoritarian structure, and they potentially had a much greater interest in harsh punishments for such violations than did a garrison commander on the home front.

As for atonement, individuals sentenced by the Berlin court to prison for violations of paragraph 175 served, on average, 7.5 months in prison before receiving front-parole. The average for all other courts amounted to only 2.5 months. Curiously, individuals who received prison sentences from the Berlin court for violations of paragraph 175a, but who ultimately were paroled, also atoned an average of 7.5 months, despite the more severe punishment provisions. For all other courts, the average came to 5.5 months. The military judicial authorities reintegrated two of the six individuals sentenced to penal servitude by the Berlin court and three of the ten individuals sentenced to penal servitude by all other courts. The remaining eleven most likely spent the entire war in detention.[72] Thirteen individuals (or 6.4 percent of the entire case file sample) were dismissed from service after failing the habitual offender review process, demonstrating the Wehrmacht's willingness to turn over to the police any human matériel that it deemed either unusable or a threat to the Wehrgemeinschaft.[73]

Finally, 62 percent of the individuals sentenced to prison by the Berlin court for violating paragraph 175 had their sentences partially suspended. In other words, 62 percent of those convicted were released from detention early for front-parole. (Given the fragmentary nature of many case files, it is possible that this figure could be considerably larger.) The Berlin garrison's commander did not parole all these individuals, however. Other authorities paroled many of those who initially fell under the Berlin court's jurisdiction. On the other hand, the Berlin garrison's commander and Gerichtsherr, General Paul von Hase, did not suspend a single sentence in its entirety. For all other courts, the partial suspension rate amounted to 81 percent, with twenty-four sentences, or 15.4 percent, entirely suspended.

A high percentage of homosexual offenders served their sentences in field penal battalions. Considering that the military judicial authorities ultimately reintegrated the majority of these individuals into the regular troops (or released them for service in the parole battalions, which had extremely high fitness standards until late 1944), the argument that the field penal battalions had been designed with the calculated destruction of "asocials" and "inferiors" in mind appears unfounded.[74]

The case files from the Sixth Infantry Division raise some interesting questions. For violations of paragraph 175 the Court of the Sixth Infantry Division imposed an average sentence of 8.25 months' imprisonment, which is significantly below the average for all other courts (10.5 months) and the Berlin court (13.4 months). Again, only eight case files for homosexual offenses from the Sixth Infantry Division survived the war, rendering any statistical comparison questionable. Obviously, with such a small sample, one additional long sentence would skew this average significantly. However, one factor reinforces the leniency implied in the Sixth Infantry Division's average sentence. The division's commanding officer (or officers) suspended the entire sentence in five of the eight cases (62.5 percent). With the average for the field and reserve courts (i.e., excluding the Berlin court) at 15 percent, it seems unlikely that cases involving wholly suspended sentences for the Sixth Infantry Division survived the war in such disproportionate numbers. Finally, those convicted for violations of paragraph 175 and 175a served, on average, less than 2 months in prison before their release for parole, which is significantly less than the overall average of 3.5 months.

The case files from the 253rd Infantry Division, despite the small sample, represent the spectrum of intensity, with punishments ranging from a few weeks' imprisonment to several years of penal servitude. Perhaps more importantly, the commander completely or partially suspended the sentences in favor of front-parole in five of seven cases.

To sum up, the Court of the Wehrmacht Commander–Berlin handed down significantly different punishments compared to the reserve and field courts. It imposed a higher percentage of men to penal servitude and imposed higher punishments for violations of paragraph 175. Perhaps most importantly, individuals convicted by the Berlin court for simple violations of paragraph 175 spent three times longer in prison before being paroled than did those convicted by other courts. Similarly, individuals convicted by all other courts for violations of paragraph 175a also received parole more quickly, despite the higher average sentence for this offense.

There are several possible explanations for these differences. First, the Berlin formation's commander and his jurists may indeed have been assisting Himmler and other fanatics in their campaign against homosexuals. Second, this court's proximity to the center of political power may have resulted in more severe punishments and thus longer periods in detention before reintegration. Several case files from this court contain correspondence from the Reich Chancellery, the ss, or the party demanding information on cases or requesting specific action by the court. No evidence exists, however, to indicate that the court responded to or complied with these requests. Nevertheless, the court and the commander may have felt compelled to demonstrate exceptional rigor in punishing violations of paragraph 175.

Third, manpower issues, though always important, may have carried less weight on the home front than on the battlefront. For this reason, the Gerichtsherr perhaps had less motivation for leniency or facilitating reintegration. Fourth, the higher percentage of penal servitude sentences might be explained by the fact that a far higher percentage of the soldiers coming before the Berlin court for same-sex intimacy had previous convictions for violations of paragraph 175: one-third compared to less than one-fourth for all other courts. Conversely, the field and reserve courts' lower penal servitude ratio might be attributed to their inability or disinclination to thoroughly investigate a defendant's civilian record. On the other hand, the higher average penal servitude sentence imposed by the field and reserve courts for violations of paragraph 175a most likely reflects the seriousness with which these courts viewed the abuse of command authority.

Finally, on the home front, soldiers had greater access to teenagers and adolescents (and perhaps more importantly, German teenagers and adolescents), which under paragraph 175a normally brought more severe punishments. Nearly one-fourth of the individuals in the Berlin court case file sample had had sexual contact with German boys age eighteen or younger.

Despite any differences in sentencing practices and incarceration periods, the previously identified trends nevertheless apply to the Berlin court. Like those convicted by the field courts, the homosexual offenders coming before the Berlin court experienced high reintegration rates. More than 90 percent of the individuals sentenced to prison for violations of paragraphs 175 or 175a ultimately rejoined the Wehrgemeinschaft.[75]

In Berlin, too, the military judicial authorities placed considerable weight on an offender's martial qualities and his willingness to subordinate himself to military order. Thus, whatever differences existed in sentencing practices and regardless of the reasons for these differences, homosexual offenders coming before the Berlin court could rejoin the Wehrgemeinschaft if they were willing to carry a weapon in good faith. Even when the Berlin court passed long prison sentences, reintegration often took place. The following case, tried by the Court of the Wehrmacht Commander–Berlin, is thus representative of the military judicial Alltag. It also highlights the Wehrmacht's perception that homosexuals could be successfully "reeducated" if sufficiently "motivated" in the penal system.

Lothar W.

In October 1942 the Berlin court sentenced Lance Corporal Lothar W. to three years' imprisonment for violating paragraph 175.[76] A suspected homosexual since 1937, the defendant had been convicted previously for two violations of paragraph 175 in 1939 and eight violations of paragraph 175 in 1940. In this case, Lothar W. befriended a twenty-one-year-old soldier on the street and invited him to his dwelling. There, the defendant embraced his new acquaintance. He then felt the soldier's genitals through his clothing and tried to unbutton his fly. The Gerichtsherr confirmed the verdict, but because he considered Lothar W. "incorrigible," he ordered the prisoner incarcerated in a Wehrmacht penal camp, where time in detention was not calculated as time served.[77]

Noting that his two previous convictions had not made any impression on him, the court stated, "The new offenses demonstrate that he has not improved, but rather has returned to his old depravity (*Laster*)." A considerable punishment, the court concluded, appeared necessary "in order to finally bring an end to the defendant's parasitic (*volksschädlingenden*) conduct." Although this bit of ideological invective might point to a Nazi fanatic on the bench, it is worth noting that the three-year prison sentence, though lengthy, is not outside the spectrum of punishments seen in this study. In addition, it was the division commander as Gerichtsherr, not the court, who ordered the punishment completed in a penal camp, the Wehrmacht's most severe punishment option. The military commanders, not the jurists, dominated the system, and they must assume most of the responsibility for any atrocities committed by the military administration of justice.

This case also demonstrates the active interest that commanders with military judicial authority took in the administration of justice in their units. In a post-trial plea, Lothar W.'s defense counsel, calling the Gerichtsherr's attention to his client's good performance evaluations and willingness to fight, proposed that Lothar W. be paroled immediately to the front. The Berlin garrison's commander, General Paul von Hase, wrote a bold "NO" in the proposal's margin. Instead, von Hase confirmed the verdict and ordered Lothar W. to a field penal camp, as outlined above.

After several months in the camp, Lothar W. required medical treatment for unknown reasons. After seven months in the hospital, he returned to the penal camp. The Torgau authorities, stating that his attitude and performance had been excellent, submitted very good conduct reports on Lothar W. before and after his convalescence. Most importantly, he showed no signs of "recidivism." In a document dated December 8, 1943, the Torgau authorities reported that Lothar W.'s detention in the penal camp "obviously has had a good effect" and recommended that he be transferred for the orderly completion of the punishment.[78] On April 5, 1944, the Gerichtsherr of the Court of Division Number 464 ordered the punishment's completion, and Lothar W. was transferred to Field Penal Battalion 18. On November 8, 1944, he was paroled to a regular unit.

This case illustrates two crucial points. First, the military judicial authorities believed that homosexuals, if sufficiently "motivated," could be successfully "reeducated" and reintegrated. Despite three convictions, Lothar W. rejoined the regular troops after detention in a field penal camp "had a good effect." Second, the Wehrmacht did not intentionally destroy potentially usable human matériel. In this case, Lothar W. received medical treatment for seven months while a penal camp inmate. If the Wehrmacht had been bent on the destruction of its penal camp detainees, as many scholars claim, one wonders why a three-time homosexual offender was provided with medical care for such a long time. At any rate, Lothar W.'s checkered past did not prevent his rejoining the Wehrgemeinschaft, even if it took two years.

Comparison to Civilian Courts

The average sentence imposed by the courts in the case file sample for simple violations of paragraph 175 was comparable to the lowest regional average calculated by Burkhard Jellonnek in his evaluation of civilian court sentencing practices.[79] On the other hand, the military judiciary's average sentence for violations of 175a was nearly twice as long as the averages calculated by Jellonnek for the civilian courts.[80]

These statistics reveal what the court transcripts themselves indicate. The courts were less concerned with the intimate contact itself than the effect it might have on the military apparatus. As a rule, they dealt ruthlessly with sexual activity between superiors and subordinates, whether coercion was involved or not. The documents show that the courts consistently regarded such violations of command responsibility as an unacceptable threat to the cohesion, stability, and effectiveness of the military apparatus, and for this reason they imposed severe punishments—punishments that were on average more severe than those imposed by the generally more ruthless civilian courts.

Many of the cases discussed in this chapter represent the extremes of the Wehrmacht's treatment of men convicted for violations of paragraph 175 and 175a. The remaining cases in the sample naturally fall somewhere in between. Although punishments could indeed be severe, this was a Prussian tradition, not necessarily a Nazi one. As in so many other aspects of the Third Reich, the political leadership's priorities regarding homosexuality proved irreconcilable with total war, which required the mobilization of every last reserve. The Wehrmacht recognized this from the outset. Despite increasing pressure from Himmler, the military continued to recycle its usable human matériel. Clearly differentiating between the "one-time blunderer" and the true homosexual, the Wehrmacht punished, "reeducated," and reintegrated the vast majority of homosexual offenders. As parolees these men then faced front-line dangers under the sword of Damocles for the war's duration. Nevertheless, even multiple offenders could rejoin the Wehrgemeinschaft if they proved during their "reeducation" that they could control their impulses and fully subordinate themselves to military order. On the other hand, the Wehrmacht had few scruples about turning over "incorrigible" homosexuals to the ss for destruction through work in concentration camps.

Comparing the methods of a democratic nation's armed forces with those of a dictatorship may be comparing apples to oranges. Although such a comparison is fraught with perils, a few words about the U.S. military's handling of homosexuals during the Second World War seem appropriate here. According to Allan Berube, the U.S. military discharged approximately nine thousand soldiers and sailors for homosexuality during the war. In addition, five thousand selective service applicants were rejected for the same reason. By comparison, the Wehrmacht not only called up known homosexuals but also generally required several homosexual violations before it discharged soldiers as habitual offenders.

Approximately 6,600 German servicemen were convicted for homosexual offenses between September 1939 and the end of June 1944. If we assume that perhaps as many as one thousand more were court-martialed before the end of the war, this would bring the total to 7,600. In the sample investigated for this study, the Wehrmacht discharged only thirteen of the 203 individuals (or 6.4 percent) convicted for violations of paragraph 175 or 175a as habitual homosexual offenders.[81] At a dismissal rate of 6.4 percent, out of the projected 7,600 individuals convicted for homosexual offenses, the total number dismissed from the Wehrmacht as "true" or "incorrigible" homosexuals would come to 486, compared to the 14,000 that the United States either rejected for, or dismissed from, service for the same reason.[82] This should not be perceived as an indication of toleration on the Wehrmacht's part with regard to homosexuality. Rather, it is an indication of the German military's recognition of its inferior human war potential compared to its much more populous opponents. Whereas the United States had a manpower pool that allowed it to discharge thousands of homosexuals, the Wehrmacht had to husband its human matériel carefully.

Although it is tempting to characterize a punishment of a few months' imprisonment with the majority of the sentence suspended for front-parole as a slap on the wrist, this would be an inaccurate assessment. Individuals receiving light punishments had to endure the harsh conditions and brutal treatment of the Wehrmacht's penal institutions and, once paroled, bear the physical dangers of combat and the psychological pressures under Damocles' sword. Exposed to enemy fire for the duration, even a light punishment could result in years of service at the front without respite. Although at least one individual punished for violating paragraph 175 did not have his parole revoked after being judged unfit for combat, he most likely represents the rare exception.

Those given more draconian punishments had to endure months

and even years of incarceration in the centralized Wehrmacht prison system, the decentralized field penal camps, or Emsland. Although only 8 percent of the individuals sentenced for homosexual activity received penal servitude sentences, 70 percent of these individuals were not reintegrated into the Wehrgemeinschaft. The case files do not reveal whether or not they survived the war. The Wehrmacht's willingness to turn over "recidivists" and the "incorrigible" to the ss demonstrates its obliging cooperation with the regime and seamless integration into the Hitler state. On the other hand, its refusal to co-operate with the party and police until it had classified an individual as a true homosexual demonstrates the Wehrmacht's determination to maintain full control over its usable human matériel, but certainly not its compassion.

In dealing with cases of sexual contact between men, the courts interpreted and applied the laws inconsistently and imposed vastly different punishments for similar infractions under similar circum-stances. Contrary to the thesis of a judiciary steered from above, the only explanation possible for the variations is the individual com-manding officers' assessments of the prisoners and the pressures that their units faced, both externally and internally. Balancing manpower requirements with the individual's potential for future offenses, the commanding officers rejected very few parole proposals on the basis of an infraction's "reprehensibility" or "loathsomeness." Rather, in attempting to avoid a repetition of the First World War, the com-manders' ultimate criterion proved to be an individual's willingness to fully subordinate himself to military order and carry a weapon in good faith. Even multiple homosexual offenders could rejoin the Wehrgemeinschaft if they were willing to bleed for the fatherland.

CHAPTER SEVEN

Sexual Assault

In cases of sexual assault, the military judicial authorities demonstrated the same pragmatic interest in recycling usable instruments of war that they had in cases of homosexuality. Prisoners' transgressions were measured closely against their service records both at trial and when being considered for reintegration into the Wehrgemeinschaft. Gerichtsherren ordered a high percentage of convicted rapists to begin their "rehabilitation" in parole battalions and field penal units rather than in prisons. Established in 1941 and 1942, these formations were created by the Wehrmacht so that the reclamation of human matériel would also serve the war effort. The vast majority of these special penal formation detainees descended the penal chain, ultimately rejoining the regular troops. As they did with homosexual offenders, the military judicial authorities generally evaluated servicemen convicted for rape on the basis of their ability and willingness to carry a weapon in good faith.

Cases of sexual assault establish more clearly than any other offense category that Wehrmachtjustiz was a military organization that had been designed to serve military interests. The Gerichtsherren, as masters of the military judicial process, harnessed the system in a relentless attempt to confront the military realities on the various battlefronts. Hence, in this chapter, the reintegration of perpetrators will be overshadowed by the commanders' and courts' focus on practical military considerations in the respective theaters of war.[1]

Sex under the Swastika

George Mosse, in *Nationalism and Sexuality*, concludes that German fascism perceived a lack of sexual control as "a characteristic of the enemies of ordered society. The enemies of society and the inferior races were identical in racist thought, while the superior race possessed the attitudes, manners, and morals of existing society." The Nazi attitude toward sexuality, according to Mosse, emphasized the home, the family, restraint, and discipline. Under National Socialism, sexual intoxication of any kind was viewed as both unmanly and antisocial. "Those who could not control their passions were either considered abnormal . . . or would inevitably drift into abnormality."

> As a form of heightened nationalism, racism supported bourgeois respectability. It emphasized the difference between virtue and vice, the necessity of a clear line between the normal and abnormal according to the rules laid down by society. . . . Those who stood apart from the norms of society were totally condemned. It was no longer the specific sexual acts alone that were considered abnormal, but the entire physical and mental structure of the person practicing these acts. Such a person was excluded from society and the nation.[2]

National Socialism's attempt to inaugurate "a new era of discipline, morality, and Christianity," in conjunction with women's special role within Nazi ideology as the propagators of the master race, leads one to expect that a military judiciary bent on societal purification would have considered perpetrators of sexual assaults against German women especially dangerous to the Volksgemeinschaft. As Mosse points out, however, the regime's priorities often proved irreconcilable with its ideals, and the case files indicate that commanders and courts were concerned about matters other than social respectability, decorum, and Nazi population policy.[3]

One also might expect that, given Nazi racial concepts, military courts would have dealt leniently with soldiers accused of raping Slavic women, as many scholars have indeed claimed.[4] Again, however, the case files reveal a different picture, with servicemen often receiving very severe punishments for assaults against east European women.

Overall, the evidence suggests that commanders functioning as Gerichtsherren and the courts subordinated to them proceeded against sexual assaults with practical military considerations rather than ideology in mind. Varying between theaters, the courts' jurisprudence and sentencing practices were geared toward meeting the specific military realties on the various battlefronts.

As in cases of homosexuality, the courts demonstrate a complex mix of moderation and ruthlessness in cases of sexual assault. In contrast to homosexual offenses, which only occasionally produced a "victim," sexual assaults created victims in the truest sense of the word. Therefore, classifying punishments as draconian or mild is problematic and contentious. Is three years' imprisonment for the violent rape of a teenager mild or draconian? Is three years of penal servitude for the rape of a grandmother moderate or harsh? Whose standards hold sway?

For the purposes of this discussion, punishments in cases of sexual assault can only be classified as harsh or mild relative to each other. This is not an attempt to avoid condemnation or exoneration of the courts' jurisprudence; rather, it is an acknowledgment that the case files reveal two sets of victims: the victims of specific crimes and the victims of a brutal military judicial system.

In the case files examined, eighty individuals received sentences ranging from several months' imprisonment for attempted rape to the death penalty for a completed rape.[5] As discussed in chapter 5, the death sentence rate for rape most likely amounted to less than 1 percent. The case file sample contained one death sentence and therefore the death penalty may be slightly overrepresented.

The Reich Criminal Code established the minimum punishment for rape under section 177 as one year's imprisonment and the maximum punishment as fifteen years of penal servitude. The courts, of course, could exceed these parameters through the application of Wartime Penal Code section 5a. Few completed rape crimes received the minimum penalty. Most attempted rapes resulted in at least six months' imprisonment. Although many perpetrators committed their crimes at night (and therefore most likely under blackout conditions) or at gunpoint, few courts bothered to invoke the Antisocial Parasite Ordinance or the Ordinance against Violent Criminals, which had been placed at their disposal for the imposition of draconian penalties.[6] Most courts failed to apply (or even discuss) the standard provisions against the unauthorized use of a weapon.[7] Furthermore, a May 1940 OKH directive calling for less-severe punishments for sexual assaults than would be indicated under normal circumstances (i.e., peacetime civilian conditions) found little mention in the case files, and even less application, as indicated by the high number of harsh punishments.

Sexual Assault: The Eastern Front
The case files do not support Maiwald and Mischler's contention that the military leadership encouraged sexual assault as part of

Hitler's racial war of annihilation in the east. In support of this position, the authors cite Field Marshal Wilhelm Keitel's demand that all means should be employed in the east, "even against women and children." Maiwald and Mischler, however, do not document a single specific order instructing the troops to commit rape as part of the military strategy.[8] In fact, by calling the reader's attention to the Wehrmacht's extensive efforts to prevent sexually transmitted diseases among the troops, the authors actually undermine their thesis.[9] In the First World War, "carnal flu" incapacitated hundreds of thousands of German soldiers. The Wehrmacht was determined to prevent any repetition. During the Second World War, it operated an extensive system of closely regulated and medically supervised brothels in order to reduce the spread of sexually transmitted diseases.[10] The Wehrmacht also introduced severe punishments for soldiers careless enough to contract a sexually transmitted disease.[11] A strategy of "sexual debasement" in the east—that is, a strategy of sexual assaults as a means of repression—would have completely sabotaged these efforts.[12]

Scholars also have suggested that the military judicial authorities did not perceive sexual assaults against Slavic women as "moral offenses" and therefore pursued such crimes as "fraternization," "racial offenses," or even "collaboration with partisans."[13] In the case files, however, it appears that the authorities did not equivocate and indeed classified sexual offenses perpetrated against Slavic women as sexual assaults. Exceptions to this rule occurred in the east, but many courts also chose to call sexual assaults against German women something other than what they were—for example, "libelous behavior."[14]

The Central Documentation Agency's Eastern Collection contains a considerable number of case files for processes against soldiers who committed sexual assaults against inhabitants of the eastern occupied areas. However, the case files do not resolve the controversy surrounding the consequences of the Barbarossa Jurisdiction Decree.[15] Instead, they only raise more questions. On the one hand, approximately 40 percent of the individuals convicted for rape crimes in the Eastern Collection case file sample had assaulted eastern inhabitants. Perhaps more importantly, the case files examined for this study contain only one specific reference to the Barbarossa Jurisdiction Decree.[16] At first

glance, this seems to suggest that the military judicial authorities ignored the Jurisdiction Decree to a large extent.

On the other hand, the Eastern Collection fell into Soviet hands
at war's end. Therefore, the case files in the Eastern Collection came
from units operating in the east. One might expect that the collection
would contain a higher number of case files for crimes committed
against eastern inhabitants if indeed the military judicial authorities
pursued them on a regular basis.

Another possibility should also be considered. The prewar provisions required the military judicial authorities to prosecute sexual assaults, even if the victims had not filed complaints. In October 1940 the
provisions were changed. Henceforth, a complaint had to be lodged
before the military judicial authorities could initiate legal action.[17]
Soviet civilians might have chosen not to report crimes committed
against them by German soldiers. In fact, experts estimate that, even
in ideal victim-friendly (i.e., civilian peacetime) environments, the
majority of rape crimes go unreported.[18] It would not be surprising
then if the war's nature in the east caused local indigenous personnel
to perceive any attempt to obtain justice as futile.[19] Or, by extension,
Soviet civilians might have considered any contact with the occupation authorities to be dangerous and therefore might have chosen not
to report crimes in general and sexual assaults in particular.

The case files nevertheless establish that the military judicial authorities did prosecute soldiers for sexual assault, even if the frequency of
prosecution cannot be established.[20] How many sexual assaults the
authorities ignored (or how many assaults civilians chose not to report) must remain a matter of speculation.

The case files also do not support Maiwald and Mischler's claim
that the Wehrmacht promoted sexual assaults in the east through the
"most extreme restraint" in prosecution. Contrary to the authors'
conclusions, the case files also reveal that when the military judicial
authorities chose to prosecute soldiers for assaulting eastern inhabitants, the courts did not impose exceptionally light punishments. The
punishments were well within the spectrum of severity seen for assaults committed against west Europeans. In fact, they often were
quite severe, with penal servitude punishments a common occurrence. The courts represented in the Eastern Collection, for example,

imposed penal servitude sentences for completed acts of rape in the eastern occupied areas at a rate that approached 50 percent, while soldiers on the home front and in other theaters received penal servitude punishments at a combined rate of 30 percent.[21] Considering the relatively small number of cases in the sample, these statistics must be taken with a grain of salt. Yet they nevertheless indicate that soldiers could (and did) receive draconian punishments for rape crimes perpetrated against east European women.

Birgit Beck effectively refutes the myth that the Wehrmacht employed sexual assault as an explicit tool of total war in the east. She nevertheless contends that courts-martial imposed much lighter punishments for sexual assaults committed against Soviet civilians than for assaults against French nationals, for example. Perceiving a link between racism and sexual assault, Beck suggests that military courts viewed the rape of Russian women as a trivial crime because, according to National Socialist ideology, the Soviet people had "no concept of female sexual integrity."[22] For this reason, the military judicial authorities ignored most sexual assaults. When the authorities did prosecute offenders, they did so in order to maintain military order and discipline. Nevertheless, mild punishments, according to Beck, proved to be the rule, rather than the exception.[23]

Again, the case files examined for this study suggest otherwise, with soldiers in the east often receiving draconian punishments and with penal servitude sentences a common occurrence rather than a rare exception.[24] Compassion for the victims, however, was not the reason for severe punishments. The courts, as a rule, demonstrated a complete lack of sympathy for east European assault victims, very often making statements such as, "She is not so frail that she has suffered any emotional damage." Despite this ambivalence toward the victims, rape crimes that endangered the military apparatus or its mission could provoke a very stern response from the military judicial authorities. It was, as Christoph Rass contends, the Wehrmacht's "existential interests" that prompted commanders to demand, and courts to impose, harsh sentences in the east.

Sexual assaults had the potential to hinder occupation tasks and aggravate the partisan problem, and thus the military judicial authorities took them seriously. In the case files, the courts regularly cited the orderly prosecution of occupation policy and the adverse impact that rape crimes had on the partisan movement as the primary reasons for severe punishments. In short, Wehrmachtjustiz punished German soldiers for crimes against Soviet civilians not for reasons of compassion but rather for the protection of immediate military interests.

Take, for example, the 1942 case of canoneer Heinz B. The Court of the 339th Infantry Division sentenced him to four years of penal servitude for raping a Russian woman four times in two days. The Gerichtsherr confirmed the verdict and ordered the punishment completed.[25]

The court heavily weighed Heinz B.'s four previous convictions by civilian and military courts and his repeated disciplinary punishments when imposing the sentence. However, it focused primarily on the crime's potential impact on the partisan movement and excoriated the defendant in a long diatribe. The severe punishment, the court stated, was less for the "protection of the sexual honor of the injured Russian" than for the fact that Heinz B. "damaged the interests of the German armed forces to the greatest extent (*auf der erheblichste*)."

Specifically, the court expressed its concern that the mistreatment of local indigenous personnel at the hands of German soldiers would drive them to join the partisans. "The village of Suglitz," the court observed, was in an area "strongly infested by partisans," and in such areas it had to be considered that civilians would be "driven into the hands of the partisans through mistreatment by German soldiers." The court declared, "Among the population of the village, there already exists the opinion, which arose from Russian propaganda, that German soldiers would fulfill their desires through the force of weapons and would mercilessly shoot women who do not comply. The defendant's conduct has strengthened that opinion."

The court continued this line of inquiry and stated that "through Heinz B.'s actions, the danger that the people will turn to the partisans and fight against the German Wehrmacht was considerably increased." Heinz B.'s crime, the court lamented, "contributed to the fact that pacification work in an area so close to the front, and thus of special significance," had been endangered. He damaged not only "the reputation of the German Wehrmacht with the civilian population" but also "immediate interests important to the war."

Although the court chastised the defendant for failing to subordinate himself to and take his place in the German community (*Gemeinschaft*), this bit of National Socialist rhetoric seems merely an afterthought when compared to the emphasis placed on the immediate military problems of pacification and the partisan threat.

The Court of the Seventh Panzer Division expressed similar sentiments during the August 1941 rape trial of tank gunner Alfred M., who received three years of penal servitude for multiple crimes that included one count of rape.[26] The court stressed the adverse impact that Alfred M.'s actions might have on the local population. His crimes, according to the court, had to be considered especially grave because "even if one considers that the sexual honor of women according to the Russian concept is valued (*gewertet wird*) differently than according to German perceptions, the defendant's actions were shameless to such an extent that they would have been, without a doubt, also regarded by the Russian women as offensive to the highest degree."

Expressing fears about the crime's potential to adversely affect both the war effort and civilian-military relations in the occupied area, the court declared, "Through his actions, the defendant has furthermore not only disrupted the friendly terms (*gute Einvernehmen*) between the German troops and the villagers of Worotyschino, but above all also damaged the reputation of the Wehrmacht to the greatest extent. This type of criminal act . . . will naturally spread like wildfire by word of mouth among the civilian population and be generalized so that what he has done will be attributed to German soldiers as a whole."

The court also took into account Alfred M.'s poor military record and deficient performance when allocating the punishment. As a soldier, the court noted, not only had he conducted himself "extraordinarily badly," he also had failed to demonstrate any kind of "military performance or merit." "All educational measures of the troops and all disciplinary measures," the court reflected, "have been without success" and "nothing came as a result of his six months in the education unit." The court concluded its assessment of the defendant by declaring, "The defendant appears subsequently as an incorrigible character who must be met with the full weight of the law."

In typical Nazi fashion the court characterized Alfred M. as a "personality that deserves no leniency," but it had no ideological agenda and its priorities are unambiguous: the maintenance of good relations with the civilian population and the protection of the Wehrgemeinschaft through the removal of disruptive elements. These practical military considerations remained the court's primary concern. Classified as an unusable instrument of war, Alfred M. was convicted, discharged as "unworthy of service," and incarcerated at Emsland, the standard procedure for those sentenced to penal servitude.

The general lack of empathy for east European victims and Wehrmachtjustiz's priority of protecting military interests are also reflected in the 1944 rape case of specialist David N. Although a particularly brutal crime, the case nevertheless conforms to these trends. The Court of the 201st Security Division sentenced David N. to ten years of penal servitude for manslaughter in coincidence with attempted rape. During a violent sexual assault, the defendant became outraged at his victim's resistance and shot her twice in the head. The commander of the Third Panzer Army, who had the power of confirmation in this case, confirmed the sentence and ordered the punishment served in a field penal battalion.[27]

As in the cases discussed previously, the court's deliberations focused primarily on practical military considerations rather than on the fate of the victim. It did characterize the crime as "extremely brutal," but the following passage reveals the court's primary concerns:

> His act was suited to damage considerably the reputation of the Wehrmacht and disturb (*erschüttern*) the trust of the civilian population in the German Wehrmacht. It also could not be overlooked that the mood in the squadron also was unfavorably influenced by the crime. The granting of mitigating circumstances therefore cannot be considered. On the other hand, in his favor is his young age and, disregarding one minor disciplinary action, he has conducted himself flawlessly and has no legal punishments. Also mitigating the punishment (*strafmildernd*) was considered the especially demanding conditions in the east. *It is known that the Russians have perpetrated numerous atrocities against German soldiers and still do perpetrate, and even act against their own population in the most extremely brutal way* [emphasis mine]. These facts, according to the opinion of the court, have surely not been without influence on the attitude of the defendant.

In the preceding passage, the recurring themes found in the east appear again, with the court focusing on the Wehrmacht's reputation, the crime's impact on the military's relationship with the civilian population, and in this case even unit morale. Inverting the war's reality on the eastern front, the court blamed Russian atrocities against Germans for David N.'s actions. Primarily preoccupied with immediate military problems, the court displayed only the slightest concern for the victim.[28]

The violent collective rape of two Russian teens by five German soldiers in 1944 provoked a similar reaction, this time from the Court of Corps Battalion (Korps-Abteilung) E. In this case, the court did display some compassion for the victims, yet the partisan threat and occupation policy remained the overriding priorities.[29] When imposing two-year penal servitude sentences on the five defendants, the court characterized their crimes as "especially reprehensible." It then declared, "The defendants have acted extremely brutally (*roh*) and vulgarly (*gemein*). They have damaged the reputation of the Wehrmacht most severely by their actions. Such conduct must contribute to the fact that the population, which is friendly to Germans, will gravitate to the partisans and bandits who create difficulties for the Wehrmacht."

The court acknowledged the defendants' outstanding service records, preventing even more harsh punishments. All five were delivered to a field penal camp at the end of June 1944. The case files contain no further information on their fate.

In addition to demonstrating the courts' consistent concern about the adverse impact sexual assaults might have on the partisan problem, this case also provides insight into the military judicial process. An army judge with the Third Cavalry Brigade provided the requisite second opinion on the court's verdict. Characterizing the punishments as too mild, he strongly criticized the judgment. "The crimes were committed with unsurpassed bestiality," he stated. The perpetrators, in his opinion, had "conducted themselves not as German soldiers, but rather as inhuman rabble (*Soldateska*)." Their behavior could not be explained by any irresistible sexual urges but could be attributed only "to the most vile inclination." The only possible mitigating circumstance, he opined, could be that "through the harshness of the war" (presumably meaning in the east), they might have been "partially clouded as to the reprehensibility of their acts." Nevertheless, in his opinion, the damage to the Wehrmacht's reputation and civilian-military relations had been so extensive that a far more severe punishment, perhaps even death via section 5a of the Wartime Penal Code, would have been appropriate.

The commander of Corps Battalion E, however, disagreed with this assessment. The defendants, he stressed, were relatively young, had served in the east since the campaign's beginning, and had conducted themselves flawlessly until their crime. He considered these facts sufficiently mitigating and recommended the verdict's confirmation.

Both opinions were sent up the military judicial chain of command to the commander of the Second Army, who had the power of confirmation in this case. The region's judge advocate also rejected the dissenting opinion tendered by the judge with the Third Cavalry Brigade. A 1940 decree, the judge advocate stressed, stipulated that the death sentence would be appropriate in such cases only if the perpetrator had "conducted himself in every way inhumanely and brutally."[30] In this case "it is a matter of soldiers who otherwise are judged as normal," he observed, and thus the death sentence would be inappropriate. In his opinion, "*Usable soldierly performance* [emphasis mine] could still be expected from them after education." For this reason, he recommended the verdict's confirmation and detention in a field penal camp. The Second Army's commander followed this recommendation.

The exchanges outlined above indicate that the jurists understood clearly the centrality of military considerations in the Wehrmacht's version of justice, with the brigade-level jurist expressing concerns about civilian-military relations and the region's judge advocate focusing on the perpetrators' potential as usable instruments of war. The process itself demonstrates the countervailing forces at work in the military judicial process. The military commanders and staff legal advisers by no means considered a court's verdict as sacrosanct, and all offered their opinion as to the appropriate punishment. According to the judge with Third Cavalry Brigade, Wartime Penal Code section 5a should have been invoked and the death penalty considered. The corps battalion commander, however, stressed the defendants' outstanding service in the field. The judge advocate also stressed their potential as usable instruments of war after "education." An officer rather than a jurist, however, had the final say, and the commander of the Second Army opted to conserve the human matériel in question rather than suspend the verdict and attempt to obtain the death penalty in a retrial.

In sum, the protection of military interests characterizes Wehrmachtjustiz on the eastern front. Pacification, the partisan threat, and the conservation of the Wehrmacht's usable human material were the specific priorities, and harsh punishments were a common occurrence rather than a rare exception. The cases described above represent some of the more severe punishments handed down for assaults against east European women. Not all courts, however, met defendants with the full weight of the law. Yet, even when eschewing penal servitude punishments in favor of "lenient" prison sentences, these courts displayed the same concerns about the problems that sexual assaults posed for the Wehrmacht and its mission.

The Court of the Eighty-second Infantry Division is a case in point. The Eastern Collection contains three case files from this division for assaults against Soviet women.[31] In all three cases, which were tried between 1942 and 1944, the court handed down prison sentences ranging from one to three years for crimes that often brought penal servitude punishments such as those in the cases described previously. It would be easy to blame Nazi racial ideology for these relatively "mild" punishments. However, several factors suggest that the punishments reflected military considerations rather than ideology.

First, the punishments were well within the normal spectrum of severity for rape crimes perpetrated against west Europeans, *including German women*, and hence they are not in any way aberrant. Second, the Eighty-second Infantry Division was heavily mauled on the eastern front during the period in question, and the perpetrators in all three cases descended the penal chain, ultimately being paroled to regular units after service in field penal battalions. In other words, immediate external pressures on this particular unit may explain the relatively lenient punishments, with the commanding officer perhaps demanding prison sentences (rather than penal servitude) in order to facilitate reintegration.

Without an in-depth investigation into this division's history, this interpretation is speculative. The salient point, however, is that Nazi racial ideology is not the only factor that might have strongly influenced Wehrmachtjustiz. Concluding that the National Socialist *Weltanschauung* explains lenient punishments in the east may be convenient, but it ignores the complexity of the issue. It also trivializes the reality of Wehrmachtjustiz as a tool of war, as a military organization designed and deployed to assist the Wehrmacht in the pursuit of its strategic tasks. Considering the obvious external stress on the Eighty-second Infantry Division and the practical military considerations consistently addressed by the court, the convenient explanation fails to satisfy the burden of proof. This is not to suggest that ideology was absent on the eastern front, just that other factors could have played a more important role in the courts' decisions.

Whatever the specific mix of phenomena behind its relatively lenient sentencing practices, the Eighty-second Infantry Division's military judicial paper trail reveals the importance of practical military considerations in this court's pursuit of justice. In June 1943, for example, the court sentenced Lance Corporal Philipp W. (b. 1920) to two and one-half years' imprisonment for raping a forty-four-year-old Russian woman. When allocating the punishment, the court identified the damage his conduct inflicted on the Wehrmacht's reputation with the civilian population as the main reason for severity. "That kind of conduct," the court declared, "cannot be tolerated in the interest of the Wehrmacht's reputation and in the interest of cooperation with the civilian population." The court nevertheless granted mitigating circumstances, citing his four combat wounds and his diligence in operations. It therefore dispensed with a penal servitude punishment but concluded that the punishment had to exceed the minimum sentence considerably for reasons of "deterrence."[32]

Entered into the court record, Philipp W.'s performance evaluation characterized him as a "primitive, unstable, asocial type." According to many scholars, fanatic judges seized upon such personal assessments and used them not only as evidence of guilt but also as justification for draconian punishments in the interest of societal purification. In this case, however, the court focused on the defendant's performance in combat. According to the very same performance evaluation, Philipp W. had "no fear before the enemy." The military commander who ultimately received jurisdiction over Philipp W. after his conviction also evidently placed greater weight on his performance in the field than on his character. He paroled Philipp W. after only a few months. His diligence in operations, demonstrated by his fearlessness in battle and four combat wounds, apparently outweighed his personal shortcomings and previous transgressions.

The court again focused on immediate military problems in the case of Walter U. He was sentenced in 1942 to two years' imprisonment for raping a sixteen-year-old Russian girl. "There are," reflected the court, "certainly more vulgar and brutal forms" of rape. Nevertheless, he had committed his crime at a time when "his comrades [were] putting their lives on the line for their Fatherland in the front trenches." For this reason, the court considered his crime especially serious and stated:

> Through his act he has severely damaged the reputation of the German Wehrmacht and *severely impaired the plans of the Wehrmacht to establish in the interest of general pacification a relationship with the population that is as trusting as possible* [emphasis mine]. . . . Finally, the prison sentence must be high enough so that it will have a deterring effect on all the defendant's comrades who have a weak nature in the interest of the maintenance of discipline, order, and the fighting power of the troops. It is the first rape case that has happened in the division. The troops must know that the strongest action will be taken against those types of cases of barbarism (*Verwilderung*) in the sexual area in the interest of the . . . honor . . . of the German soldier.

The Gerichtsherr confirmed the verdict, ordered the punishment completed in a field penal battalion, and stipulated that the prisoner be reviewed for parole after four months.[33]

Walter U. was in fact paroled six months later. He subsequently committed a new offense (which could not be identified from the available documents). After returning to Field Penal Battalion 9 to serve the new sentence as well as the remaining portion of his initial punishment, he had to be disciplined several times in the following months. In January 1944 the Gerichtsherr of the Court of the Senior Engineering Commander (Höheren Pionier Kommandeurs) 3 ordered him transferred to a field penal camp because he "repeatedly gave cause for complaint."

In contrast to Philipp W. in the preceding case, Walter U. proved unable or unwilling to fully subordinate himself to military order. The military judicial authorities determined that he was no longer a usable instrument of war and moved him up the graduated penal chain to a field penal camp, the Wehrmacht's most draconian punishment option. Whether or not he received a third chance to rejoin the Wehrgemeinschaft is not clear from the case file. However, despite his unsuitability as a soldier, Walter U., as valuable human matériel, nevertheless served the war effort as a field penal camp inmate.

Although no firm conclusions can be made on the basis of just three case files, little evidence exists of ideologically based jurisprudence in the Court of the Eighty-second Infantry Division. Despite the comparatively lenient sentences, the divisional commander (and the jurists subordinated to him) evaluated the crimes and the perpetrators according to the same criteria encountered in cases that resulted in severe punishments. Their points of orientation were the same, and their priorities were immediate military considerations and the reclamation of usable instruments of war.[34]

Cases involving east European victims share other commonalities. The courts generally evaluated the testimony and depositions of east Europeans, both victims and eyewitnesses, without extreme prejudice and with only occasional qualification or reference to their descent. In fact, specific racial slurs generally were not part of the military judicial vocabulary.[35] Furthermore, even in cases when the military judicial authorities betray a certain bias toward eastern inhabitants, their bias did not necessarily preclude convictions.[36] It should also be stressed that all plaintiffs, victims, and witnesses were regarded with a certain degree of suspicion, regardless of their nationality or ethnicity.[37]

On the other hand, the courts in the east often expressed their belief that the victims had suffered little emotional damage because the "Russian concept of a woman's sexual honor is different than that of the German perception," or words to that effect. Whether this prejudice had its basis in Nazi racial ideology or simply reflects traditional German condescension toward east Europeans is difficult to determine. According to Birgit Beck, the courts' consistent denigration of the Soviet people's lack of "sexual integrity" suggests the jurists' adherence to Nazi racial concepts. Noting that combatants in the American Civil War seldom raped white women, yet frequently assaulted African American and Native American women, Beck perceives a link between racism and sexual assault on the eastern front.[38] She does not reconcile this conclusion with the fact that German soldiers raped French, Italian, and even German women in substantial numbers during the Second World War, and no evidence suggests that non-Slavic women were assaulted at a significantly lower rate than Slavic women. The link she suggests, then, seems rather tenuous.

When dealing with sexual assaults against French nationals, the courts often denigrated French sexual mores. The fact that prejudices were at work in different regions does not refute the importance of ideology in the east, but it does demonstrate the complexity of the issue. One very significant difference, however, indeed existed between the courts' handling of sexual assaults committed against east European women, on the one hand, and west European women, on the other. The courts frequently attempted to defame the reputation of west European victims. German and French women often became the objects of intense scrutiny by the courts, which went to great lengths to uncover evidence of promiscuity for the purpose of imposing lighter punishments.[39] In the east, it simply sufficed for the court to refer to "the Russian people's different concept of sexual honor" in order to achieve this. East or west, however, the courts' purpose was the same. Nonetheless, it is not clear whether the bias seen in the east had its origins in traditional German anti-Slavic attitudes or in Nazi racial concepts. The possibility exists that many courts combined the two forms of anti-Slavic prejudice, creating various and unique strains of German racial bigotry.

Most importantly, the Wehrmacht did not "promote" rape on the eastern front through the imposition of lenient sentences. In fact, the courts frequently stated that severe punishments were necessary for reasons of "deterrence." Although the Court of the Eighty-second Infantry Division handed down relatively light punishments, it did not promote rape through its sentencing practices. It imposed sentences ranging from one year to three years' imprisonment. Many courts imposed sentences within this range for sexual assaults against French, Italian, *and even German* women.[40]

Sexual Assaults against French Nationals

Among the eighty individuals in the case files who were convicted for rape or attempted rape, sixteen were prosecuted and punished by the military judicial authorities for assaults against French women. The courts imposed penal servitude sentences in six of these cases (37 percent). The partisan problem, mentioned so frequently by courts on the eastern front, received little mention by courts operating in France, which is most likely explained by the resistance movement's quiescence until relatively late in the occupation.

The courts nevertheless were very conscious of civilian-military relations and the maintenance of discipline. Assaults that grievously disrupted the quiet routine of occupation for the civilian population were met with the full weight of the law. Indeed, trespassing or forced entry in the commission of a rape crime virtually guaranteed the perpetrator a draconian punishment.[41] Additionally, the military judicial authorities frequently exhibit paternalism, often blaming the victims for their misfortunes, a phenomenon that was also encountered in cases involving German woman. The denigration of the French national character is another prominent theme encountered in the case files, with French morals and integrity frequently assailed.

In occupied France, however, the most prevalent trend was the maintenance of good relations with the civilians in the occupied area. The Court of the Ninety-fifth Infantry Division in 1941, for example, focused on civil-military relations when imposing a severe punishment on Lance Corporal Christian S. He received three years' penal servitude for raping two French women. The court demonstrated a bit of compassion for the victims, declaring that "all the circumstances show that he seized the opportunity to commit these rapes without any regard for the women," but it was mainly outraged at the impact of the crimes on civilian-military relations. "He has shown by his acts," the court ranted, "that he in no way took the Wehrmacht's reputation into account. He has aided enemy propaganda in the worst way. He is also old enough to know that in the First World War even occasional indecent sexual offenses (*Sittlichkeitsdelikte*) by German soldiers were exploited by enemy propaganda in the crudest manner to agitate against the entire German people." The Gerichtsherr confirmed the verdict and ordered the punishment completed.[42]

The Court of the First Panzer Division in August 1940 articulated similar concerns when sentencing Lance Corporal Werner K. to three years' imprisonment for raping a thirty-one-year-old French woman. Werner K.'s transgression, the court determined, was the result of youthful indiscretion rather than any "criminal inclination." His crime was nevertheless especially serious because he and all of the troops had been instructed repeatedly about the "correct conduct in sexual relations with the French civilian population." Despite these instructions, he committed a crime that "endangered the reputation of the Wehrmacht in an occupied enemy area." The division, the court noted, had already experienced several rapes. The punishment, therefore, would have to be severe in order to "effectively deter others" from similar crimes.[43]

The following two cases, examined in detail, are particularly instructive regarding the military judicial process.

In the case of Viktor G., the defendant's intoxication receives close scrutiny. Viktor G. received the most severe punishment imposed by the courts in the case file sample for a sexual assault against a French woman. The case further demonstrates the military judicial process's complexity, as well as the dominance of military officers (rather than the jurists) in the process. Although a high percentage of the perpetrators in the case files assaulted women under the threat of a weapon, Viktor G.'s case represents one of the few instances in which a court invoked section 1 of the Ordinance against Violent Criminals, which was placed at the courts' disposal in December 1939 for arriving at more draconian penalties. It did so, however, only during a retrial after a judge advocate had criticized the court for not invoking the ordinance. Although the court engages in Nazi rhetoric, referring to the perpetrator as an "evil parasite," ideology ultimately had little influence in the outcome of the case.

Victor G.

On May 22, 1940, the Court of XV Army Corps sentenced Private Victor G. to death on one count of rape and one count of coercion in coincidence with breaking and entering. After consuming two bottles of wine in approximately two hours, the defendant forced his way into two separate homes and threatened the families with his rifle. He even discharged the weapon on the street and inside the dwellings. In one home, he fondled four young women, ages thirteen to twenty-two. In the second house, he raped the sixteen-year-old daughter of the French peasant Paul L. After the assault, he fell asleep and remained sleeping until nine o'clock the next morning when a patrol arrested him.[44]

When allocating the punishment, the court characterized the crime as "an especially severe offense against Manneszucht" that "assisted enemy propaganda regarding shameful and violent conduct of German soldiers towards the inhabitants of enemy lands." The court continued:

> He has damaged the honor and reputation of the German soldier so severely in an operational area so that only the harshest punishment comes into consideration. The highest planned punishment for rape of fifteen years penal servitude, however, does not seem sufficient. A more severe case of damage to military Manneszucht can scarcely be imagined. The accused is such an evil parasite (*übler Schädling*) for Manneszucht in the troops that he must be mercilessly exterminated (*rücksichtslos ausgemertzt*).

For these reasons, the court invoked section 5a of the Wartime Penal Code in order to exceed the regular punishment parameters and impose the death penalty.[45]

The commander of XV Army Corps (Victor G.'s commanding officer) supported the verdict and recommended that the punishment be carried out. On May 23, 1940, a judge advocate with the Fourth Army characterized the crime as "loathsome," but based on the amount of alcohol consumed, he did not deem the crime worthy of death. After contemplating these opinions, the commander of the Fourth Army suspended the sentence and convened a second hearing.

When the defendant was retried on May 24, 1940, by the same court but with a different judge presiding, his alcohol consumption received greater scrutiny. Conceding that the defendant might have been impaired, the court imposed a penal servitude sentence of ten and one-half years.[46] Victor G.'s commanding officer, however, recommended to the commander of the Fourth Army that he not confirm this new verdict. In his judgment, the original sentence of death had been the appropriate punishment. Referring to the points covered in the first trial, he voiced his concern that the crime had indeed severely damaged discipline.

In contrast to his earlier assessment of the matter, the judge advocate with the Fourth Army noted in the requisite second opinion that Victor G. had used a weapon to commit the assaults. The court, in his estimation, should have invoked section 1 of the Ordinance against Violent Criminals, which provided for the death penalty for crimes committed under the threat of a deadly weapon. For this reason, he recommended that the verdict be suspended and a new trial ordered. The Gerichtsherr followed this advice and ordered a third trial.

On May 30, 1940, the Court of XV Army Corps, which presided over the first two trials, condemned Victor G. to death for rape in conjunction with the use of a deadly weapon as per section 1 of the Ordinance against Violent Criminals and Wartime Penal Code section 5a. Victor G.'s commanding officer, just as he had after the first trial, supported the death penalty and recommended confirmation. Once again, however, the judge advocate changed his position and criticized the application of section 5a, stating that the defendant's alcohol consumption undoubtedly must have had some effect on him, and therefore the normal punishment parameters provided for a sufficient punishment. He nevertheless recommended the verdict's confirmation but suggested converting the death sentence into a lengthy penal servitude punishment.

The commander of the Fourth Army confirmed the verdict but refused to grant clemency as the judge advocate had recommended. In the commander's opinion, the crime had indeed greatly damaged the Wehrmacht's reputation. Victor G., however, petitioned for clemency. On June 17, 1940, the OKH informed the Court of XV Army Corps that the army's commander-in-chief had granted clemency and converted the death penalty into a five-year penal servitude sentence.[47] According to the document, the commander-in-chief did not consider the crime worthy of death (*todeswürdiges Verbrechen*). In his opinion, the prerequisites for neither the Ordinance against Violent Criminals nor section 5a of the Wartime Penal Code had been met. This must have been a disappointment to Victor G.'s commanding officer, who lobbied for the death penalty from the beginning.

First incarcerated at Emsland, Victor G. was transferred to Siegburg Penitentiary in August 1942. In January 1943, the OKH ordered him transferred to Torgau for the parole battalion exam. On April 19, 1943, the Torgau commandant reported that Victor G. had demonstrated his willingness to become a "usable soldier." The commandant therefore recommended service with a parole battalion. For unknown reasons, however, Division Number 464's commanding officer ordered Victor G. released to a regular front-line unit. Dismissed from detention on May 13, 1943, and sent to his new unit, Victor G. became a British prisoner of war sometime in 1944.

This case demonstrates how difficult it would have been for a fanatic presiding judge to turn his court into a lethal assembly line in the service of ideology. The Nazi rhetoric, a phenomenon encountered rarely in sex offense cases, certainly puts the court in a bad light. The possibility exists that the presiding judge in this case was indeed a fanatic Nazi. Yet too many countervailing forces existed, preventing an individual jurist from imposing his own brand of justice. In addition to potential conflicting opinions from judge advocates and staff legal advisers, a military commander's power as Gerichtsherr rendered it impossible for a judge to dispense terror-justice solely by his own efforts. Note that it was two officers (Victor G.'s commanding officer and the Fourth Army's commander) who consistently advocated the death penalty while the jurists vacillated throughout the process.

In the end, an officer had the final say, with the army's commander-in-chief granting clemency and thus conserving the human matériel in question. Despite the damage that Victor G.'s crime allegedly inflicted on Manneszucht, he received the opportunity to prove in detention that he could become a "usable soldier," and the military judicial authorities ultimately reintegrated him into the Wehrgemeinschaft— from the precipice of death to reintegration in less than three years.

The preceding case represents the most extreme example in the case files of a draconian punishment handed down for sexual assaults against French women. The following case reveals the traditional paternalistic attitude that courts often displayed when prosecuting rape crimes against west European women. Just as important, this case demonstrates the Gerichtsherren's interest and influence in the military judicial process.

Ludwig D.

On June 16, 1940, the Court of the Seventh Panzer Division sentenced Private First Class Ludwig D. to eighteen months' imprisonment for raping a fifteen-year-old French girl. The defendant approached a home after noticing the attractive teenager and informed the family he would be lodging there that evening. When the girl escorted him inside, he threw her on the floor. He covered her mouth when she began screaming and raped her despite vigorous resistance. After a post-trial investigation of the family's reputation, the Gerichtsherr confirmed the verdict *but mitigated the sentence to one year*. He then ordered only three months of the sentence served, with the remainder suspended for front-parole.[48]

Ludwig D. committed his crime after the establishment of orderly conditions in the occupied region of France. He also "damaged the Wehrmacht's reputation." These two facts, according to the court, justified the imposition of the sentence under aggravating circumstances. The court, however, granted mitigating circumstances for the following reasons: first, in war, soldiers face long periods of abstinence that "seduce" men with "violent sexual urges" to commit "rash acts"; second, the French sense of morality "is not as strongly impressed upon them as with the Germans"; third, the defendant had no previous punishments and submitted a remorseful confession. Nevertheless, the court deemed a considerable punishment necessary in order to deter others from committing similar offenses, which the court noted were occurring more frequently.

Suggesting that the court could have weighed the French people's "lower morals" more heavily when allocating the punishment, the staff legal adviser characterized the sentence as a bit excessive. In addition, Ludwig D.'s regimental commander wrote to General Irwin Rommel, the Gerichtsherr and commander of the Seventh Panzer Division. In an attempt to obtain a reduction in the punishment, the regimental commander informed Rommel that "it appears doubtful that this is an incontestable (*einwandfrei*) case of rape, since it has been established in the meantime that the reputation of the girl is not good (*kein gutter*) according to the Burgermeister . . . and the administrator of the local hospital. . . . The witness, Frau J. is also of questionable reputation. . . . These new facts cause me to request a renewed examination of the matter."

Based on this information, Rommel not only directed the local authorities to depose the *Burgermeister* and the hospital administrator but also ordered a medical examination for the girl in order to establish her sexual history. Although the medical examiner could not come to any definite conclusions about her previous sexual activity, the Burgermeister reported that she allegedly had many boyfriends. The hospital administrator testified in his deposition that he did not know her personally, but that the whole family had a poor reputation. Rommel therefore decided to confirm the verdict but mitigate the sentence, as outlined above.

Due to an extended hospital stay while incarcerated, Ludwig D. could not be released for front-parole until February 11, 1941, approximately five months after his conviction.

As often seen in the western theater, the victim's reputation (as well as her family's) influenced the ultimate outcome of this case, with General Rommel mitigating the sentence. In addition, the court (as well as the staff legal adviser) displayed a national prejudice not unlike that seen in the east, remarking on the deficient morals of the French. In this case, however, the bias most likely had its foundation in traditional German anti-Gallic sentiment.

Despite the frequent denigration of the French national character, the military judicial authorities were nevertheless prepared to deal ruthlessly with soldiers who assaulted French women, imposing penal servitude penalties at a rate of nearly 40 percent. The commanders and the courts subordinated to them considered the disruption of the quiet routine of occupation a serious threat to German interests and the indiscipline that sexual assaults represented a grave threat to Manneszucht.

The Court of the Twenty-ninth Panzer Grenadier Division and Italian Nationals

The Eastern Collection contains six case files for sexual assaults against Italian nationals from the Court of the Twenty-ninth Panzer Grenadier Division, presenting a rare opportunity to obtain a fuller picture of a single court's jurisprudence.[49] In contrast to courts dealing with assaults against French and east European women, the Court of the Twenty-ninth Panzer Grenadier Division often held the morals of the Italians in high regard. It punished soldiers for assaults against Italian women rather mildly, however, when compared to the sentences imposed for sexual assaults against east European and French women. The court did not impose a single penal servitude sentence against the ten individuals convicted for rape or attempted rape of an Italian woman. Although the sample is small, several of these assaults were "collective or gang" (*gemeinschaftlich*) rapes, which elsewhere consistently brought penal servitude sentences. All of the trials occurred after Italy switched to the Allied camp.

Engaged in all the major battles for Italy after the Allies landed in September 1943, the Twenty-ninth Panzer Grenadier Division was completely destroyed by the British Eighth Army in April 1945.[50] The case files give a hint at the considerable stress the division experienced in the last months of its existence. The courts-martial for the six cases in question took place from February through October of 1944. The military judicial paper trail provides an interesting snapshot of the Wehrmacht's adaptation of the penal system to the demands of total war. The Gerichtsherr and division commander, Major General Fritz Polack, ordered nine of ten prisoners immediately to field penal battalions so that their "rehabilitation" would also serve the war effort.[51] These case files, in other words, indicate the serious manpower problems confronting the Wehrmacht in 1944, with the division commander ordering the perpetrators of even violent rape crimes to the special formations.

The penal and parole battalions, of course, had been created so that convicted servicemen would serve rather than sit during their punishment, but further evidence suggests that the Twenty-ninth Panzer Division was under severe external stress. Most of the case files end rather abruptly, most likely due to the complete destruction of the division in early 1945. Although sketchy, the case files reveal the following about the ten soldiers in question: Four were paroled relatively quickly and rejoined regular units. One penal battalion detainee became a British prisoner of war, while another was wounded so severely by a grenade that he had to be treated in Germany. The paper trails for the remaining four prisoners end with their delivery to the field penal battalions. In other words, within weeks of their "monstrous" crimes, ten out of ten convicted rapists were either fighting in regular units or serving the war effort in the specially created penal battalions, or they had become casualties of war. By 1944 Wehrmachtjustiz had become very proficient at recycling the Wehrmacht's human matériel.

In addition to this snapshot of manpower mobilization, the military judicial paper trail also reveals the specific military realities confronting the division from mid- to late 1944. The military judicial authorities consistently identify sexual assaults as a prominent explanation for the rise in anti-German sentiment among the Italian people. Much like their counterparts on the eastern front, the courts consistently stressed the growing partisan threat when punishing rapists.

In September 1944, for example, the court sentenced two noncommissioned officers to two years' imprisonment each for the collective rape of an Italian woman.[52] Decorated and proven in combat during several campaigns, the defendants also had received good performance evaluations. The court therefore granted mitigating circumstances. Although it refrained from imposing penal servitude sentences, the court nevertheless determined that the punishments had to be considerable, given that the defendants "injured the sexual honor of the Italian woman . . . in the most selfish manner" and "severely damaged the reputation of the Wehrmacht." Severity was indeed urgent, noted the court, because, "above all," the crime directly promoted the partisan movement. "It is clear," the court stated, "that through such monstrous crimes as has been committed, the Italian *Bands* will procure new adherents, a fact that has consequences that other decent German soldiers will have to suffer."

In another case of collective rape from February of the same year, the court likewise focused on the crime's potential impact on the partisan movement. In this case, the three perpetrators brutally raped a sixteen-year-old Italian teenager. When deliberating the defendants' fates, the court declared, "They have conducted themselves badly. That is . . . they have injured the young girl physically and mentally through the three consecutive rapes . . . and most heavily damaged the reputation of the Wehrmacht in the eyes of the Italian people, who place great worth on the sexual discretion of young women." The court did not end there but issued the following warning: "*If Italians, who have hitherto been friendly to Germans act hostilely toward German soldiers (einstellen sich gegen feindlich) or even join the Badogliobanden, then people such as the three defendants will have that on their conscience* [emphasis mine]."

The Gerichtsherr confirmed the two-year prison sentences and ordered the punishments served in a field penal battalion.[53]

In another striking example, Corporal Willi P. came before the court in August 1944 for attempted rape. When imposing a one-year prison sentence, the court explained its decision to exceed the legally established minimum punishment in this case. The defendant, declared the court, "not only severely damaged the reputation of the Wehrmacht" but "above all . . . produced a justifiable hate against the German soldier with the Italian population," bringing "new adherents to the Badoglio *Banden*."[54]

In the following March 1944 case, the court again dwells primarily on the partisan problem and lauds Italian sexual mores. The case also provides one of the few examples in which a court applies legal codes against the unauthorized use of a weapon.

Alfred K.

On March 7, 1944, the court sentenced Sergeant Alfred K. to two years' imprisonment for usurping command authority and attempted rape in coincidence with the unauthorized use of a weapon. Late one evening the defendant approached a bunker housing civilians with the intention of finding a sexual partner. He explained to the civilians that he had been given the order to check identification papers. When he found a young woman without any identification, he informed her that she would have to accompany him to the command post. Approximately two hundred meters from the bunker, he tried to rape her, drawing his pistol to silence her screams. Alfred K., however, could not overcome her resistance, and he fled the scene. The Gerichtsherr confirmed the verdict and ordered the punishment atoned in a field penal battalion.[55]

In contrast to many other cases in which perpetrators professed to be acting in some official capacity in order to gain access to their victims, in this case the court convicted Alfred K. for usurpation of command authority. Also in contrast to most cases, the court convicted him for the unauthorized use of a weapon. Under the procedural guidelines, the Gerichtsherr submitted the indictment. Why some commanding officers failed to include secondary charges such as those lodged against Alfred K. is difficult to explain. Perhaps many did not receive close counsel from their legal staff on the many possible technical violations of the law. Most likely, however, the majority of commanders simply did not care about technicalities—desiring instead a fast investigation, short trial, and swift punishment—and therefore focused on the main issue. Indeed, most transcripts are relatively brief and concise, suggesting that the commanders wanted to get to the bottom line without wading through tedious legalese or lengthy technical points of law when reviewing judgments at the time of confirmation.

Acknowledging Alfred K.'s clean record, the court granted mitigating circumstances in order to "protect him from a dishonorable penal servitude sentence." However, Alfred K. had transgressed in a very severe manner. The court thus considered a severe punishment absolutely necessary:

> By the usurpation of command authority, he has most grievously (*aufs gröblichste*) abused the defenselessness of the Italian civilian population and their trust in the legality of official actions undertaken by German soldiers. Through the attempted rape with the use of a weapon he has severely damaged the reputation of the Wehrmacht and undermined the trust of the Italian civilian population in the German soldier. Through an act such as the one committed by the defendant, the civilian population is rising against (*wird aufgebracht gegen*) the German Wehrmacht and drifting into the camp of the *Badogliobanden*.

In the performance evaluation submitted for the trial, Alfred K.'s commanding officer described him as a "weak, fickle character" who simply was unqualified to be a superior officer. On the basis of this assessment, the court declared, "He has not demonstrated any kind of merit that could speak in his favor. On the contrary, he is a badly judged soldier and an incompetent officer." Despite this unfavorable evaluation, Alfred K. ultimately received parole after approximately five months. He rejoined a unit with the Sixteenth Army.

Overall, the Court of the Twenty-ninth Panzer Grenadier Division consistently focused on immediate military considerations when passing judgment, and the commanding officer ordered the punishments atoned in field penal battalions, with only one exception.[56] The penal battalions, by this point in the war, had replaced prisons as a primary destination for convicted soldiers, demonstrating the military judicial system's adaptation to an increasingly perilous military situation. The prisoners thus did not escape the war's harsh realities after committing their crimes but instead soon found themselves back at the front. They either rejoined their comrades in regular units or they labored under fire in the penal battalions, with two individuals quickly becoming casualties of war.

The total number of prisoners ultimately reintegrated into the regular troops is impossible to determine. Due to the war's late stage and the division's ultimate destruction, the case files end abruptly. It is highly likely that the military judicial authorities eventually paroled the four penal formation members whose fates could not be determined. After assuming command of the reserve army, Heinrich Himmler ordered prisoners of all stripes and fitness ratings paroled whenever possible. Thus the chance that the perpetrators in question were reintegrated remains very high.

One final thought: The Court of the Twenty-ninth Panzer Grenadier Division praised the moral chastity of the Italian people on several occasions, in great contrast to courts operating in France. Whether these expressions represented the court's genuine sentiments or simply were hopeful expressions of fascist unity between the German and Italian people is a matter of speculation. The latter seems unlikely, however, considering that the trials took place after Italy switched to the Allied camp.

Sexual Assaults: The Home Front

Before analyzing sexual assaults on the home front, it is worth considering again the role of German women as the propagators of the "master race." Although the wartime reality for women under Hitler did not correspond to the Nazi ideal, the protection of women remained an ideological underpinning of population policy. Despite the courts' slightly heightened sense of empathy for the victims, their handling of assaults against Aryan women proved to be not altogether different from their approach to assaults against foreign nationals, including occasional displays of paternalistic attitudes.[57] Although the courts frequently emphasized a crime's reprehensibility, military considerations remained high on their list of priorities, and individuals' service records were crucial to their fates. Manpower requirements also influenced the process.

Even those perpetrating fairly violent assaults against German women frequently found themselves quickly reintegrated if their records indicated they were willing instruments of war. The military judicial authorities regarded Sergeant Ernst S. as just such an instrument. Convicted by the Court of Division Number 159 in June 1941, Ernst S. received a one-year prison sentence for raping a young German woman. The Gerichtsherr confirmed the verdict and ordered the punishment completed, but he stipulated that the sergeant would be reviewed for parole after two months.[58]

Ernst S. had a clean record, and the court therefore granted mitigating circumstances. It also acknowledged his good conduct and, based on his commanding officer's assessment that Ernst S. was a "daredevil under fire," his bravery on the battlefield. Addressing the difficulties that enforced abstinence posed for soldiers, the court announced, "Furthermore, for a long time before the crime he had not had the proper opportunity for sex, so that his reckless behavior appears understandable, even if it cannot be sanctioned." His consumption of alcohol (which, according to the court, most likely increased his libido) and his last-minute confession were also considered as mitigating circumstances.

For these reasons, the court imposed the minimum sentence for a completed act of rape and concluded its deliberations, declaring, "Members of the Wehrmacht who conduct themselves in such a violent manner against German woman must generally be met with severe and deterring sentences." On June 17, 1941, the region's judge advocate amended the verdict with an "opinion of the field court," informing the Gerichtsherr that the court supported an early parole for Ernst S. "because of his bravery before the enemy." Although the case file becomes fragmentary at this point, one document indicates that Ernst S. was indeed eventually paroled.

In this case the court imposed the minimum sentence for a fairly violent assault against a young German woman, and the Gerichtsherr provided for Ernst S.'s quick reintegration. Considering the court's emphasis on his demonstrated bravery, which it lauded during the oral hearing and in its post-trial opinion, it appears that martial virtues held sway over a German woman's virtue, at least for this court.

If Ernst S.'s fine record as a soldier saved him from languishing in prison, manpower requirements could also trump "justice." In October 1939 the Court of the 251st Infantry Division sentenced Sergeant Ernst F. to eight months' imprisonment for the attempted rape of a German housewife. The Gerichtsherr confirmed the verdict and ordered the punishment completed.[59] Throughout the fall of 1939 and the spring of 1940, the prisoner lodged multiple parole petitions, which the Gerichtsherr repeatedly rejected. However, on May 16, 1940, just five days after the beginning of the Western Offensive, Ernst F. was paroled to the front.[60] He rejoined his unit with the 251st Infantry Division, which participated in the campaign.[61]

Codified before the war, the requirements for parole had been written with manpower considerations in mind, and in practice the Wehrmacht's penal system functioned as a ready reserve. It did so even before the creation of the special penal formations, as demonstrated by the case of canoneer Fritz V. He too was released early from detention after assaulting a German woman. Sentenced by the Court of the 253rd Infantry Division to one year in prison for the attempted rape of a fifteen-year-old German girl in January 1940, Fritz V. was shortly "sprung." The commander and Gerichtsherr of the 253rd Infantry Division on May 13, 1940, granted immediate parole for "military reasons" to Fritz V. and forty-one other division members sitting in various penal institutions. The 253rd, which participated in the French campaign, obviously needed all available hands. Released on 21 May, Fritz V. returned to the regular troops.[62]

Based on the experiences of Ernst S., Ernst F., and Fritz V., one could draw the conclusion that the Wehrmacht considered attacking a German woman a serious crime that merited punishment, but not so serious a crime that soldiers should miss operations. This is a gross oversimplification of the issue, of course, but the case files contain numerous examples of this phenomenon.

The Court of the Wehrmacht Commander–Berlin

The Central Documentation Agency's collection of six thousand case files from the Court of the Wehrmacht Commander–Berlin surprisingly contained only a handful of rape cases. Compared to the six rape cases found in the Eastern Collection from the Twenty-ninth Panzer Grenadier Division for the last eighteen months of the war in Italy, the low number for the Berlin court for the entire war seems significant. The Berlin court imposed punishments that covered the spectrum of severity. In the final analysis, military considerations and the needs of the Wehrgemeinschaft superseded the needs of the Volksgemeinschaft, even for this court near the center of Nazi power. The case files largely conform to the established trends already discussed. The following three cases, reviewed in depth, are representative of the Berlin court in particular and the military judicial Alltag in general.

Stanislaus B.

In October 1941 the Berlin court sentenced Technical Sergeant Stanislaus B. to three years of penal servitude. A noncommissioned officer in the Great War, the defendant attacked a unit member's fourteen-year-old daughter as she did his laundry. Muffling her screams with a blanket, he raped her. Although he never fully penetrated her, he did ejaculate. The Gerichtsherr confirmed the verdict and ordered the punishment completed.[63]

Previously fined on two occasions for sexual misconduct, Stanislaus B.'s disruptive sexual past led the court to deny him mitigating circumstances.[64] Asserting that mildness would be inappropriate in this case, the court stated, "He has not shied away from attacking a fourteen-year-old girl for the satisfaction of his carnal desires, even though there are women in the area who, according to testimony, were willing to oblige him to the utmost." In the absence of mitigating circumstances, the criminal codes required the imposition of penal servitude.

Damaging the reputation of the noncommissioned officer corps, assaulting a subordinate's daughter, and undermining this subordinate's trust in his superior officers earned Stanislaus B. aggravating circumstances. The staff legal adviser emphasized these same points in the requisite second opinion. The Gerichtsherr confirmed the verdict, and Stanislaus B. was delivered to Penal Camp II, Aschendorfermoor (Emsland).

Despite a favorable appraisal from the penal camp superintendent, the reserve army commander rejected a petition lodged in mid-1942 for service with a parole battalion. The crime, in his opinion, demonstrated a "considerable deficiency of character." He also pointed out that Stanislaus B. was not fit for employment at "the foremost part of the front." The reserve army commander, however, ultimately ordered Stanislaus B. transferred to Torgau in mid-1943 for a determination of his fitness to serve. Although he received a not too flattering report from the Torgau authorities, they acknowledged his "willingness to prove himself" and recommended parole with a regular unit. On September 20, 1943, approximately two years after his conviction, he was dismissed from custody and sent to his new unit. Stanislaus B. was reported missing in action on April 18, 1944.

One suspects that the reserve commander's initial refusal to approve Stanislaus B.'s transfer to a parole battalion was based more on his limited fitness than his character. The order transferring him to Torgau states explicitly that he was not to be considered for the parole battalions, which required the highest fitness rating (at least until late 1944), but rather for a regular unit, which could make use of soldiers with limited fitness ratings. It therefore appears that at this point in the war, the reserve commander was simply concerned with getting him back into action in some useful capacity. Despite a "considerable deficiency of character," his service in the Great War and his fairly good performance evaluations evidently made him a usable soldier—one willing to prove himself—which throughout the war remained the primary criterion for inclusion in the Wehrgemeinschaft.

The following case provides a fine example of how the military judicial authorities hoped the system of front-parole (and the sword of Damocles) would motivate convicted soldiers.

Wilhelm R.

In January 1942 the Berlin court sentenced Secretary Wilhelm R. to two and one-half years' imprisonment for indecent assault in coincidence with attempted rape. The defendant, who supervised perhaps twenty-five female clerks, accosted three staff members. On several occasions, he made inappropriate contact with twenty-seven-year-old Miss S., fondling her breasts and, on two occasions, attempting to pull down her panties. He ejaculated during one episode. The defendant accosted two other young female staffers in the same manner on multiple occasions. Field Marshal Keitel confirmed the verdict and ordered Wilhelm R. dismissed from military service, the standard procedure for military civil servants convicted of serious crimes.[65]

Protesting his innocence, Wilhelm R. characterized the accusations as an elaborate attempt by the women to frame him. The court, based on the consistent testimony of the women, rejected this alibi. During the sentencing phase the court acknowledged his clean record and good conduct, and thus granted mitigating circumstances. It nevertheless considered the following factors as aggravating circumstances: first, he stubbornly lied to the end; second, he sought revenge against one of his victims for reporting the incidents by trying to get her fired; finally, he committed all infractions during duty shifts. "His debauchery," according to the court, demonstrated that this "aberrant inclination" was part of his character, as indicated by the fact that he "has not shied away from showing the girls pornography . . . at the office."

The court concluded its deliberations, stating, "He has damaged the reputation of the Wehrmacht most severely. The fact that no lasting emotional damage has remained for the victims from the sexual attacks is insignificant when compared to the need to strongly condemn this type of transgression in the interest of protection."

Although dismissed from service, Wilhelm R. had not been convicted dishonorably, so he was incarcerated in a mobile military prison unit and not Emsland, where those receiving penal servitude sentences were sent. His lawyer immediately lodged a parole petition, which the army medical inspector (*Heeres-Sanitätinspecteur*) rejected as premature in March 1942, despite a plethora of glowing reference letters from former commanders.[66] In May 1943 the reserve army commander ordered Wilhelm R. transferred to Torgau for the parole battalion exam. He arrived at Torgau in late July. In early August prison officials gave him a good report, characterized him as a "usable soldier," and based on his limited fitness rating, they recommended that he be sent to a parole battalion construction unit. Division Number 464's commanding officer accepted this recommendation and paroled Wilhelm R. on August 31, 1943.

In a textbook example of how the military hoped the parole system would function, Wilhelm R. apparently was well motivated by the sword of Damocles hanging over his head. He performed above and beyond the call as a parolee. He lodged a petition in 1944, requesting remission of the remainder of his sentence and restoration to his former rank. The parole battalion construction unit reported on March 18, 1944, that Wilhelm R. had been a "model soldier." "Despite his physical limitations," the unit noted, "he has done his duty" and "given his best," proving himself "under direct enemy fire." According to another report he played a decisive role in "securing the Atlantic Coast in November 1943" and "helped defend a bridgehead in February 1944."

Based on his performance as an "earnest soldier," the commander of the Ninth Army recommended remission of the remainder of his sentence. In the classic two-stage model for remission and rank restoration discussed in chapter 3, he did not advocate rank restoration. Senior Engineering Commander (Höheren Pionierführers) 10 also supported remission, basing his decision on Wilhelm R.'s very good conduct and "model performance in battle operations in the area of the Thirty-first Infantry Division." He too, however, did not support rank restoration, citing the severity of the crime. The petition was sent up the chain of command, and Field Marshal Keitel indeed ordered the remission of the remainder of Wilhelm R.'s prison sentence on May 15, 1944. He did not, however, restore Wilhelm R. to his former rank. Whether the sword of Damocles inspired Wilhelm R. to further heroic action could not be determined.

In the last case, an eleventh-hour military judicial inquiry, the defendant assaulted a German teenager.

Emil S.

The Berlin court in December 1944 sentenced Corporal Emil S. to two years' imprisonment for attempting to rape his fifteen-year-old sister-in-law. Four years previously, the defendant, after drinking heavily one evening, persistently pursued the young girl. He tried to remove her pajamas and fondled her. When his wife intervened, he struck her several times, rendering her unconscious. He again attacked the girl. Due to her stiff resistance, he failed to penetrate her, although he did penetrate her digitally. At one point, he threatened to shoot her if she refused to say that she loved him. The wife intervened a second time, successfully calming him and getting him to bed. The Gerichtsherr confirmed the verdict and suspended the sentence for front-parole.[67]

The court rejected Emil S.'s claim that he had been senselessly drunk and had no memory of the incident, yet nevertheless considered his consumption of alcohol as a mitigating circumstance. The court also accepted as mitigating his good conduct, good behavior in the interim, and the fact that the act did not "correspond to his inclination." In January 1945, Emil S. was sent to a field unit.

Given the late date in the war, it should be no surprise that Emil S. was sent directly into combat. After assuming command of the reserve army in September 1944, Himmler ordered commanding officers to parole to the front immediately upon conviction all soldiers who were physically fit. Those who might pose a discipline problem were sent to a field penal battalion. In this case, based on Emil S.'s performance in France and Russia and his good service record, the military judicial authorities apparently considered him a reliable instrument of war and sent him to a regular unit.

The great lengths to which the military judicial authorities went in order to prosecute a four-year-old crime can only be described as amazing. At seventy pages in length, the case file indicates the considerable effort that the authorities expended on this case, with the vast majority of the documents pertaining to the pretrial investigation. Even with the Allies closing in, the Wehrmacht's version of justice invested considerable man-hours, collecting the facts it required to determine an individual's fitness for inclusion in the Wehrgemeinschaft.

When dealing with sexual assaults against German women, the courts as a rule did not heap verbal abuse or Nazi insults on the defendants. This finding lies in great contrast to scholars' frequent reports of Nazi rhetoric and ideological invective in cases of desertion and subversion.[68] Again, the finding raises the question of why the courts regarded soldiers convicted of raping German women as less despicable than deserters or "subversives." Given the preeminent place of women in Nazi population policy and Nazism's emphasis on sexual restraint and decorum, one would expect that assaults against "Aryan" women would have truly outraged a fanatic judge. Yet, other than frequently characterizing sexual assaults as "reprehensible" (which they obviously were), the courts appear to have been rather restrained, more often than not weighing the perpetrators' future military usefulness quite heavily, as did the commanding officers who had the final say.

In general, if a rape crime's reprehensibility prevented quick reintegration, manpower considerations in the long run proved overpowering, leading the military judicial authorities to reintegrate the majority of offenders after the partial atonement of their sentences. A minimum of 60 percent rejoined regular units, while 9 percent were mobilized in parole battalions. Due to the fragmentary nature of many of the case files, the ultimate fates of the remaining 31 percent are not clear. However, the likelihood that the majority rejoined the regular troops or parole battalions should not be underestimated.

Very little in the sexual assault case file sample suggests ideologically based jurisprudence. Rather, the evidence indicates an organization guided by practical military considerations: the partisan movements in the east and Italy, civilian-military relations in France, and the perpetrator's value as a combatant in cases of assaults against German women. If the courts imposed harsh punishments (even a short time within the labyrinth of the Wehrmacht penal system could be lethal), the courts did not impose them for ideological reasons or for the purpose of societal purification. Instead, immediate military interests guided both jurisprudence and the reintegration phase, and most convicted rapists were allowed to rejoin the Wehrgemeinschaft. Very few commanding officers locked up the perpetrators and threw away the key, even though the door could remain locked for a considerable period of time.

CHAPTER EIGHT

Child Molestation and Incest

The Central Documentation Agency's Eastern Collection contains relatively few case files for processes against individuals molesting children. Therefore, the case files for this chapter were supplemented with child molestation cases handled by air force courts (also contained in the Eastern Collection). The Eastern Collection contains an even smaller number of case files related to incest, so they are analyzed here alongside child molestation cases.[1] Only a few individuals in these cases committed crimes against foreign nationals, so it is not possible to analyze the case files on a national basis.

Few commonalities in jurisprudence emerge in these case files. However, the documents contain far too many examples of class bias, caste consciousness, and paternalism from the jurists to be ignored. Especially in cases of child molestation, the courts scrutinized the behavior and reputation of the victims and their families in an obvious effort to justify lesser penalties for the perpetrators.[2] Molested children from lower socioeconomic backgrounds sometimes received the courts' sympathies, but they just as often received the court members' disdain.

Sentencing practices, however, varied considerably. Nearly identical crimes committed by individuals with similar records and backgrounds often resulted in widely disparate punishments.

Incest
Although it is difficult to assess the significance of children in Nazi ideology, there can be little doubt that incest would have been regarded as an exceptional threat to racial purity. In the case file sample, thirty-six individuals were convicted for child molestation, while twelve were convicted for incest. Seven of the twelve individuals convicted for incest had molested a stepchild or legal ward, while only five individuals had had sexual contact with a blood relative. The average prison sentence for an incestuous relationship with a blood relative was approximately 8.25 months. The average prison sentence for nonincestuous child molestation came to sixteen months. The one

penal servitude sentence imposed for incest between blood relatives was eighteen months, while the courts handed down penal servitude sentences of 22.5 months, on average, for child molestation.

With such a small sample of incest cases, no definite conclusions can be drawn from these statistics. They do, however, suggest the potential for considerable discrepancies in punishments imposed for these two offenses, and at least raise an interesting question. Given the Nazi emphasis on racial purity, it seems significant that the average punishment for incest, even in this smallest of samples, would be so much lower than the average sentence for simple cases of child molestation. If the jurists had exploited their position to conduct societal purification, would they not have considered incest a serious threat to racial purity and therefore dealt with it ruthlessly? Again, the sample is small, but the case files tell a rather interesting story. The court that appeared most outraged by an incestuous relationship, lashing out at the defendant in a long diatribe, imposed the lightest punishment handed down by any court *for either child molestation or incest in the sample*. The case of Hans L. therefore deserves special scrutiny.

Hans L.

The Court of the Air Defense Commander–Crete in March 1942 sentenced Nazi Party Motor Corpsman Hans L. to three months' imprisonment for having intercourse with his teenage sister on several occasions. She gave birth to his child in December 1941. According to the defendant, he could not find a suitable partner in his village and was simply overcome by an "irresistible urge" (*unwiderstehlichen Trieb*). The Gerichtsherr confirmed the verdict and ordered the punishment completed.[3]

The court, citing Hans L.'s young age, good conduct, open confession, and clean record, granted mitigating circumstances.[4] However, the court also berated the defendant, stating, "To the disfavor of the defendant must be considered his grievous violation of the racial laws raised by National Socialism to a fundamental principle of the state." The court continued:

> Because the defendant, as a member of the Hitler Youth, knew fully that children produced by the sexual union of such close relatives as they

represent as brother and sister receive almost always only the bad genes, and later as a consequence of mental and physical hereditary defects that make them incapable of work, these children do not represent useful members of the Volksgemeinschaft. For such children, the state must spend huge sums unprofitably during their whole lives, which deprives the healthy offspring of the German people.

After this tirade, one would have expected a draconian punishment. Despite its apparent anger, however, the court imposed the lenient three-month prison sentence. It then blithely characterized this mild punishment as "necessary" but "sufficient" atonement. Hans L. was released to a regular unit in July 1942 after fully serving his sentence.[5]

In this case the court easily recapitulated the Nazi racial state philosophy and the regime's position on the burdens that "life unworthy of life" placed on the Volksgemeinschaft, and then slapped the defendant on the wrist. Did the court engage in its vitriolic discourse in order to satisfy the political leadership but then rule according to its conscience, as many apologists have claimed? Or did the isolated Crete garrison face a severe personnel shortage? The latter remains a possibility if one considers that the prosecutor, who was obligated to follow the Gerichtsherr's instructions, requested the three-month prison sentence upon Hans L.'s conviction. Whatever the court believed or felt about Hans L.'s conduct, it nevertheless complied with the commanding officer's wishes.

The possibility also exists that the court members were fanatic National Socialists—individuals who perceived themselves as agents for the Volksgemeinschaft's purification. If so, then the Gerichtsherr's dominance and control of the military judicial process remains the only possible explanation for the outcome of this case. In short, the court either would not or could not make an example of Hans L. for his "grievous violation" of the regime's "fundamental" racial principles.

Hans L., however, was not alone in violating such principles "raised by National Socialism." Sergeant Ernst S. was also prosecuted and punished in 1942 for impregnating a sibling. His transgression, however, did not even rate a trial but instead was settled by a punishment decree.[6] Ernst S., like Hans L., received the proverbial judicial slap on the wrist. The Gerichtsherr and commander of the 377th Grenadier Division sentenced him to four months' imprisonment for his offense against racial purity, and then granted an immediate parole.[7]

While the court in the case of Hans L. easily articulated the Nazi racial state philosophy, the Court of Military Government Area Headquarters 379–Lublin failed to even allude to the dangers that incest posed to the Nazi racial state in the 1941 case of Private Paul B. The court sentenced him to eight months' imprisonment for carrying out a consensual sexual relationship with his sister. Separated at a young age, Paul B. and his sister made contact after a fifteen-year separation. Quickly falling in love, they began an intimate relationship that eventually destroyed their marriages. The court granted mitigating circumstances, acknowledging the fact that the siblings had not seen each other since childhood. This, according to the court, had greatly diminished the "natural inhibitions" against such a liaison. Otherwise, the court offered little commentary in its deliberations and gave no indication of outrage over the incestuous relationship itself. It thus imposed a relatively light punishment when in fact the criminal codes allowed for penal servitude.[8]

Lance Corporal Franz H., another practitioner of incest, avoided punishment altogether for his disregard of National Socialist racial precepts.[9] Arrested for having intercourse with his twelve-year-old sister, Franz H. was sentenced in June 1943 by the Court of the Ninth Infantry Division to eighteen months' imprisonment for child molestation and incest.[10] The Gerichtsherr, when confirming the verdict, suspended the entire sentence in favor of front-parole, with the proviso that Franz H. remain on the eastern front with his own unit. Decorated and described as "dependable" and "duty conscious" by his immediate superior, Franz H. had also proven himself in combat. His dedication to martial concepts, rather than racial ones, apparently counted for more in the eyes of his commanding officer. Franz H., after violating fundamental Nazi racial principles, did not serve a single day for his crime.[11]

In the following case, the Court of the Wehrmacht Commander–Berlin imposed the only penal servitude sentence for incest in the case file sample. Ideology, however, had little impact on the ultimate outcome of this case.

Siegfried H.

The Court of the Wehrmacht Commander–Berlin in April 1943 sentenced Siegfried H. to eighteen months penal servitude for child molestation and incest. In 1941 the defendant attempted to have sex with his thirteen-year-old daughter, Anneliese. She resisted, which prevented penetration and caused Siegfried H. to ejaculate prematurely. After drinking one evening in 1943, the defendant climbed into bed with his sixteen-year-old-daughter, Hedwig, and had sex with her. She complied out of fear. According to a medical exam, he never fully penetrated her. After each incident, he warned the girls not to tell anyone. The Gerichtsherr confirmed the verdict and ordered the punishment completed.[12]

Refusing to make any confession, Siegfried H. contested the girls' testimony. The court therefore refused to grant mitigating circumstances. "The defendant makes the worst impression through his undisciplined and untruthful conduct," the court fumed, "in fact, so bad that his good performance evaluation seems hardly understandable. Only a severe punishment can make him understand." Siegfried H. received one year of penal servitude for each offense, which according to the prescribed formula came to eighteen months. He was incarcerated at Penal Camp II, Aschendorfermoor (Emsland), on May 13, 1943.

Shortly after his conviction, Siegfried H.'s wife petitioned for clemency, requesting that he be granted front-parole. Asked to assess Siegfried H.'s potential for reintegration, the penal camp superintendent reported, "He makes the impression of a man who is reluctant to serve (*wehrunwilligen Mensch*) and unprepared for combat (*nicht einsatzbereiten*). He is not useful as a soldier in the foreseeable future." The petition was sent up the military judicial chain of command, and the deputy chief of staff of VI Corps rejected it on July 4, 1944.[13]

If the documents accurately summarize the court's deliberations, it deemed a severe punishment necessary because of his "undisciplined and untruthful conduct," rather than the nature of the crime. Characterized as "unwilling" and "unprepared" for operations, Siegfried H. apparently refused to conform in detention, and the military judicial authorities therefore refused to reintegrate him, at least not before mid-1944 when the paper trail ends. Nothing in the documents, however, indicates indignation by the authorities over the crime itself. Siegfried H. was measured primarily by his martial qualities, both in court and in detention; the exact nature of his transgression was a secondary consideration compared to his usefulness as a soldier.

Overall, courts adjudicating incest cases imposed rather mild sentences for an offense that fanatic judges would have considered very dangerous to the Volksgemeinschaft. The incestuous activities documented in the case file sample, as a rule, did not provoke any special outrage from the courts. Although one court easily recapitulated the Nazi racial state philosophy, it handed down the lightest punishment found in the files for a crime that seriously threatened genetic health. In Siegfried H.'s case, the Court of the Wehrmacht Commander–Berlin imposed by far the most severe punishment for an incestuous relationship with a blood relative.

At twenty months per conviction, the Berlin court also imposed higher prison sentences, on average, for simple child molestation when compared to all other courts, whose average prison sentence came to approximately fourteen months per conviction. In addition, the Berlin court imposed penal servitude sentences for child molestation 40 percent of the time, with all other courts averaging 17 percent. Whether these statistics can be attributed to the Berlin court's proximity to the center of political power or its commander's views is unclear. The average period between a verdict's confirmation and parole (when applicable) was approximately 6.5 months for individuals convicted by the Berlin court, while the average for all other courts came to 3.25 months. The majority of the individuals convicted by the Berlin court had no apparent physical limitations that would have prevented parole, so the discrepancy is hard to explain. Many convicted soldiers entered another commander's jurisdiction when incarcerated, so the discrepancy cannot be attributed solely to the Berlin commander's standards for parole.

The Court of the Wehrmacht Commander–Berlin

Few discernible patterns in sentencing practices emerge in the cases of child molestation. Soldiers receiving the most draconian punishments, for example, included first-time offenders as well as previously convicted pedophiles.[14] The jurists nevertheless betray a certain class bias, with caste consciousness frequently perceptible in the courts' deliberations. Paternalism, frequently encountered in cases of sexual assault, also appears to have influenced jurisprudence in child molestation cases. Conversely, little evidence supporting the thesis of ideologically based jurisprudence emerges in the documents. In great contrast to the ideological invective and insults reported in cases of desertion and subversion, child molestation as a rule provoked only minor irritation from the bench.

The molestation case that most strongly suggests the influence of ideology on jurisprudence raises more questions than it answers. Ironically, the Nazi Weltanschauung in this revealing proceeding worked in favor of the accused, rather than against him. The case of Hugo B., in fact, turns the thesis of Wehrmachtjustiz as an agent of societal purification on its head.

Hugo B.

The Court of the Wehrmacht Commander–Berlin in September 1943 sentenced Sergeant Hugo B. to one year's imprisonment. Although indicted for child molestation, the defendant was convicted for public indecency. On several occasions, Hugo B. allegedly exposed himself to his neighbor's daughters, aged ten and eleven, as they played in their backyard. On one occasion, he purportedly masturbated and called to the children, "Pull on this!" The defendant contested the children's version of the events, testifying that he had urinated in his backyard one afternoon but most certainly had not masturbated in public. The Gerichtsherr refused to confirm the verdict for the reasons discussed below.[15]

According to the court, the young girl, Erika B., made a "good and credible impression." The court characterized her testimony as "halting" but believed her story, which was "free of any kind of fantasy-like embellishments." If her testimony had been contrived, the court noted, then "it would be a matter of a very clever and calculated liar, which one would not expect from an eleven-year-old girl." The court summarily rejected Hugo B.'s alibi, refusing to believe that he simply relieved himself behind his house.

When allocating the punishment, the court determined that Hugo B.'s spotless reputation could not be considered authoritative but that the impact of his alleged behavior on the girls should be. According to the court:

> The two girls come from the simplest circles and from a family with many children. The simple social conditions (*Verhältnisse*) and the multitude of children prevent the mother from supervising the emotional (*seelische*) welfare of the children in the same measure as in higher social classes. Besides, children from this social class come relatively earlier in professional life than children from the higher classes. The dangers in a moral respect are therefore here essentially greater. Obscene (*unsaubere*) experiences could therefore influence the childlike imagination essentially stronger than with children who are more protected and have more supervision.

The court concluded its deliberations, stating, "The protection of youths must under all circumstances be valued more highly than the defendant's integrity, which has until now been irreproachable (*die bisherige Unbescholtenheit des Angeklagten*)."

Hugo B.'s wife, in a letter dated one week after the trial, informed the court that the children's mother had filed similar complaints against others, complaints that proved to be unfounded. One of the children had been arrested for stealing and had to spend time in a youth home. Mrs. B. also described two family members as "imbecilic creatures" (*blöde Geschöpfe*) and informed the court that all eight of the children attended special schools for the mentally challenged (*Hilfsschule*). The children's testimony therefore should not be believed. She pointed out that, under the law, testimony was only admissible in court if the witness had full control of his or her faculties. For this reason the children should never have come before the court as witnesses in the first place. Not only had the mother been sterilized, but she also had been refused the Mother's Cross "because she only brought feebleminded inferior (*schwachsinnige, minderwertige*) children into the world." In conclusion, Frau B. made the following statement:

> According to the statements of the whole neighborhood, the family . . . stands morally at the lowest level, is only a burden to the German state, and through an unsubstantiated claim has achieved it that a decent and irreproachable person was convicted. Neither my husband nor I will

ever be able to overcome this vilification. No person acknowledges the justice of this harsh judgment and no decent person will take offense if a soldier relieves himself on a bush once in passing, moreover a soldier who had to spend more than seventeen months in Russia, more or less bringing uncultivated manners home.

Based on this letter, the reserve army commander, General Fritz Fromm, suspended the verdict and ordered a new trial.

The Berlin court convened for the retrial on November 3, 1943, and acquitted Hugo B. of the charges. Demonstrating that the value of evidence is often in the eye of the beholder, the court based its decision largely on the mother's "congenital feeble-mindedness." According to the court record, she could not understand a map (presumably of her neighborhood) displayed in court. She also failed to comprehend the criminality of giving false testimony and prevaricated on several issues, including the reason for her sterilization. She spoke far too quickly, the court members observed, to have given her answers proper consideration, as is "required with testimony before a court." The court thus rejected her testimony altogether and concluded that she had lodged the complaint from a self-serving need for thrills and recognition (*Sensationlust und Geltungsbedürfnis*).

The court conceded that the older child's testimony had been free of any contrived embellishments but now discounted her testimony altogether. It based this contradictory decision on a report from the Hilfsschule outlining the child's poor academic performance and truancy, and the mother's ambivalence. The report concluded, "The children . . . strike one as unpleasant overall because of their uncleanliness (*Unsauberkeit*). The credibility of the child absolutely must be doubted." Because the younger child had been arrested for theft and therefore was a "delinquent," the court likewise discounted her testimony.

Based on the family's poor reputation, the court turned its previous interpretation of the evidence on its head. It now accepted Hugo B.'s alibi that he had simply relieved himself in his backyard, then hurried off because he had to make it to a dental appointment on time, not because he was trying to avoid apprehension. Acquitted of all charges, Hugo B. subsequently received 370 Reichsmark (RM) for damages and court costs.

This case illustrates the risk in accepting a court's interpretation of the facts, as recounted in the documents, as the actual "truth." In this case the court interpreted the facts from two different perspectives and arrived at two different versions of history, rendering any conclusion on Hugo B.'s guilt or innocence impossible. The court during the first trial emphasized the need to protect children, especially those from lower socioeconomic circumstances who receive "less protection and supervision" from their parents. Yet it rejected the children's testimony during the second trial as soon as the family's genetic health was called into question.

The court appears to have been very much at home in the Nazi racial state. But was Wehrmachtjustiz in service of ideology, as the critics would have it? When examined more closely, this case highlights the difficulty in gauging the extent to which National Socialist ideology influenced jurisprudence, and perhaps more importantly, for what purpose.

In the first trial, the court dispassionately examined the evidence and convicted an alleged pedophile, yet little that can be characterized as reflecting National Socialism emerged during its deliberations. In fact, class bias proved to be more germane to the court's assessment of the evidence, with stereotypical observations about families from lower socioeconomic backgrounds prominently articulated. It is not until the second trial that Nazi racial ideology and the attendant clichés materialize. As soon as evidence calling into question the family's genetic health surfaced, the court quickly acquitted the defendant.

Why did the court not show its National Socialist stripes in the first hearing? If jurists perceived the function of Wehrmachtjustiz as societal purification, then why did the court in the first trial not immediately label an alleged child molester an asocial element that had to be purged from the Volksgemeinschaft, according to the pattern reported by many scholars in cases of desertion? Why did this court exhibit an affinity for National Socialist ideology only in the second trial, and then only for the clear purpose of rationalizing the acquittal of an alleged pedophile? Put more simply, the National Socialist Weltanschauung became the defendant's salvation, rather than his doom. According to the critics, the jurists were in service of ideology. In this case, ideology appears in service of the war effort, with National

Socialist racial concepts justifying the exoneration, rather than the elimination, of a soldier with a fine service record.

This case neither proves nor refutes the influence of ideology on jurisprudence. Rather, it demonstrates once again the issue's complexity. While the case of Hugo B. raises as many questions as it answers, the following case further supports the thesis that class bias, caste consciousness, and paternalism may have had a greater impact than National Socialist ideology on Wehrmachtjustiz.

Paul B.

On May 27, 1943, the Berlin court sentenced Lance Corporal Paul B. to five years' imprisonment for child molestation. Convicted twice by civilian courts for molestation, the defendant in this case encountered an eight-year-old girl, sat with her on a bench, and coaxed her to put her head on his lap, which excited him greatly. He then convinced her to see a movie with him. In the theater, he placed her hands on his genitals. Another theater patron observed their activity, which led to his apprehension. The Gerichtsherr confirmed the verdict and ordered the punishment completed in a field penal battalion.[16]

Paul B. made a full confession before the court. In his own defense, however, he testified that he had not approached any children since his last conviction. In this case, he explained, the youngster had actually approached him.

Before the trial, doctors at the University Institute for Forensic Medicine and Criminality evaluated the defendant, and the attending physician's diagnosis was submitted as evidence. Paul B., the report noted, had been in full command of his faculties. According to the attending physician, however, he was not a habitual offender; nor were the prerequisites for castration present. A second medical expert also testified before the court. He emphasized that Paul B. had successfully battled his "psychopathological inclination" since his last conviction, and thus "security measures" were unnecessary.

Acknowledging Paul B.'s ability to resist his desires since his 1939 conviction, the court fully subscribed to the two medical experts' assessments of the defendant. It also lauded Paul B.'s performance in combat and noted that he had performed well enough to be promoted. For these reasons, the court refrained from imposing a penal servitude sentence.

Perhaps most important in its decision, the court, in a display of both class bias and paternalism, held the victim partly responsible for Paul B.'s conduct. In a long discussion of the girl's background and character, the court justified the imposition of a prison sentence rather than a penal servitude punishment. Asserting that the twice-convicted pedophile had not actually relapsed (*ist nicht rückfällig geworden*), the court determined that he had not taken the initiative but instead had been overpowered by the girl's enticing behavior:

> Criminal assistant R., who has interrogated the girl, has remarked that the girl does not make a very good impression. The domestic conditions are very bad (*übel*), she does not know her father's first or last name, the mother lives with a friend or fiancé, the child is often left to her own devices. It is known to the Berlin criminal courts that girls from this type of environment are frequently precocious to such an extent that they are prematurely depraved (*verderben*), that they approach men and tempt them to actions that fall under the criminal code against child molestation in order to receive money, sweets, or trips to the cinema.

The court later continued its condemnation of the girl's behavior:

> According to the credible description by the defendant . . . made much more credible by the remarks from the Women's Criminal Division official, the court has come to the conviction that the defendant would not have come to his criminal act without the stimulating conduct of the girl. The court believes that the defendant has learned to control himself in so far that he no longer attacks small children, and that here chance played a role, a chance arising from a distinct class of children in whose circle that kind of thing often happens and who themselves for the most part are responsible for such incidents.

Despite the long-winded defamation of the girl's character and conduct, the court nevertheless concluded that the punishment would have to be severe in order for it to exercise an educational effect on Paul B. Sentenced to five years' imprisonment; he was paroled after approximately fifteen months. There the paper trail ends.

In this case, a three-time offender's behavior received less scrutiny than that of his victim. Although his prison sentence was certainly lengthy at five years, Paul B. could have been sentenced to penal servitude. As in Hugo B.'s case, the class bias encountered in this case is intriguing. In conjunction with the paternalism often encountered in cases of sexual assault, it appears that caste and gender were at least as important as ideology in jurisprudence, if not more so.

Caste and gender also may have influenced the outcome of the case of Otto G. He was convicted by the Court of the Wehrmacht Commander–Berlin in May 1942 to six months' imprisonment for molesting a twelve-year-old girl. The court took his good conduct and clean record into account, but it focused primarily on his seduction by "special circumstances." The girl appeared "precocious" and her demeanor indicated that she was "experienced sexually." For these reasons, the court placed most of the blame on her. "She loafs around on the street in the evenings," the court lectured, "and met repeatedly with the defendant who, as a simple man from the country, was overpowered by the big city."[17] The Gerichtsherr confirmed the verdict and ordered the punishment completed.[18]

In addition to demonstrating the potential influence of class and gender on jurisprudence, this case shows the vast differences in the Berlin court's sentencing practices in cases of child molestation. The six-month prison sentence handed down by the court in Otto G.'s case contrasts sharply with the sentence imposed against Lance Corporal Bernhard V., who also came before the court on molestation charges.[19] In each case the defendants fondled twelve-year-old girls. Each had clean records. The court tried Bernhard V. in June 1942, while Otto G. came before the court just one month earlier. Yet Otto G. received a six-month prison sentence, while Bernhard V. received two years of penal servitude. Although different judges presided over the cases, greater diversity in sentencing can hardly be imagined and is difficult to explain. Rendering an explanation even more elusive is the fact that the same commander, General von Hase, confirmed both verdicts.[20] If the political authorities attempted to steer jurisprudence in order to obtain uniform (and presumably draconian) punishments, they clearly failed here.[21]

Predicting the severity of punishments imposed by the Berlin court based on the defendant's background and the nature of the abuse is indeed largely impossible in molestation cases. The court-martial of gunner Franz J. is a prime example. He sexually abused a stepdaughter over a period of four years, yet he received a relatively brief one-year prison sentence, which in fact he never atoned. The Gerichtsherr ordered the punishment served as six weeks of intensified arrest upon confirmation of the verdict. The remainder of the punishment was suspended until after the war.[22]

Franz J. also may have benefited from the court members' class bias and paternalism. The evidence gathered during the investigation strongly suggests that the child had been molested over an extended period. The court rebuked the defendant for his actions but also condemned the victim for her behavior. She testified that she endured the years of abuse because she feared her stepfather and had no faith in her mother. The court nevertheless minimized the defendant's responsibility and trivialized the victim's years of suffering, remarking, "It is surprising that she never told anyone" and never "resisted him." Furthermore, the court characterized her as "not overly intelligent," as a girl who made an "awkward impression." When granting mitigating circumstances, the court ruled that she had greatly facilitated Franz J.'s actions through her conduct.

If the evidence does not fully support characterizing the Berlin court's jurisprudence as class justice, one cannot deny its frequent displays of contempt for underprivileged youths and their families. The Court of the Wehrmacht Commander–Berlin was prepared to deal ruthlessly with pedophiles on occasion, but little evidence suggests punishments were imposed for ideological reasons.

Child Molestation: Field and Reserve Courts

Other than paternalism and an apparent class bias, few perceptible trends in jurisprudence emerge in the documents of child molestation cases tried before field and reserve courts. As with the Berlin court, sentencing practices varied considerably. The military judicial authorities consistently exhibited the same concern with practical military considerations as seen in cases of rape and homosexuality, with Manneszucht and military order their points of orientation. Courts and commanders carefully weighed the perpetrators' offenses against their service records both at trial and during the reintegration process. A soldier's (or prisoner's) willingness and ability to fully subordinate himself to military order remained the primary criterion when evaluating convicted child molesters for inclusion in the Wehrgemeinschaft.[23]

Illustrating the dearth of perceptible trends in the cases, the nationality of the victims proves to be a poor barometer for predicting the severity of a punishment. Molesting a foreign national rather than a German youth, for example, did not visibly influence the courts during the sentencing phase. In the case file sample, three of the most draconian punishments handed down by field and reserve courts were for the sexual abuse of non-German children.

The Court of the 346th Infantry Division, for example, imposed one of the most severe punishments for the molestation of a French boy in March 1943, sentencing Organization Todt foreman Franz K. to eighteen months of penal servitude.[24] The Court of the 319th Infantry Division imposed the same sentence against Otto H. for molesting a British national in the same year, while the Court of the Garrison Commander–Sofia in 1941 sentenced physician's assistant Kurt P. to two years' imprisonment for accosting two Bulgarian teens.[25] These punishments fall easily within the spectrum of severity encountered in cases involving German youths. The two harshest punishments handed down for the violation of German children were eighteen months of penal servitude imposed by the Court of the 52nd Division in 1940 and a three-and-one-half-year prison sentence imposed by the Court of the 253rd Infantry Division.

Despite the inconsistency in punishments, the military judicial paper trail nevertheless reflects many of the patterns encountered in cases of sexual assault and homosexuality. The reintegration process, for example, was predictable, with the Gerichtsherren, prison and penal unit commanders, and other military officers assessing convicted pedophiles in terms of their value as combatants and willingness to conform to military order—in short, in terms of their "usability" as soldiers.[26]

Ideological invective and Nazi rhetoric seldom appear in the case files, although examples can be found.[27] The case of Private Heinrich T. is a prominent example. Labeled an "antisocial parasite" at trial, he was convicted for accosting a German lad. If the National Socialist Weltanschauung influenced the court members, it had little practical impact on Heinrich T.'s fate. Indeed, upon close inspection, military interests, not ideological ones, ultimately determined the course of events. Heinrich T. committed one of the more reprehensible acts of molestation against a German child in the case file sample, yet he soon found himself back with his comrades.

Heinrich T.

In May 1940 the Court of the 253rd Infantry Division sentenced Private Heinrich T. to three and one-half years' imprisonment for molesting a six-year-old child. Previously convicted by civilian courts for child molestation and violations of paragraph 175, the defendant in this case befriended a German boy and took him for a walk in the woods. There he fondled the lad's genitals. After an unsuccessful attempt to penetrate the boy, Heinrich T. masturbated himself and the boy simultaneously until he (i.e., the defendant) achieved orgasm.[28]

Outraged over the defendant's reprehensible crime, the court labeled the twice-convicted pedophile as an "antisocial parasite" who deserved no mercy. The court, however, imposed a prison sentence rather than the more severe punishment of penal servitude. Penal servitude, the court observed, was automatically accompanied by mandatory discharge. This, the court lamented, allowed perpetrators "to spend the war far from the front in safety, even if under severe physical hardship," while their comrades risked their lives "before the enemy." By sentencing him to prison, the court explained, Heinrich T. would remain in uniform, giving the Wehrmacht the chance to exercise the appropriate "educational influence" during his punishment.

The court members in this case might have been party fanatics. The Nazi slur and implicit reference to "counter-selection" is quite striking. It is also largely irrelevant, because Heinrich T.'s future was determined by the Gerichtsherr. The Gerichtsherr's immediate post-trial decisions impressively illustrate the considerable power commanders exercised over those who became ensnared in the military judicial machinery. On May 8, 1940, the Gerichtsherr confirmed the guilty verdict and, based on the severity of the crime, ordered Heinrich T. directly to a Wehrmacht penal camp.[29] He rescinded this order one day later, however, and issued a temporary parole. The Gerichtsherr granted this reprieve so that Heinrich T. could participate in the Western Offensive, which began on May 10, 1940. A permanent decision regarding parole, the Gerichtsherr decreed, would be made based on Heinrich T.'s performance in the campaign.[30]

Heinrich T. returned to his unit and accompanied the 253rd Division as it thrust across the Belgium frontier. On May 18, however, he was caught hiding in a chateau. This attempt to avoid combat came on the heels of another unexplained absence from the troops twenty-four hours earlier. Therefore, after the conquest of France, the Gerichtsherr revoked Heinrich T.'s parole. He was sent to a Wehrmacht penal camp as per the Gerichtsherr's original completion order.

Heinrich T. spent the next three years in various Wehrmacht penal institutions. He refused to conform. Prison authorities reported in July 1941 that he had been disciplined eight times, receiving a total of thirty-four days confinement between January and June 1941. His violations included talking back to superiors (on one occasion, telling his foreman to "lick my ass"), punching a fellow prisoner, and shirking work. Bruchsal Prison in January 1942 reported that Heinrich T. had been disciplined twelve times and punished with a total of sixty-four days confinement. According to the report, he performed badly on work details and had an unmilitary appearance, and therefore would be transferred to a mobile prison unit at Regensburg.

Although Heinrich T.'s location after January 1942 is not clear, he was disciplined five more times between February and April of that year, receiving a total of forty-three days of confinement. For this reason he was sent to Field Penal Camp II in July 1942 and then to Field Penal Camp III in February 1943. Six weeks later, Heinrich T. was transferred to a prison in Germany (*Heimatgefängnis*) for medical reasons.[31] He spent the next year recuperating in various hospitals and convalescence units. He was ultimately classified as medically incapable of incarceration (*haftunfähig*) and dismissed from service on May 11, 1944. The civilian authorities in Köln subsequently received jurisdiction over him. Because he was officially classified as a penal camp inmate, none of the time that Heinrich T. had spent in the Wehrmacht penal system had been credited as time served. The Köln County Court, on September 8, 1944, thus notified the Wehrmacht that he had been subpoenaed and would serve his sentence in Anrath Prison.

Heinrich T.'s odyssey demonstrates several important points. First, the Gerichtsherren largely controlled the defendants' fates, and manpower considerations very often influenced their decisions. Second, the Gerichtsherren could be utterly pragmatic when dealing with sex offenders. Heinrich T.'s transgression was apparently reprehensible enough to merit a stiff punishment, yet not so horrible that he should miss operations. The "parasitic" pedophile Heinrich T. rejoined his unit with an opportunity to prove his value as a combatant.

But Heinrich T. refused to carry a weapon in good faith, and the Gerichtsherr revoked his parole. Still refusing to conform, he was disciplined repeatedly over the next three years. Only his failing health prompted his permanent exclusion from the Wehrgemeinschaft. Especially noteworthy is the fact that as a penal camp detainee, he received extensive medical care. According to many scholars, the penal camps were designed with the destruction of the "asocial" in mind. If that were the case, one wonders why a molester of German youths received medical treatment over an extended period. One might also ask why he ultimately was discharged for medical reasons if destruction was the purpose of the penal camps.

Heinrich T.'s violation of a German child was truly reprehensible, and the court imposed a fairly severe multiyear prison sentence. And, in all fairness, not all Gerichtsherren proved as pragmatic as this one in their handling of pedophiles. Military considerations, however, normally trumped all others.

Although nearly identical crimes committed under similar circumstances resulted in disparate punishments, one area of consistency in sentencing practices is found in cases involving young women approaching the age of majority. Although the case files are too few to establish a trend, they nevertheless contain several interesting examples.[32] In such cases, the courts imposed lenient sentences for contact between soldiers and teenage girls.

The Court of the 189th Reserve Division, for example, sentenced Michael H. in August 1943 to three months' imprisonment for child molestation. He had engaged in heavy petting with a thirteen-year-old German girl, and the contact included reciprocal manual stimulation of the genitals. The Gerichtsherr confirmed the verdict and immediately suspended the sentence for front-parole.[33] In another striking example, the Court of the 253rd Infantry Division in January 1941 sentenced Corporal Willi G. to six months' imprisonment for his carnal knowledge of a German teen. His intimate contact with the thirteen-year-old included intercourse. The Gerichtsherr confirmed the verdict but then suspended the entire sentence, and Willi G. rejoined the troops.[34] By punishment decree the commander of the 214th Infantry Division in 1942 sentenced Private Karl G. to six months' imprisonment for having consensual sex with a thirteen-year-old *Mädchen*. The sentence was suspended in its entirety, and Karl G. remained with his unit as a parolee.[35]

In addition to immediate parole for the perpetrators, these three cases have something else in common. They all suggest the potential influence of paternalism and class bias in jurisprudence. In the case of Michael H., the girl's reputation did not escape the court's scrutiny. With a case pending against her for consorting (*Umgang*) with French prisoners of war, the court described her as a "wanton and precocious girl with no sense of shame" and concluded that Michael H. had "not damaged her morally." For these reasons the court granted mitigating circumstances.

Willi G.'s underage partner likewise became an object of scorn. The court considered the defendant's fairly clean record and performance as a "capable soldier" when allocating the punishment, but it focused primarily on the girl's character and conduct. The court noted that the girl "hung out on the streets" and had been punished for disturbing the peace, and characterized her as a physically developed girl whose reputation was no longer "flawlessly respected." It could not therefore be assumed, the court ruled, that the defendant had seduced her. The court granted mitigating circumstances and imposed the minimum punishment.

In Karl G.'s trial, paternalism also appears crucial to the outcome of the case. He was granted mitigating circumstances, and hence a milder punishment, because evidence suggested that his victim had other sexual partners.

In these three cases, the jurists laid a good portion of the blame on the victims and slapped the defendants on the wrist. All three soldiers, having had their sentences suspended, returned to their duties and apparently never served any time. These examples indicate the courts' general tolerance of sexual relations between soldiers and young women approaching the age of majority, especially if the victims had "questionable reputations" or appeared physically well-developed for their ages. Class bias and paternalism, not Nazism, appear to be the most likely explanation for the courts' forbearance in such cases. In the five specific examples found in the case files, only one of the five perpetrators served any time: six weeks of a six-month sentence.[36]

Very little in the case files suggests ideologically based jurisprudence in cases of child molestation and incest. On the contrary, class bias, caste consciousness, and paternalism appear far more influential than the Nazi Weltanschauung in the courts' decisions and thus had a far greater impact on the defendants' fates. Cases of child molestation also reflect, to varying degrees, patterns encountered in cases of homosexuality and sexual assault, with practical military considerations guiding the overall process.

In incest cases, only one court used the bench as a forum to warn against incest's danger to the Volksgemeinschaft and racial purity. After proselytizing, however, the court imposed the lightest punishment found in the case files for either incest or child molestation. The court may have been truly outraged at the defendant's conduct, but nevertheless it bowed to the Gerichtsherr's wishes and imposed a negligible punishment. It also is possible that the court simply paid lip service to the Nazi racial state philosophy and imposed the light sentence without any qualms, placing the war's prosecution above ideological goals.

Finally, of the forty-eight individuals convicted for child molestation or incest, thirty-six were immediately paroled by the Gerichtsherr at the time of confirmation or received parole after atoning a portion of their sentence. In seven cases, because the case files are fragmented, no definite conclusions can be drawn as to whether the prisoners served their full sentence or were granted parole. Given the high parole rate for the individuals whose fates have been determined with certainty (thirty-six of forty-eight, or 75 percent), it is likely that the military judicial authorities ultimately sent four or five of these individuals back into action in one form or another. Two individuals atoned their punishment, while three others either were dismissed from service or, most likely, remained in custody until the end of the war.

Altogether, the evidence suggests that as many as forty-three child molesters and individuals convicted for incest out of a total of forty-eight rejoined the troops. Apparently, it took more than the sexual abuse of children or sexual contact with a relative to be permanently excluded from the Wehrgemeinschaft.

CHAPTER NINE

Racial Defilement and Bestiality

Two categories of sex offenses deserve scrutiny, despite their apparently infrequent occurrence. The first, racial defilement (*Rassenschande*), or sexual contact between "Aryans" and Jews, is obviously important for this investigation. Anti-Semitism and racial purity were the cornerstones of Nazi ideology and the "blood laws" were the most important legislative pillars of the National Socialist state. The second category, bestiality, is difficult to analyze within the context of the Nazi Weltanschauung, but the case files nevertheless provide insight into Wehrmachtjustiz. The Eastern Collection contains very few case files for these two offense categories, and thus any conclusions must be regarded as tentative at best. The small number of case files also renders general interpretative discussions problematic, and hence the most important cases are discussed in detail in this chapter in order to highlight the salient points.

Racial Defilement

The Nuremburg Laws of September 1935 represent a significant milestone along the twisted road to Auschwitz. Outlawing sexual contact between "Aryans" and Jews, the blood laws threatened racial defilement with very stiff penalties.[1] With anti-Semitism and racial purity at the very heart of Nazi ideology, cases of racial defilement should, in theory, provide compelling evidence of the true nature of Wehrmachtjustiz. The Eastern Collection contained only four case files for processes against violations of the blood laws, while only three case files from the Court of the Wehrmacht Commander–Berlin survived the war. The Central Documentation Agency's computer database contains six additional case files from various units. Whether this small number of surviving case files indicates extreme restraint in prosecution in defiance of Nazi law and ideology is not clear from the documents.

The evidence from this small sample suggests, as do the cases in the other categories of sex offenses, a military judiciary driven by practical military considerations. The case files indicate that when confronting racial defilement, the military judicial authorities generally considered the war's prosecution and martial virtues as more important than a soldier's dedication to racial purity. This is not to suggest that there are no examples of overt anti-Semitism in the documents. However, the military judicial authorities, even when punishing "racial defilers," made the prosecution of the war their priority. Indeed, blatant anti-Semitic expressions and slurs appear fairly frequently in the documents, yet what mattered most to the Gerichtsherren was how an individual's punishment could best serve the war effort.

The most important discovery in the case files is the apparent divergence in jurisprudence between the civilian and military courts in racial defilement cases, a difference that benefited those in the Wehrmacht (and civilians falling under its jurisdiction). Michael Ley, in his investigation of civilian Rassenschande cases tried before the Vienna County Court, demonstrates the potential fanaticism with which the civilian authorities pursued racial defilement. He concludes that many defendants were convicted on flimsy evidence and very few were acquitted.[2]

In the thirteen case files examined for this chapter, the opposite held sway on both counts. Military courts required hard evidence, and acquittals were numerous. In addition, the Vienna court consistently rejected as exculpatory defendants' claims that they had been unaware of their partners' descent. In Ley's survey of 150 cases, the Vienna court cited ignorance of descent as the justification for an acquittal on only one occasion.[3] By great contrast, in the thirteen cases examined for this chapter, five defendants avoided convictions by pleading that they had not known their lover was Jewish, as the following two cases demonstrate.

Erich D.

In April 1942 the Court of the First Flak Division refrained from conducting a judicial inquiry against Private Erich D. for racial defilement. The defendant met the girl, Eva, a "full Jew" (*Volljüdin*), while on leave. They spent the night in a hotel and had sex. The court accepted the defendant's explanation that he had been misled by his Jewish lover regarding her descent. During her interrogation she confirmed that she had not been wearing the Jewish star. She also admitted that she had presented fake identification at the hotel. She further acknowledged that her plan of deception included claiming Italian ancestry in order to explain her dark features to the defendant. Under these circumstances, the court dropped the charge of "criminal racial defilement" against the defendant. Erich D. returned to his unit, where he likewise avoided any disciplinary action over the incident. On parole for a previous (but unrelated) offense, Eva was incarcerated in a women's prison. Her records were subsequently transferred to the state police (*Stapo*) for the initiation of "preventive measures" (*vorbeugender Maßnahme*).[4]

In stark contrast to the judicial Alltag in the civilian courts reconstructed by Michael Ley, the court in this case did not consider Erich D.'s violation of the blood laws as criminal because he had not known his partner's true heritage. Ignorance was bliss, as the saying goes, for Erich D. According to Ley, "Aryans" as a rule could only escape conviction in the Vienna civilian court when the accusations were completely misguided. In this case, there was no question that sexual contact occurred. Had Erich D. come before a civilian court, he might have indeed been punished severely.

In the following case the defendant also escaped punishment after pleading that he had been unaware of his partner's descent.

Josef L.

The Court of the Sixth Army in July 1941 dismissed racial defilement charges against Lance Corporal Josef L. The defendant admitted having sex with Erika G., a polish Jew. The court, however, stated that it "could not be refuted" that he considered her to be non-Jewish. Erika G., the court observed, wore no arm band, spoke German, and posed as an "ethnic German" (*Volksdeustche*). Furthermore, the prosecution could only offer the testimony of the "unreliable Jew" as evidence. For these reasons, the charge of racial defilement was dropped.[5]

As in the first case, there was no doubt that intimate contact occurred, and the defendant conceded that he had indeed committed racial defilement. The Court of the Sixth Army, like the Court of the First Flak Division, nevertheless ruled that a crime had not been committed. The court's use of the term "unreliable Jew" indicates anti-Semitism, yet other than this slur, the court does not express any revulsion or outrage at the intimate contact itself.

In contrast to Erich D. and Josef L., the defendant in the following case was convicted for his violation of the blood laws. Karl S.'s sentence also represents the harshest punishment imposed for racial defilement found in the case file sample, and the court displays considerable wrath. Karl S., however, was simultaneously convicted for evading military service, and thus the source of the court's anger is not completely clear. In fact, the court's fairly compassionate attitude toward the defendant's Jewish wife muddles the issue considerably.

Karl S.

The Court of the Commanding Officer of Greater Paris in April 1942 sentenced Karl S., an expatriate German national, to death on charges of subversion for his evasion of military service and four years of penal servitude for racial defilement. He met his wife, Flora, in 1936. Unable to marry in Germany because of her Jewish descent, they emigrated in 1938. Before their departure, Karl S. was summoned for an induction examination. He applied for, and was granted, an extension. Additional extensions were denied. Married in France in 1940, the two fled to the unoccupied area of France after the German invasion in May of that year. They were apprehended after Germany occupied the remainder of the country in 1942.[6]

The court acrimoniously castigated the defendant for "renouncing the Fatherland for a Jew." However, it is not clear from the documents whether the court was more outraged by the defendant's marriage to a Jewish woman or his evasion of military service. Indeed, the court imposed draconian penalties for both offenses. For his "treacherous" evasion of military service, which prosecutors pursued as subversion of fighting power with the attendant draconian circumstances, the defendant received the death penalty. For racial defilement, the court imposed four years of penal servitude, the highest punishment in the racial defilement cases examined here.

The court, during its deliberations, simultaneously addressed both the defendant's marriage and evasion of service:

For the crime of subversion of fighting power [i.e., his act of desertion], paragraph 5 section 1 of the wartime penal code provides for the death penalty. The court has not been able to establish a mitigated case under section 2 of this provision; on the contrary the crime appears extraordinarily severe. The defendant . . . as a German citizen of German blood, has in spite of one of the fundamental principles of the new German Reich and in spite of clearly defined laws threatening imprisonment wanted to and did marry the Jewish woman and has, based on his plan, put all his duties as a German citizen aside and deserted his Fatherland. For this treachery, he deserves death. . . . For the marriage itself, a further punishment of four years penal servitude appears commensurate with the guilt.

The court is indignant about the defendant's actions, but which ones? Did the defendant's violation of the blood laws or his evasion of service cause more outrage? The court members could very well have been rabidly anti-Semitic, but that conclusion is difficult to sustain if one considers their fairly sympathetic attitude toward the defendant's wife. Close scrutiny of the documents indeed renders a firm conclusion on the issue problematic. When sentencing Karl S.'s wife, Flora, the court neither disparages nor vilifies her and even displays a bit of compassion. The court concluded that she had violated the blood law in full consciousness of the ban against intimate relationships between Germans and Jews, and therefore a severe punishment was necessary. However, they also granted mitigating circumstances, stating, "In her favor is considered that as a consequence of an ailment, she will have to suffer more in confinement than a healthy person."

Although the four-year penal servitude sentence indeed represents a severe punishment, it could have been much higher had the court rejected any mitigating circumstances. The absence of any anti-Semitic insults or aspersions during the sentencing phase may or may not be relevant, but it might suggest that it was indeed Karl S.'s evasion of military service that outraged the court, rather than his intimate relationship and marriage to a Jew.

While the primary issue for the court in this case is not clear, the following case demonstrates one court's preference for pursuing martial goals, rather than racial ones.

Ernst R.

In December 1943 the Court of the Wehrmacht Commander–Berlin sentenced Lance Corporal Ernst R. to four years' imprisonment for violating the blood laws. The defendant had taken an eighteen-year-old girl, Ingeborg J., into his home in December of the previous year. The teenager, who had fled her parents dwelling to avoid "resettlement" (*Umsiedlung*), testified that the defendant had provided her refuge in exchange for sex. The court refused to accept the defendant's claim that he had not been aware of her heritage.[7]

Although four years' imprisonment is a relatively harsh punishment, the court concluded its deliberations with a recommendation for early parole. The "abominable" (*verabscheuenswert*) crime, the court noted, was not a one-time blunder but rather a "cunningly camouflaged" (*raffiniert getarntes*) year-long affair in which the defendant passed off "the Jew" as his wife. The court nevertheless emphasized that the defendant deserved leniency:

> As far as his behavior otherwise (*sonstigen Verhalten*), the defendant, whose only previous punishment is not worth mentioning and who has understood to overcome all difficulties in life that defy him with energy and diligence, deserves a milder judgment, namely in the direction that he could be protected from penal servitude and the exclusion from society that goes with it. However, a high punishment must be passed and four years' imprisonment appears appropriate. . . . The court recommends for the remorseful defendant who makes an orderly and militarily smart impression (*ordentlichen, strammen militärischen Eindruck*) the possibility of parole at the front or, in case of limited fitness, one such in an operational area.

The Gerichtsherr confirmed the verdict but mitigated the sentence to three years. Ernst R. remained in a local detention center in Berlin for only eight weeks before he was sent to a parole battalion.[8] There the case file ends.

It seems obvious in this case that the court members had little interest in severely punishing this soldier, despite his premeditated and "cunningly camouflaged" year-long relationship with a Jew. Instead, the court, in feigned anger, gave the soldier a gratuitous tongue lashing and then advocated an early parole, which the Gerichtsherr ultimately granted. Thus, within weeks of being convicted for his "abominable" crime, Ernst R., a "cunning" racial defiler, was free on parole. This case also raises a topic worthy of further investigation: to what extent did German soldiers exploit (sexually or otherwise) desperate Jews hoping to avoid "resettlement"?[9]

The fact that the courts in the preceding four cases do not appear rabidly anti-Semitic does not necessarily mean that the military judicial authorities sympathized with Jews or viewed them as equal under the law. As the fate of Eva in the first case illustrates, the military judicial authorities had no reservations about handing Jews over to civilian police agencies. Further evidence also suggests that the rights and welfare of Jews were irrelevant for Wehrmachtjustiz. In the following case, a German soldier is prosecuted for crimes against a Jew, but protecting the Jewish victim's civil liberties was not part of the equation. The court-martial of Ernst H. suggests that the Wehrmacht punished indiscipline in the form of criminal behavior, even if the victim was Jewish. The loss of a Jewish life stemming from such indiscipline, however, was immaterial.

Ernst H.

In June 1942 the Court of Military Government Area Headquarters 379–Lublin sentenced Corporal Ernst H. to four years' imprisonment under section 330a for rape, the unauthorized use of a weapon, plundering, and racial defilement. While heavily intoxicated, the defendant forced his way into a Jewish dwelling where he raped a Jewish woman at gunpoint. Previously convicted for an alcohol-related offense, Ernst H. did not dispute the charges but claimed that he had absolutely no memory of the events. The Gerichtsherr confirmed the verdict and ordered the punishment served in a field penal battalion. Ernst H. spent approximately sixteen months with the formation before he was paroled to the Seventy-third Infantry Division in late 1943.[10]

The court, in its deliberations, showed no outrage about the defendant's violation of the blood laws. In fact, it had nothing at all to say about Ernst H.'s racial transgression, the blood laws, or their importance to the Nazi state. Instead, the court focused primarily on the defendant's over consumption of alcohol in this particular case and his abuse of alcohol in general. Perhaps the most revealing aspect of this case, however, is the crime for which Ernst H. was not prosecuted. During the assault a large pane of glass was shattered. Flying shards killed a four-day-old Jewish infant. The prosecution did not pursue murder or manslaughter charges.[11] This would seem to suggest that the Gerichtsherr wanted to impress upon his command that indiscipline would not be tolerated and that, if one chose to rape and plunder, there would be severe consequences. The death of a Jew can be overlooked, but not indiscipline. Put another way, the military judicial authorities tolerated the death of a Jew at the hands of a German soldier, but not the behavior that caused the death.

In the following case, the war economy takes precedence over the rigorous enforcement of racial purity.

Anton B.

In April 1943 the Court of the Commanding Admiral–Black Sea (Bucharest) sentenced the civilian machinist Anton B. to twenty-one months' imprisonment for racial defilement and military theft.[12] Stationed in the Romanian city of Galatz, the highly decorated former soldier carried out a fifteen-month-long intimate relationship with Fani M., a twenty-six year old Jewish woman. Despite learning about her Jewish heritage just a few weeks after the affair began, the defendant continued seeing the young woman.[13] The Gerichtsherr confirmed the verdict, expressly rejected immediate parole, and ordered the punishment completed.

A Sudeten German, Anton B. explained in his own defense that his parents were dead, his first marriage had failed, and he had never had a fulfilling family life. The woman understood him and cared for him, providing him with joy for the first time in his life. He fell in love with her and was subsequently unable to break off the relationship after discovering her descent.

When allocating the punishment, the court acknowledged the existence of the loving relationship and in fact cited it as a compelling reason for imposing a prison sentence rather than penal servitude. Anton B., the court concluded, did not "belong to that category of racial defilers who from the very beginning and consciously protest against the law and commit racial defilement." Anton B, the court reflected, had been treated badly by fate, receiving "little love" and being denied a "harmonious and dear family life." For these reasons, the court declared, he had been too weak to break off the relationship. The woman, however, was also to blame. Despite her cognizance of the ban on intimacy between Germans and Jews, she nevertheless "understood how to draw him to her" (*ihn an sich zu ziehen verstanden*).

The court did not stop there but continued to find reasons to justify a lenient sentence:

> The court has further considered in the defendant's favor that he has lived in a foreign state up until the addition of the Sudeten region to the Reich and has not been schooled or educated in the basic principles that have led to the enactment of the blood laws. Finally, the defendant has committed the act in a country in which Aryans and Jews live peacefully side-by-side and the racial principles of the German people have still not found acceptance (*noch keinen Eingang gefunden haben*).

Having concluded its repertoire of mitigating circumstances, the court, noting that the affair stretched over a considerable period of time, asserted that a severe punishment was still necessary. Receiving twenty months for his crime of racial defilement, Anton B. was incarcerated on May 5, 1943, in a civilian prison at Landsberg am Lech. He was paroled less than five months later. His professional skills as a machinist, the Gerichtsherr explained on August 27, 1943, were in great demand, and his placement in the economy was vital to the war effort due to a great lack of individuals with such qualifications.

The remarkable thing about this case is that it is completely unremarkable. A fifteen-month intimate relationship violating the basic tenets of the Nazi racial state brought neither personal recriminations nor condemnation but instead an extensive review of the perpetrator's previous hardships. The court did not express shock or disapproval at the relationship but instead empathized with the defendant. The court did impose a fairly stiff punishment, but the Gerichtsherr paroled Anton B., the convicted racial defiler, after only five months for reasons related to the war economy.

The court in the following case, by contrast, readily recites Nazi racial principles and easily articulates the contemporary anti-Semitic clichés during its deliberations.

Karl D.

In July 1942 the Court of the Commanding Admiral of Auxiliary Naval Forces–France sentenced seaman first class Karl D. to one year's imprisonment for conducting an extended affair with a Belgian woman of Jewish descent. The defendant met the woman in Antwerp where he rented a room for their liaisons, which occurred two or three times per week from the spring of 1941 until the fall of that year. Convicted during a subsequent trial on a related charge, Karl D. received an additional ten months. Together, the total punishment came to twenty months. The Gerichtsherr confirmed the verdicts on September 26, 1942, and ordered the punishment completed in a field penal battalion.[14]

Citing multiple clichés as the basis for its decision, the court rejected the defendant's alibi that he had not known his lover's ancestry. Her "physical appearance," the court noted, made her "easily recognized" as a Jew, and "many Jews live in Antwerp." In addition, the defendant knew that the woman's father was a diamond broker, "a typical Jewish profession." He even visited his lover's son's barbershop, located in a "typical Jewish quarter" of the city. The son, like the woman's ex-husband, had a "typical Jewish last name." These facts, declared the court, could not have been overlooked by the defendant, and he should indeed have reckoned that she was a Jew.

During the sentencing phase, the court condemned the defendant for his involvement with a Jewish woman. "As an SA man," the court lectured, Karl D.'s actions represented a "breach of loyalty (*verletzt die Treuepflicht*) toward the German people," and the court considered this the primary aggravating circumstance. Despite this breach of loyalty, however, the court expressly rejected a penal servitude punishment as too harsh because it was accompanied automatically with the loss of worthiness to serve. Described by his commanding officer as "a willing soldier with a good military bearing as well as an open and honorable character," Karl D.'s good conduct earned him mitigating circumstances. The court also considered as mitigating the defendant's sexual vulnerability, explaining that Karl D. had been carried away by his "strong sexual bondage" (*sexuelle Hörigkeit*) to the woman.

The court began the sentencing phase by berating Karl D. for his "breach of loyalty," but it concluded the session by lauding the defendant's ultimate strength of will in ending the relationship. In an incongruous change of perspective from its initial determination that Karl D. should have reckoned that his partner was Jewish, the court brought the hearing to a close by remarking that the defendant found the strength to break the sexual relationship once he was "clear about . . . her racial membership." Thus, the court reasoned, a one-year prison sentence, rather than penal servitude, represented a just and appropriate punishment.

Karl D. spent approximately one year with Field Penal Battalion 15. During his tenure with the formation, he was twice hospitalized. He first required treatment for a glandular abscess (*Achseldrüsenabzess*) and later for wounds received in a grenade attack. These medical problems prevented an early transfer to a parole battalion, despite good conduct reports. Karl D. was in fact still recovering in a Lublin infirmary on December 31, 1943, when the Gerichtsherr ordered his transfer to a parole unit. Only after physicians declared Karl D. fit for combat was he released and sent to the parole battalion reserve formation at Skierniewice on March 31, 1944. His ultimate fate could not be determined.

In this case the court displays a considerable degree of anti-Semitism through its assertion that Karl D.'s relationship with a Jew constituted a breach of loyalty to the German people. Nevertheless, Karl D.'s racial offense, which stretched over several months, did not provoke the level of wrath and acrimony so often reported in desertion and subversion cases. Most importantly, the court ultimately had nothing but praise for Karl D., the racial defiler. The court not only lauded his ability as a soldier but also gave Karl D. more credit for ending the relationship than condemnation for beginning it.

The contrast between these seven cases and the civilian cases reported by Michael Ley is indeed striking. Whether the general tolerance displayed by these seven courts-martial would be substantiated by a broad-based investigation of cases files is anyone's guess. Like the small number of surviving case files, the jurisprudence in the cases might indicate restraint in prosecution in defiance of Nazi law and ideology. Again, however, this conclusion must be considered tentative at best.

Bestiality and Violations of Paragraph 175b

Although it is perhaps the greatest taboo with regard to sexuality, bestiality nevertheless must be discussed. It is difficult to estimate the number of soldiers who engaged in this type of sexual activity, but the Eastern Collection contained enough examples to warrant their examination. Overall, the documents reveal that the courts could be as capricious when prosecuting individuals for "indecency with animals" (*Unzucht mit Tieren*) as they were when prosecuting other classes of sex offenders.

The frequency of this offense was apparently very low, and few case files survived the war. The Eastern Collection contains only sixteen case files for the prosecution of violations of paragraph 175b, the criminal code against sodomy.[15] The short average sentence of six months' imprisonment is largely explained by the low legally mandated punishment parameters. All but one individual were released early for parole. Nearly one-quarter had their entire sentences suspended by the respective Gerichtsherren at the time of verdict confirmation.

Curiously, the majority of offenders in this category had no previous record of engaging in this form of sexual activity. As frequently seen with rape crimes and homosexual offenses, many perpetrators had consumed significant quantities of alcohol and claimed little or no memory of the events. Also of interest, 40 percent of the perpetrators had poor performance evaluations or were characterized by their commanding officers as "unstable" or "mentally limited."[16]

Most importantly, the military judicial authorities seldom expressed outrage or revulsion over acts of bestiality. Instead, they focused primarily on practical military matters, most often the defendants' records as soldiers. Take, for example, the August 1944 case of August S. He was caught sodomizing a mare and was sentenced by the Court of the 214th Infantry Division to fifteen months' imprisonment. The Gerichtsherr confirmed the verdict, ordered the punishment served in the division's penal platoon, and decreed that the prisoner should be paroled after three months.[17]

August S. had a poor service record, and the court considered his repeated disciplinary punishments and two previous military judicial convictions as evidence of a "deficient sense of duty."[18] In short, the court imposed the relatively severe punishment because of his undisciplined and unmilitary conduct. His deviant sexual behavior received hardly any scrutiny, but his performance as a soldier did. The court granted mitigating circumstance because August S. was "mentally limited." It did not exploit this "mental weakness" as a justification for purging him from the Volksgemeinschaft, a phenomenon reported by scholars in cases of subversion, desertion, and other militarily obstructive acts. Despite his apparent intellectual limitations, August S. rejoined the Wehrgemeinschaft after serving his abbreviated punishment.

In contrast to August S., Lance Corporal Franz N. received a relatively mild punishment for the very same transgression. In March 1942 the Court of Military Government Area Headquarters 379–Lublin sentenced him to three months' imprisonment for copulation with a horse. The Gerichtsherr confirmed the verdict and ordered the punishment served as four weeks of intensified arrest, followed by parole.[19] During the sentencing phase, the court acknowledged Franz N.'s clean record and dependable service and granted mitigating circumstances.[20]

As in the preceding case, the court had little to say about the deviant nature of Franz N.'s transgression, nor did it ponder his suitability for membership in the Volksgemeinschaft. Instead, the court emphasized Franz N.'s clean record and, more importantly, his dependability as a soldier. He soon rejoined the Wehrgemeinschaft as a parolee and, perhaps motivated by the sword of Damocles, performed above and beyond the call of duty. He was wounded in the battle to relieve the garrison at Welikije-Luki on January 4, 1943.

Private Richard G., another practitioner of sodomy, did not serve a single day for his crime. In August 1941 the Gerichtsherr of the Fifty-second Infantry Division, via a punishment decree, sentenced him to six weeks of confinement for having intercourse with a mare. He was immediately paroled.[21] In the late summer of 1941 the Fifty-second Infantry Division was half-way to Moscow. Apparently the division commander could forgive such behavior, even from an "undependable" and "uncomradely" soldier like Richard G., during the high point of the Barbarossa campaign. As seen throughout this study, manpower considerations could have a tremendous influence on a defendant's fate.

Also conforming to previously discussed trends is the August 1944 case of Lance Corporal Hans R. The defendant, who previously had been convicted for homosexual activity, was sentenced by the Court of the 169th Infantry Division to nine months in prison for sodomy and animal cruelty. The Gerichtsherr ordered the punishment served as four weeks of intensified arrest.[22] With violations of both paragraphs 175 and 175b on his record, Hans R. was nevertheless reintegrated after four weeks. Despite his sexual proclivities, Hans R. had demonstrated his willingness to carry a weapon in good faith, having been wounded in 1943.[23] He was a usable soldier.

Two cases provide special insight into the military judicial authorities' handling of sodomy cases. Although individuals such as Hans R. were allowed to rejoin the Wehrgemeinschaft, the Wehrmacht nevertheless still had high standards for its leadership strata, as the first case illustrates.

Franz C.

In April 1940 the Court of the 169th Division sentenced Sergeant Franz C. to six months' imprisonment for violating paragraph 175b. After drinking heavily at a tavern, the defendant entered a barn on the way home in order to relieve himself. Once there, he stood on a stool and had intercourse with a young bovine. The Gerichtsherr confirmed the verdict but suspended the entire sentence for service with the field army.[24]

The crime came to light when the calf's owner noticed that the animal was experiencing vaginal swelling. Franz C. had been so intoxicated that he lost his gloves and identification papers after a pratfall in the barn. These items naturally led the authorities to him.[25] The court refused to grant the defendant the protection of section 330a, the provision for diminished responsibility due to psychological impairment, even though Franz C. had consumed eight glasses of wine, four beers, and as many as four cognacs. The court did, however, consider his drunkenness as a mitigating circumstance.

Although Franz C. never served any time, the court demoted him to the lowest conscripted grade "in the interest of the noncommissioned officer corps." This, the court concluded, was necessary "in view of the crime's despicableness." Despite an unblemished record that stretched back to 1928, Franz C. no longer qualified for a leadership role in the Wehrmacht, which required impeccable credentials from its officers and NCOs. Anything less posed a serious threat to the Wehrgemeinschaft's integrity, functioning, and authoritarian structure.

In the last and most compelling case, pilfering provoked more outrage from the bench than did sodomy.

Alois S.

In June 1943 the Court of the 214th Infantry Division sentenced Private Alois S. to a total of two years' imprisonment for sodomy and theft. On two occasions in the spring of 1943 the defendant, while intoxicated, tried to carry out coitus with a sow that was in heat. After several failed attempts, Alois S. penetrated the hog digitally while he masturbated with the other hand. The defendant also admitted that he had stolen approximately one-half pound of coffee as a member of the kitchen staff. He also stole 80 RM from a comrade and attempted to steal cigarettes from the canteen. The Gerichtsherr confirmed the verdict, ordered the punishment completed in a field penal battalion, and provided for a parole hearing after six months.[26]

The court failed to express any shock or amazement at the defendant's method of finding sexual satisfaction, but it berated Alois S. at length for the adverse impact his larceny had on unit cohesion. The most "severe crime," the court asserted, was the theft of his comrade's money, which necessitated an investigation of his barrack mates. The defendant stole from a comrade, the court fumed, even though he had been "instructed repeatedly" on the topic and "knew the consequences," and thus the act "weighed heavily against him." The court also roundly condemned the defendant for absconding with the coffee, "a scarce commodity," and for exploiting "the position of trust in the kitchen" to misappropriate "a scarce luxury item." The attempted theft of the cigarettes, also a scarce commodity, the court concluded, likewise damaged the whole unit.

This case clearly points to a military judicial organization concerned about military effectiveness. The court had little to say about Alois S.'s sexual proclivities but did lash out at him for the damage his crimes caused to the band of brothers. The Wehrmacht considered pilfering a military offense, one that damaged the war effort. Detrimental to unit cohesion and morale, pilfering hindered the material mobilization for war, particularly because individuals generally misappropriated scarce commodities such as coffee. Perhaps most important, stealing from a comrade violated the bond between brothers in arms at the most basic level, the level of trust. Illustrating its military priorities (and by extension, those of the Gerichtsherr), the court imposed fifteen months for stealing from a comrade (*Kameradediebstahl*), three months for pilfering the coffee, and only two months for the barnyard antics.

Alois S. did not arrive at Field Penal Battalion 13 until late November 1943, more than five months after his conviction. He was paroled to a regular unit just three months later.

Very little in the sodomy cases suggests ideological jurisprudence. As with other categories of sex offenses, the courts focused primarily on issues of direct military interest. Many defendants in sodomy cases were characterized by their commanders as "mentally limited," which broaches the issue of "diminished responsibility before the law," the subject of chapter 10.

CHAPTER TEN

Intoxication and Diminished Responsibility

According to Stephen Fritz, German soldiers endured the cold Russian winters only by consuming alcohol.[1] Indeed, the heavy use of intoxicating beverages apparently was a widespread problem for the Wehrmacht and was not limited to the eastern front. A high percentage of the defendants in the case files had consumed alcohol before their crimes. Nearly 30 percent of the individuals convicted for sexual assault or homosexual activity, for example, had been drinking at the time of their infractions.

Section 51 of the Reich Criminal Code codified the principle of diminished responsibility and provided parameters for the punishment of crimes committed by mentally impaired individuals. Section 330a, which was inserted into the criminal code in 1934 as an adjunct to section 51, established guidelines for the punishment of individuals committing crimes in a state of complete intoxication, and therefore under diminished responsibility as defined by section 51. The provision established the maximum punishment for any crime, including murder, at two years' (and later five years') imprisonment, thereby excluding penal servitude.

As initially promulgated in 1934, section 330a read in part as follows:

Complete Inebriation (*Volltrunkenheit*)

Whoever intentionally or negligently puts oneself in a state of intoxication that precludes the capability to reason (Section 51, number 1) through the consumption of alcoholic beverages or other intoxicating means is punished up to two years imprisonment or fined if in this condition he commits an act threatened with punishment.[2]

The criminal codes threatened homosexual activity, rape, child molestation, and incest with penal servitude. Therefore, soldiers who were convicted for these offenses, but who were granted diminished responsibility and punished according to section 330a, more often than not received far more moderate punishments than they would have under the normal punishment parameters. The courts, however, granted diminished responsibility reservedly. Among the more than eighty individuals in the case files who consumed alcohol before committing their crimes, only nineteen received the protection of section 330a, primarily for rape crimes and violations of paragraph 175.

A comparison of fifteen case files for nonsexual offenses in which the courts granted diminished responsibility shows that with nonsexual offenses, as with sexual offenses, individuals had to be very intoxicated in order to receive the provision's protection.[3]

In fact, when hearing cases of sexual offenses, the courts very often refused the application of 330a, despite considerable evidence of extremely high levels of intoxication, such as falling asleep or passing out at the scene of the crime after committing a sexual assault.[4] Only on rare occasions did the courts not require extensive evidence before concluding that an individual had been impaired beyond the capacity to reason. On the other hand, the courts appear to have been inconsistent in their perception of what constituted complete inebriation and, on occasion, accepted the testimony of a single witness as sufficient proof that an individual had been completely inebriated.

Despite the military judiciary's preoccupation with practical military considerations, no evidence suggests that "good" soldiers received the protection of section 330a more often than "bad" soldiers. Nevertheless, as with the other categories of sex offenses, individuals' service records could be crucial to their fates during the sentencing and reintegration phases.

The case files also reflect and reinforce many other previously encountered trends. For example, the military judicial authorities prosecuted and punished German soldiers for alcohol-related crimes against eastern inhabitants.[5] The case files also reflect the high reintegration rate for homosexual offenders, even those with previous convictions for violations of paragraph 175.[6] Operations frequently took precedence over justice, with at least three offenders released early from detention specifically for that reason.[7]

Two issues not yet considered make intoxication cases particularly important to this discussion. The first concerns the authoritarian structure of the Wehrgemeinschaft. A high percentage of the defendants were noncommissioned officers, and upon conviction these individuals were stripped of their rank and reenrolled at the lowest conscripted grade. This phenomenon is not unique to those punished under section 330a, but Gerichtsherren and the courts subordinated to them considered the over-consumption of alcohol as a grievous violation of command responsibility. The NCOs (and in one case, an officer) were demoted and barred from positions of authority within the Wehrgemeinschaft, which had high standards for its leadership strata. The case files clearly illustrate the desire on the part of the commanders and courts to be certain that those in positions of authority had unblemished records and reputations.

The second and perhaps more important issue in inebriation cases is the nature of the inquiry itself. The courts proceeded in a painstaking and methodical fashion to determine a defendant's degree of drunkenness at the time of a crime. The level of effort expended on this line of inquiry could be quite extraordinary. There was no arbitrary rush to judgment, even though the courts were often confronted by particularly asocial behavior in the form of very drunken soldiers committing very heinous acts. The burden of proof for what constituted "complete intoxication" often varied from court to court, but the thorough nature of the inquiry did not. Despite the alcohol-fueled asocial antics, the focal point in such cases remained the defendants' degree of intoxication, not the degree of danger a defendant's asocial behavior posed to the Volksgemeinschaft. The courts may indeed have been packed with fanatics, but in inebriation cases, toxicology rather than ideology dominated the process, despite the outrageously easy targets on the docket.

Indeed, the image often painted by scholars of fanatic courts arbitrarily dispensing terror-justice in an effort to purify the Volksgemeinschaft is very difficult to sustain in cases of inebriation. The transcripts instead give the impression of a workaday and, at times, even mundane Alltag as the military judicial authorities try to make sense of alcohol-induced deviance. Despite the wartime conditions, the often reprehensible nature of the crimes, and the difficulty posed by conflicting testimony, the courts endeavored to determine precisely how drunk the perpetrators had been, at least as far as the available evidence permitted. Although the courts were not completely dispassionate, they remained indifferent to the needs of the Volksgemeinschaft. The defendants were treated to occasional tongue lashings, yet in such instances the courts' anger generally was directed at officers and NCOs for their failure to conduct themselves appropriately as part of the Wehrgemeinschaft's command structure.

Demonstrating the divergent burdens of proof and the level of effort invested by the courts requires a detailed review of a spectrum of inebriation cases. The following cases provide an interesting look at the abuse of alcohol by men at war.

Paragraph 175 and Section 30a: Reintegration versus Habitual Offender Status

Two cases in particular demonstrate the phenomena discussed above and the trends encountered in chapter 6. In the first case, a repeat homosexual offender is reintegrated into the Wehrgemeinschaft after committing a new infraction under the influence of alcohol. In the second case, the military judicial authorities discharge a soldier as a habitual homosexual offender.

Ferdinand B.

The Court of the Wehrmacht Commander–Berlin in January 1941 sentenced Private First Class Ferdinand B. to two years and three months' imprisonment for three violations of paragraph 175 and three counts of indecent effrontery (*Beleidigung*). As a collateral punishment, he was stripped of his rank.

The court punished two of the defendant's violations of paragraph 175 under section 330a. With a previous civilian conviction for homosexual activity, Ferdinand B. in this case accosted several members of his unit on seven occasions between September and November 1940. His approaches generally were limited to attempts to fondle his comrades' genitals.[8] Ferdinand B. had been drinking on each occasion, but after extensive deliberation the court ruled that only in two instances had he been inebriated beyond the capacity to reason. Eyewitness testimony, in the court's opinion, indicated that on the other occasions he had not been appreciably impaired. The Gerichtsherr confirmed the verdict and ordered Ferdinand B. maintained in a field penal camp.[9]

When allocating the punishment, the court concluded that Ferdinand B.'s conduct could only be attributed to a same-sex orientation and, for this reason, characterized the defendant as a "considerable danger to discipline among the troops." Noting that his prior civilian 175 conviction had not restrained his "unnatural (*widernaturlich*) activities," the court concluded that a strong punishment was necessary.

To impress upon the defendant that his use of alcohol, which excited him to the point of committing "debauchery," would be punished severely in the future, the court imposed four months' imprisonment under section 330a for each violation of paragraph 175 committed while inebriated. Considering it "authoritative" that Ferdinand B.'s three acts of indecent effrontery could only be attributed to his "unnatural" inclination, the court also imposed four months in prison for each offense committed while legally sober. Concluding its deliberations, the court added insult to injury, declaring that pretrial detention would not be calculated as time served. His conduct and personality, the court declared, made him unworthy of such a gesture.

As per the Gerichtsherr's completion order, Ferdinand B. was maintained as a penal camp inmate, and therefore his time in detention was not calculated as time served. He was transferred after twelve months to Brückenkopf Prison (Torgau) to begin atoning his punishment, and he received positive evaluations from prison officials. Despite his "orientation," which had been so obvious in the court's eyes, the Gerichtsherr and commander of the Berlin garrison paroled Ferdinand B. to the front in mid-1942. Sent to Supply Company 292, he performed well as cook, according to a report dated September 29, 1942.

In this case, as in many of the cases discussed in chapter 6, the military judicial authorities reintegrated a soldier with multiple homosexual offenses after he proved in detention that he could and would restrain his inclination and fully subordinate himself to military order. In great contrast, the military judicial authorities in the following case dismissed the defendant from service as a habitual homosexual offender.

Hans S.

The Court of the Third Panzer Army in April 1944 sentenced Sergeant Hans S. to two years' imprisonment under section 330a and loss of rank for violating paragraph 175 on three occasions while completely intoxicated.[10] Previously convicted by a civilian court for two violations of paragraph 175 and investigated by the Berlin police for other homosexual activity, the defendant in this case attempted to kiss and fondle two comrades. In addition, he kissed two Russian *Hiwis* during a week-long drinking binge in February 1942. Despite the role played by alcohol in the incidents, the court classified Hans S. as a habitual homosexual offender. The Gerichtsherr confirmed the verdict and ordered Hans S. dismissed from service and turned over to the civilian authorities.[11]

Due to the degree of his inebriation at the time of the infractions, Hans S. testified that he could not contest the events recounted during the trial. He nevertheless denied that he had acted from a homosexual orientation. He attributed his conduct instead to the fact that, as an actor and artist, he possessed an impulsive personality with a strongly shaped sentimental life (*Gefühlsleben*). He also stated that he enjoyed a normal sex life and was presently engaged. His previous civilian conviction for violating paragraph 175, he asserted, should not be considered as proof of a homosexual orientation. His past offenses, he explained, had simply been the result of a whim, a desire to experience "this other life."

Rejecting this explanation, the court concluded that even if he were a sentimental artist, the facts indicated a homosexual inclination or, at the very least, a bisexual one.[12] On the other hand, multiple eyewitnesses testified that he had been conspicuously drunk on every occasion, and the court accepted the defendant's claim to total intoxication.[13] Hans S. therefore was punished under section 330a for negligently placing himself in a state of total inebriation through the over consumption of alcohol.

The court also addressed his failure as an NCO, demonstrating the military judicial authorities' interest in preserving the integrity of command authority and the Wehrgemeinschaft's authoritarian structure. With his previous conviction for violating paragraph 175, the court noted, the defendant should have been better supervised as a noncommissioned officer. In addition, for the same reason, he was completely unsuited to serve as a superior officer in the first place. The court conceded that these "special circumstances" had "facilitated" Hans L.'s transgressions, and it granted mitigating circumstances. On the other hand, his previous conviction, multiple transgressions in the current case, and classification as a habitual offender led the court to impose the sentence under aggravating circumstances. It considered the defendant's sexual contact with the Russian Hiwis in the presence of other local indigenous personnel as especially aggravating. These acts, according to the court, had been "suited to severely damage the reputation of the German Wehrmacht."

Dismissed from service and sent to Wartenburg Penitentiary in May 1944, Hans L. was transferred to a juvenile detention facility (*Straf- und Jugendgefängnis*) at Stuhm on September 6, 1944. His ultimate fate could not be determined.

The court devoted considerable effort toward determining the defendant's degree of intoxication, and Hans L. received the protection offered under section 330a of the Reich Criminal Code. This did not, however, prevent his permanent exclusion from the Wehrgemeinschaft. Whether or not the civilian authorities ultimately placed him in a concentration camp remains a matter of speculation. Although the military judicial authorities reintegrated many of the repeat offenders encountered in the case files, Hans L. had the misfortune of committing his crime after June 1943 when the habitual offender classification process was implemented. If he had committed his new transgressions before the new process was introduced, chances are high that he would have remained in the military. If not reintegrated into the regular troops, he would have been employed for military purposes in a penal unit. Yet, even if he had remained in uniform, his days as a noncommissioned officer were over. The Wehrgemeinschaft, of course, had its standards.

Paragraph 175, Section 330a, and Eastern Inhabitants

Several of the individuals sentenced under the guidelines provided under section 330a were taken into custody for accosting Soviet civilians. The following two cases involved inhabitants of the eastern occupied areas.

Karl H.

In March 1943 the Court of the 299th Infantry Division sentenced First Sergeant Karl H. to two years' imprisonment under section 330a for two violations of paragraph 175a, number 2. The court also imposed the collateral punishment of loss of rank. In early January 1943, after drinking heavily at a party, the defendant ordered a Russian Hiwi to manually stimulate his (i.e., the defendant's) genitals until he achieved orgasm. In March, again after drinking, he twice fondled a subordinate in the unit's orderly room. Characterizing the defendant as a man unaccustomed to alcohol, the court accepted Karl H.'s claim that he could not remember either incident. Based on eyewitness testimony, the court concluded that his complete inebriation had been "clearly demonstrated." The Gerichtsherr confirmed the verdict and ordered the punishment completed in a field penal battalion.[14]

Karl H.'s company commander submitted a performance appraisal, dated March 7, 1943, for the court's edification. Describing Karl H. as physically and mentally very gifted, the company commander informed the court that Karl H. had conducted outstanding service, possessed excellent organizational talent, and labored tirelessly in the company's interest. The only son of a Great War veteran who was killed in action, Karl H. had remained with the company at his own request, very often visiting the men employed at the foremost part of the front. Based on his flawless conduct and the role that alcohol played in his transgressions, Karl H.'s company commander considered a severe punishment unnecessary.

Although acknowledging this glowing testimonial, the court still considered severity imperative. "The acts," the court fulminated, "are so sordid and vulgar and *have so damaged the reputation of superior officers* [emphasis mine] and the German Wehrmacht that in spite of his excellent record a considerable punishment must be imposed." Karl H. therefore received eighteen months' imprisonment for his offense against his subordinate and one year for the incident involving the Russian Hiwi. Combined, the two sentences totaled two years' imprisonment under the predetermined formula.[15]

Karl H. arrived at Field Penal Battalion 2 in early April 1943. Asked to assess the reintegration potential of a large group of prisoners, the battalion reported in an undated document that the specified individuals, including Karl H., had all performed well. Many of the individuals in question, the battalion noted, had even engaged in a heavy defensive battle in the 293rd Infantry Division's sector.[16] The battalion commander therefore recommended parole for the individuals in question.[17] Based on this report, the commander of Military Administrative Headquarters 184 (Briansk) paroled Karl H. on July 30, 1943. He was ordered to rejoin his old unit, the 529th Grenadier Regiment with the 299th Infantry Division.

Karl H., presumably a model soldier, committed two homosexual acts under the influence of alcohol. Indeed fortunate to have received the protection offered by section 330a, Karl H. could have received a penal servitude punishment for his violations of paragraph 175a, number 2. Ordered to a field penal battalion, he rejoined the Wehrgemeinschaft just four months after committing his "sordid and vulgar" crimes. Heavily wounded after being released, Karl H. apparently remained on parole despite a limited fitness rating.[18] He was, however, denied restoration to his former rank. His drunken offenses, according to the Gerichtsherr, made him unworthy of clemency in this matter.[19] Note also the penal system's role as a de facto ready reserve, with Karl H.'s field penal battalion evaluating a large number of detainees for parole simultaneously.

Among the case files, these three cases resulted in the most severe punishments imposed by the courts for violation of paragraph 175 or 175a while inebriated beyond the capacity to reason. The courts' sentencing practices could vary greatly in intoxication cases, and many defendants, despite even the most outrageous drunken antics, received fairly mild punishments under section 330a. In the following case, an officer made a rare appearance before the bench. The case of Rudolf T. also provides an outstanding illustration of the exceptional standards demanded from those belonging to the Wehrgemeinschaft's leadership strata.

Rudolf T.

In May 1942 the Court of the Twenty-ninth Infantry Division sentenced Lieutenant Rudolf T. to nine months' imprisonment under section 330a for violating paragraph 175a. The court recused itself on the question of service grade reduction, leaving the issue of rank to military administrative channels. After binge drinking with other unit members one afternoon in January 1942, the defendant attempted to force a fifteen-year-old Russian lad, at gunpoint, to perform oral sex on him. Rudolf T., however, lost his balance during the assault and fell down a flight of stairs. His pratfall allowed the boy to gather his clothes and escape. The Gerichtsherr confirmed the verdict, ordered three months completed, and suspended the remainder of the sentence for front-parole.[20]

The other men present during the afternoon party had all been drunk, and considerable evidence supported the court's application of 330a. During their drinking session, for example, the men destroyed furniture in an uninhabited house. Rudolf T.'s comrades unanimously characterized him as the most intoxicated. While assaulting the boy, the defendant even threatened Sergeant B. with his pistol when the sergeant appeared on the scene to investigate the noise. After the boy escaped, Rudolf T. reentered the abandoned dwelling and became very violent, snapping the head off an unlucky chicken. When his comrades tried to disarm him, a brawl ensued. After he had been subdued, Rudolf T. vomited.

Rudolf T. claimed to have no memory of the incident. He further stated that he had never had homosexual relations. He explained before the court that he had been involved with girls since the age of twelve or thirteen and that he had begun having sex at the age of eighteen. He said that although he had very intense sexual relations, he had never participated in anything perverted. Previously engaged, Rudolf T. testified that his fiancé had broken off the engagement, married another, and had recently given birth. In fact, he had received a letter from his former fiancé about the birth on the day in question. This information, he confessed, drove him to the bottle.

In its deliberations, the court noted that under normal circumstances, the defendant's violations of paragraph 175a would merit penal servitude. In light of Rudolf T.'s drunkenness, however, the court concluded that his ability to reason most likely had been precluded. Citing the unanimous eyewitness testimony and noting that the defendant vomited, the court declared that, in all probability, he really could not remember the incident.[21] The court still chastised the defendant, characterizing his conduct as "grotesque." It is "unworthy of an officer," the court declared, "to find himself in such a state of complete inebriation that he cannot remember what he did. *One does not expect this from an officer. He is forcefully reproached for this* [emphasis mine]."

The court did not stop there but continued to berate the defendant for his irresponsible alcohol consumption. It was "especially shameful" for an officer to violate paragraph 175, the court lectured, and it lambasted Rudolf T. for his drinking binge, which put him in "a very bad light." Becoming so inebriated bordered on premeditation because he "reached for the bottle" out of anger and irritation over his ex-fiancé's letter. His behavior, the court declared, indicated "a special weakness of character" because officers did not allow themselves to be overwhelmed by "such things."

Twice wounded and a recipient of the Purple Heart, Rudolf K. had also been decorated with the Iron Cross, both first and second class. Promoted steadily since entering service in 1938, he was characterized by his commanding officer as not only a fine youth but also a diligent, eager, and passionate soldier who had proven himself in combat. The court acknowledged Rudolf T.'s outstanding bravery but nonetheless pointed out that *good conduct from an officer should be self-evident.* Although ruling that his actions represented a "one-time blunder," the court, citing the bad impression he made in public, deemed nine months' imprisonment necessary. The court refrained from reducing him in rank. It left this collateral punishment to be handled through military administrative channels.

After the verdict's confirmation, the documents become fragmentary, offering little information as to when or where Rudolf T. served his abbreviated punishment. However, one document, dated May 27, 1942, indicates that Rudolf T. was drummed out of the officer corps for his transgression and reenrolled at the lowest conscripted grade. According to the document, he could never again be employed as a superior officer (*Vorgesetzter*).[22] The case file contains few clues as to Rudolf T.'s employment after his punishment and ignominious dismissal from the officer corps. One document, dated February 20, 1945, suggests that he was involved in counterespionage in Düsseldorf.

Given that Rudolf T. had decapitated a chicken and vomited, he probably had been very drunk, and the highly decorated and apparently exemplary officer received the protection of section 330a, more than likely preventing a penal servitude sentence. Despite his demonstrated bravery, diligent performance, and four decorations, the Wehrgemeinschaft had extraordinarily high standards for command, and Rudolf K. was drummed out of the officer corps.[23]

Section 330a and Expert Medical Testimony

In the following case, the court enlisted the help of a medical expert to determine the defendant's state of mind at the time of his crime, again illustrating the level of effort invested in inebriation cases.

Wilhelm B.

The Court of the 169th Infantry Division in October 1940 sentenced Master Sergeant Wilhelm B. to one year's imprisonment under section 330a for violating paragraphs 175 and 175a. A former professional soldier and railway civil servant, the defendant encountered Sergeant L., a recent arrival to Wilhelm B.'s unit, while drinking in a pub. Inviting the newcomer to join him for a drink, Wilhelm B. admitted to Sergeant L. that he was quite drunk and asked his new comrade to help him home. En route to Wilhelm B.'s lodgings, he asked the sergeant to address him by the familiar "du." When they arrived at his quarters, Wilhelm B. suggested the sergeant spend the night so that he would not violate the impending curfew. He then demanded a kiss to seal their new friendship. Sergeant L. complied, believing it was only a pledge of camaraderie and departed, assuring the defendant that he had ample time to return to his quarters before taps.

Eight months later, Wilhelm B. ordered twenty-year-old Lance Corporal A. out of bed one evening and demanded that he follow him. Obeying this order, the young soldier stopped to pull on clothes, but Wilhelm B. instructed him to "come as you are." In the defendant's room, Wilhelm B. rubbed Lance Corporal A.'s chest and grabbed his genitals. He then ordered the corporal to remove his sleeping attire and get into the bed. Wilhelm B. then fondled the corporal's genitals and haunches. After a short time, Lance Corporal A. leapt out of bed and ran. The Gerichtsherr confirmed the verdict and ordered the punishment completed.[24]

The court determined that, in the first incident, the defendant had not misused his authority, as stipulated under paragraph 175a, number 2, when obtaining the kiss from Sergeant L. The defendant, the court explained, had made the request as a friend, not as a superior officer. In the second case, however, the court concluded that not only had Wilhelm B. attempted to seduce a man under the age of twenty-one, a violation of paragraph 175a, number 3, he also had abused his authority. Lance Corporal A., the court noted, only complied because of the defendant's superior rank.

Based on the deposition of an expert medical witness, the court ruled that the defendant had been intoxicated beyond the ability to reason. He was therefore punished under section 330a. The medical expert, a university professor, had the following to say about the defendant: "It is a matter of a masked (*lavierten*) homosexual; that is, a homosexual who in a condition of sound mind can control his natural instincts (*Triebleben*). In an inebriated state, this latent homosexuality is activated. For this activation, it requires merely an uninhibited condition in the sense of a light alcohol contamination and not total inebriation. This explains the goal-oriented nature in the execution of the crime."

The medical expert added that under certain circumstances, Wilhelm B. suffered bouts of *Narcolysie* [sic] in the form of frequent attacks of a sleep-like state without loss of affect.[25] Judging by the eyewitness testimony, the medical expert concluded that Wilhelm B. found himself in just such a state on the evenings in question. His conduct, therefore, had to be attributed to psychological impairment as defined under section 51, number 1.[26]

During the sentencing phase, the court acknowledged Wilhelm B.'s clean record, good conduct, and "soldierly bearing," but stated that the crimes' severity and "destructive effects" on his unwilling partners also had to be considered.

Initially incarcerated in Wehrmacht Prison Gemersheim on November 10, 1940, Wilhelm B. eventually was transferred to a mobile prison unit. In mid-March 1942 the Gerichtsherr of the Court of Division Number 172 granted parole after prison officials reported that Wilhelm B. was suitable for front-parole as per OKH decrees of January 9 and 17, 1941. He was released from detention on April 29.[27]

Wilhelm B. was subsequently mustered out of service for employment with the German Federal Railway (Reichsbahn) in compliance with OKH decrees.[28] His professional qualifications were apparently vital to the railway's wartime operations. Before his discharge he nevertheless had been reintegrated into the Wehrgemeinschaft after serving six months of a one-year sentence. If he had not been granted the protection of 330a, the chances are that he would have received a much longer prison sentence or even a penal servitude punishment. The military judicial authorities, as seen in chapter 6, dealt particularly harshly with individuals violating paragraph 175a, number 2.

Sexual Assault and Section 330a

In the following three cases, the defendants were convicted for sexual assault after excessive alcohol consumption.

Richard E.

In December 1944 the Court of the 214th Infantry Division sentenced Master Sergeant Richard E. to five years' imprisonment under section 330a and imposed a loss of rank for rape and attempted rape. Starting the day with a hearty breakfast of toast and schnapps, the defendant continued drinking throughout the morning. While supervising a civilian work detail, Richard E. led a Polish woman, Mrs. K., to a farm house, ostensibly to fetch tools. At the farm he discharged his weapon into the ground three times and demanded that she have sex with him. He took her into the house where a ninety-year-old woman, her sixty-four-year-old daughter, and another middle-aged woman resided.

Taking advantage of his intoxication and the confusion upon their entrance into the house, Mrs. K. and the sixty-four-year- old woman escaped. Richard E. then attacked the other middle-aged woman, feeling her body and pulling out his penis. He threatened her with his pistol and struck her. She nevertheless also managed to escape. Richard E. now turned his attention to the ninety-year-old mother. He forced her to perform oral sex on him and then raped her. A patrol, which had been notified by Richard E.'s former captives, apprehended him in the act. The Gerichtsherr confirmed the verdict, ordered the punishment served in a field penal battalion, and stipulated that he should be evaluated for parole in no less than six months.[29]

Testifying that he could not remember anything, the defendant claimed that he had no recollection of events after mid-morning. His arrest, however, shocked him back to reality. He could not explain his actions but suggested that the schnapps must have had an extremely high alcohol content. According to the apprehending officer, Richard E. indeed appeared shocked and was incapable of understanding why he had been arrested; even after being taken into custody shocked him out of his stupor, he was still very drunk.

The court, after considerable deliberation, concluded that the amount of alcohol consumed more than likely had been sufficient to induce a state of complete inebriation. The alcohol produced by the locals, the court conceded, had a very "powerful" and "destructive effect," as demonstrated by the "countless cases" involving the local moonshine that were coming before courts-martial. The court invoked section 330a and characterized the defendant as a thoughtful man who had never committed a crime before.

In a rare discussion of the provisions for intensified punishments that had been placed at the jurists' disposal, the court ruled that the Ordinance against Violent Criminals of December 5, 1939, would not be invoked because, according to "the will of the lawmakers and the jurisprudence of the Reich Supreme Military Court," it should be applied only against a certain type of offender, "the gangster." Richard E., in the court's opinion, was not that type. The court also discussed the applicability of Wartime Penal Code section 5a, which allowed the courts to exceed the normal sentencing parameters if required for the maintenance of discipline or the security of the troops. Section 5a, the court explained, should be invoked only for crimes subject to imitation by others, something that it considered unlikely in this case. Raping a ninety-year-old woman, the court concluded, was far removed from "normal contemplation."

An obviously thorough court, it further addressed the OKH guidelines established in 1940 for the judicious handling of sexual offenses committed in operational areas. The guidelines stipulated that during the war, condemning one-time blunders of a moral type (*einmalige Entgleisungen auf sittlichen Gebiet*) as otherwise dictated under normal conditions would not be practical. According to the court, "no special circumstances" warranted exceeding the normal punishment parameters. Therefore, the OKH guidelines would be followed, with the sentencing parameters contained in section 330a (up to five years' imprisonment) providing for sufficient punishment.

During the sentencing phase, the court took into account Richard E.'s "irreproachable character" and good conduct during his long military career, which included a twelve-year stint after the First World War.[30] Under section 330a, punishments were imposed for "negligently" or "intentionally" becoming completely intoxicated, but the court chose to partly blame the local population for the defendant's transgression. "It should not be forgotten," the court stated, "that according to the experience of the military courts in recent times, the civilian population bears a great part of the blame for this kind of offense by the fact that they again and again sell this type of alcohol to soldiers at exorbitant prices."

On the other hand, when handing down the maximum allowable punishment under section 330a, the court emphasized the damage Richard E.'s actions had caused to the army's reputation in the occupied area.

Expressing doubts about the defendant's degree of drunkenness, the staff legal adviser did not recommend the verdict's confirmation. Perhaps, he suggested, the defendant had not been dead-drunk but rather just overwhelmed by his libido, which went out of control due his alcohol consumption. The adviser also criticized the court for not applying section 5a. The Gerichtsherr rejected this opinion and confirmed the verdict. Richard E. was sent to Field Penal Battalion 5 in early January 1945. There the file ends.

Richard E. more than likely had been very drunk. If not, it would be hard to explain how three middle-aged women managed to escape from an armed soldier who not only brandished his weapon but also discharged it more than once. As demonstrated in chapter 7, sexual assaults committed in the eastern occupied areas often brought lengthy penal servitude sentences. Richard E. was most fortunate that the court invoked 330a.

The court surprisingly did not chastise the defendant, a master sergeant, for his blatant disregard of the impeccable standards of conduct required of noncommissioned officers, although the criticism is certainly implied. Whether his long and distinguished military career influenced the court is not apparent in the documents. It might have influenced the Gerichtsherr, who rejected his staff legal adviser's advice and confirmed the verdict rather than ordering a new trial and demanding a harsher punishment under Wartime Penal Code section 5a. Once again, military officers, not jurists, controlled the military judicial process.

Peter G.

In May 1943 the Court of the First Panzer Division sentenced Sergeant Peter G. to two years' imprisonment under section 330a and imposed the collateral punishment of rank loss for molesting a ten-year-old French girl. Drinking with other company members at a pub one evening, the defendant consumed so much alcohol that he staggered and babbled incoherently. At nine o'clock at night he left the pub. A short time later he was apprehended nearby after he sexually assaulted a young girl in a latrine. He was found sitting undressed in the toilet. A bystander reported that he had observed the girl sitting on Peter G.'s lap, facing him, with her legs apart. A medical examination determined that the girl had been penetrated. The Gerichtsherr confirmed the verdict and ordered four months served, with the remainder of the punishment suspended until after the war.[31]

Peter G. testified that he had no memory of the incident. The pub patrons, the bystanders at the crime scene, and his comrade Sergeant A. all testified that Peter G. had been staggering and slurring his words. According to the bystanders, he seemed oblivious when apprehended. In the opinion of a medical expert, Peter G. most likely had been impaired to irrationality, and the court invoked section 330a.

When allocating the punishment, the court, as usual, emphasized not only the crime's damage to the Wehrmacht's reputation but also the crime's impact on the reputation and honor of the noncommissioned officers corps, which were damaged "most severely." As a noncommissioned officer, the court noted, Peter G. had been "*especially obligated to conduct himself impeccably* [emphasis mine]" and remain in control of his senses when drinking. His "reprehensible act" thus deserved a severe punishment. On the other hand, having participated in various campaigns, Peter G. had proven himself in combat, been wounded, and had four decorations to his credit.[32] Acknowledging this excellent service record, the court granted mitigating circumstances.

Incarcerated in Wehrmacht Prison Bruchsal on June 1, 1943, Peter

G. was paroled four months later on September 25. Released from custody on that day, he rejoined the First Panzer Division.

The court had plenty of evidence to support the application of section 330a. Although Peter G.'s excellent service record prompted the court to grant him the protection of 330a, they nevertheless berated him for failing as an NCO to maintain leadership standards and then ordered him striped.

Poor service records or previous convictions, however, did not preclude the possibility of receiving the protection of 330a. The military judicial authorities showed a surprising amount of tolerance for the following defendant, who committed two alcohol-related offenses in succession.

Gerhard D.

On September 15, 1941, the Court of the 319th Infantry Division, stationed on the occupied island of Guernsey, sentenced Private Gerhard D. to eighteen months' imprisonment under section 330a for attempted rape. He had recently been convicted by the same court for drunk and disorderly conduct and had received a six-month prison sentence for that conviction. Although the Gerichtsherr confirmed that verdict, he suspended the sentence for service with a parole battalion.

Sergeant P., assigned to escort Gerhard D. to the parole battalion reserve formation at Fulda, permitted his charge to do some shopping after arriving on the continent. Entering a leave center (*Soldatenheim*), the defendant met a group of soldiers and accompanied them to a pub. After a few beers and six or seven cognacs, Gerhard D. followed his new comrades to a brothel, where he promptly fell asleep at a table. A medical corpsman attempted to assist the drunken soldier, but Gerhard D. fled.

Entering a nearby dwelling, he attacked a fifty-three-year-old woman as she returned from church. He ripped off her clothes, bit her, and threw her to the ground. The corpsman heard her screams and intervened just in time. The victim required medical treatment for bite marks on her breasts and cuts on her face. The Gerichtsherr confirmed the verdict, ordered six months of the punishment completed, and provided for subsequent service in a parole battalion if the defendant conducted himself well in detention.[33]

Gerhard D. did not contest the incident but claimed that he had no memory of the events. Although the amount of alcohol consumed had not been too great, the court concluded that he had been completely intoxicated. Gerhard D., the evidence showed, had had only coffee for breakfast, had endured a rough three-hour sea passage, and had eaten only a few biscuits for dinner before drinking beer and a considerable quantity of cognac. These circumstances, in the court's opinion, could certainly have induced an intoxicated state sufficient to prevent his ability to reason. According to the medical corpsman, Gerhard D. had been incapable of standing. Perhaps most compelling of all, he attempted to rape a woman when a brothel operated right next door. The court considered this behavior sufficient evidence of a high level of intoxication.

Committing another alcohol-related offense so soon after his conviction on a drunk and disorderly charge earned the defendant aggravating circumstances. The previous punishment, the court stressed, obviously had not made any impression on him: as a parolee, Gerhard D. knew full well that he was supposed to conduct himself impeccably. Convicted nine times for theft, Gerhard D. was characterized by the court as "an unstable man who especially under the influence of alcohol inclines to brutal acts (*Roheitshandlungen*)."

Winding up its deliberations, the court stated, "He is too weak to resist the temptation of alcohol." For this reason, it considered a severe punishment necessary so that he would exercise restraint in the future.

Admitted to Wehrmacht Prison Gemersheim in mid-October 1941, Gerhard D. eventually was transferred to a mobile prison unit. In March 1942 the unit submitted a very good report on him. His character appeared "flawless" and "no deficiencies" had been observed. Based on this information, the commander of the 319th Infantry Division paroled Gerhard D. on April 6, 1942, and he rejoined the 319th Infantry Division on Guernsey. This reintegration violated the parole provisions because the 319th was not engaged at the front and, in fact, hardly ever fired a shot in anger during the war.[34]

If this case suggests leniency on the Wehrmacht's part, it most likely reflects increasing manpower problems rather than any general tolerance for poorly motivated soldiers. Gerhard D. had been convicted nine times as a civilian (primarily for theft), receiving prison sentences as long as two years. Military courts convicted him twice after his induction for alcohol-related infractions. With the military's perceived requirements for the Wehrgemeinschaft's proper functioning, one wonders how Gerhard D. ever became a soldier at all, slipping through the plethora of filtering mechanisms. This thought is reflected in an opinion submitted on August 25, 1941, by Gerhard D.'s battalion commander:

> A detailed evidentiary summary (*Tatbericht*) already had to be submitted against Gerhard D. on 20 May 1941 because of an unauthorized absence from service, drunkenness on duty, insubordination, resistance and an actual attack on a superior officer, undermining Manneszucht, and destruction of property.
>
> I consider D. to be a soldier who performs his service only with strong supervision and even then only grudgingly. He inclines to the over consumption of alcohol and has demonstrated through his previous criminal acts that he is capable when he is intoxicated of committing any crime. His frequent punishments before his entrance into service in the Wehrmacht and the two criminal acts committed after his entrance into the Wehrmacht make it necessary to eliminate D. from the ranks because his conduct undermines Manneszucht in the troops.

The Wehrmacht's tolerance of Gerhard D., a private with no apparent specialized skills, is indeed difficult to explain. One wonders why the military judicial authorities did not, after his second conviction, order him to a field penal battalion or one of the other less pleasant punishment options. Gerhard D. most likely survived the war and went into captivity when the unmolested Guernsey garrison surrendered only hours after Germany's official capitulation.[35]

The final case demonstrates how individual courts often adjudicated cases of inebriation according to their own perceptions of what constituted total intoxication. Such cases raise further doubts about the theory of a military judiciary steered to uniformity from above. Despite the various burdens of proof for the application of section 330a, the court in this case still exerted considerable effort in arriving at its decisions.

Heinz M.

Refusing to invoke section 330a, the Court of the Senior Flight Training Commander 17 (Sudeten District) on March 1, 1942, sentenced Private Heinz M. to one year's imprisonment for bestiality and cruelty to animals. After consuming six or seven beers and six schnapps one evening, the defendant followed some young women home. Climbing a ladder to an upper window, Heinz M. attempted to gain entry to their dwelling. The objects of his affection greeted him with a bucket of cold water dumped over his head. He abandoned this less than subtle attempt to obtain a date.

Returning to his quarters, he headed for the latrine. Hearing hens cackling in a nearby henhouse, Heinz M. recalled that his mother had always probed her hens with a finger in order to determine whether or not the fowl would soon lay eggs. It occurred to him that if one could introduce one's finger into a hen, then the same could be done with one's penis. He grabbed a hen, entered the toilet, and attempted to satisfy himself in this manner at the expense of the unfortunate bird. A second hen met the same fate. Due to his drunkenness, one of the birds fell into the latrine pit. He now repeated his actions with a goose, which likewise wound up at the bottom of the outhouse. The birds' owner discovered the wounded animals near death the following morning.

Desiring further clarification on Heinz M.'s alcohol consumption, the Gerichtsherr refused to confirm the verdict and ordered a new trial.[36] The same court, chaired by a different judge, presided over the retrial nearly five months later on July 23, 1942. Reviewing the evidence from the first hearing, the court this time concluded that Heinz M. had committed his transgressions while intoxicated beyond the ability to reason. It sentenced him under section 330a to three months' imprisonment. In the first trial, the court had considered Heinz M.'s ability to climb a ladder, recall his mother's egg-checking technique, and maintain an erection as indications that he had not been completely inebriated. During the retrial, the court noted that the amount of alcohol consumed had been considerable and could not have been without effect on the twenty-year-old defendant. The fact that he mixed champagne, beer, and schnapps, the court noted, indeed led to the assumption that Heinz M. had been intoxicated, an assumption supported by the testimony of the young women whom the defendant had followed home.

Most importantly, the court also heard testimony from an expert medical witness in the second trial. Assuring the court that Heinz M. possessed a heterosexual orientation, the medical expert stated that the slightly built defendant's mental faculties had been disrupted to a high degree as a result of the alcohol consumption. If the defendant could recount the events, the witness explained, this was because the police had reconstructed the evening for him. Finally, the medical expert rebutted the court's conclusion regarding the defendant's ability to maintain an erection, explaining that an erection does not preclude the possibility of inebriation.

Based on the totality of evidence, the court determined that Heinz M. had been completely intoxicated. When allocating the punishment, the court expressed concern about this "type of moral mistake" and the harm inflicted on the animals, but it nevertheless granted mitigating circumstances, citing his clean record and remorse. Characterizing Heinz M.'s transgression as an alcohol-induced one-time blunder, the court imposed the three-month prison sentence, which it considered atoned by pretrial detention.

In the first trial the court discussed at long length the suffering that the animals endured at the hands of Heinz M. He had "unnecessarily tortured and brutally abused" the animals, the court lamented, causing them "considerable enduring pain and suffering." For these reasons, the court considered severe punishment necessary in order to impress upon Heinz M. the reprehensibility and repugnance of his crime, a crime that placed him "outside the circle of honorable national comrades."

The disparity between the Wehrmacht's concern for animal welfare and the ruthless war it conducted in the east may invite incredulous dismay, but the true importance of this case lies in the inconsistent interpretations of what constituted complete inebriation. The initial verdict rested on the court's conclusion, apparently based on its own perceptions, that an erection and the ability to climb a ladder indicated sobriety. During the second trial, the court arrived at a completely opposite interpretation of the evidence. Despite the commentary accompanying the criminal codes and the Reich Supreme

Military Court's interpretation that an individual's thinking only had to be "muddled" in order for section 330a to be invoked, the court in the first trial ruled otherwise.

Most courts required extensive evidence before concluding that an individual was impaired beyond the ability to reason; only a few considered the statements of the perpetrator or a single eyewitness as sufficient proof of complete intoxication. Nevertheless, the divergent burdens of proof encountered in the case files lead one to wonder how many perpetrators managed to fool the courts, escaping with significantly less severe punishments than might have been warranted. If one also considers that many courts in the case files refused to invoke section 330a despite considerable evidence of intoxication, it seems possible that many individuals received the normal sentencing provisions' full weight when they might have received milder punishments had the courts possessed the time or ability to solicit the expertise of medical experts.

Despite the frequent divergent burdens of proof, the courts nonetheless made impressive efforts to discern a perpetrator's degree of inebriation. They did not simply go through the motions. Right or wrong, their conclusions generally rested on a thorough review of the available evidence. The needs of the Volksgemeinschaft never intruded into the inquiry. The commanders and courts were far more interested in the Wehrgemeinschaft's needs, stripping those punished under section 330a of their rank and thus removing them from positions of authority.

Diminished Responsibility: Section 51

Messerschmidt and Wüllner conclude that Wehrmacht courts often refused to grant mentally incompetent individuals the protection offered by section 51 of the Reich Criminal Code. The authors contend that not only was this customary protection often denied, but the courts, as agents of societal purification, frequently used a perpetrator's intellectual shortcomings as the justification for imposing draconian punishments, if not societal exclusion.[37] Fritz Wüllner expands this scenario in his solo effort to include individuals with poor educations, bad childhoods, or dysfunctional families. Both authors are able to document examples of these phenomena.[38] These cases, however, primarily involve deserters, "subversives," and perpetrators of other militarily obstructive acts.

The case files for sex offenses tell a different story. When prosecuting sex offenders, the courts as a rule considered a perpetrator's mental weakness, poor education, or dysfunctional childhood as mitigating circumstances and hence as reasons for leniency. Take, for example, the 1942 case of Adolf S. The Court of the 210th Infantry Division sentenced him to four months' imprisonment for public indecency. The son of an alcoholic mother, Adolf S. had been sterilized for feeble-mindedness (*geister Schwäche*). The court therefore granted the protection provided for diminished responsibility under section 51 of the Reich Criminal Code. He rejoined his unit after serving just three weeks of confinement, as per the Gerichtsherr's confirmation order.[39]

Richard P. likewise came before a court-martial in 1942. He was convicted by the Court of the Wehrmacht Commander–Berlin and sentenced to eighteen months' imprisonment for violating paragraph 175. Citing the defendant's "considerable feeble-mindedness," the court granted Richard P. mitigating circumstances. A repeat homosexual offender, Richard P. was ordered to a Wehrmacht field penal camp. He was subsequently hospitalized for epilepsy. Nevertheless, he fully atoned his sentence in September 1944 and rejoined the regular troops.[40]

In this case not only did the court grant mitigating circumstances on the basis of Richard E.'s feeble-mindedness, but the military judicial authorities reintegrated him into the regular troops despite his epilepsy—a disease the regime targeted under its racial policies and treated by castration. In the Nazi universe, Richard P. indeed had three big strikes against him. Yet this "feeble-minded," epileptic, multiple homosexual offender remained part of the Wehrgemeinschaft.

In the final case, a psychiatric assessment of the defendant Edgar S. was weighed by the court.

Edgar S.

On August 31, 1942, the Court of the Wehrmacht Commander–Berlin sentenced medical corpsman Edgar S. to fifteen months' imprisonment for violating paragraph 175 and resisting arrest. The defendant, who had two previous convictions for violating paragraph 175 and a history of suicide and depressive disorders, was caught in a public restroom in a compromising situation with another man. His attempt to flea from the crime scene failed. Based on a psychiatric evaluation, the court considered Edgar S.'s history of mental disorders and suicide attempts as mitigating circumstances. The Gerichtsherr confirmed the verdict and ordered the punishment completed.

Subsequently mobilized in a field penal battalion, Edgar S. had to be hospitalized for unknown reasons in March 1943. While he was still convalescing in September 1944, the military judicial authorities decreed that the time spent in the hospital would be calculated as time served. The authorities therefore considered his punishment atoned and ordered the three-time homosexual offender to a regular unit after his release from the hospital.[41]

According to Messerschmidt and Wüllner, the medical profession had been in league with the military jurists in the pursuit of societal purification.[42] In this case, and in the few other cases in which psychiatric assessments were submitted in evidence, the opposite was true with sex offenders, which again raises the question of why deserters and subversives were considered more despicable creatures than sex offenders. The answer: Sex offenders had not demonstrated by their crimes any opposition to the war or unwillingness to fight. They could be forgiven.

CHAPTER ELEVEN

Conclusion

According to Lothar Walmrath, continuity existed in the sentencing practices of naval courts during the interwar period, yet they changed markedly after September 1939. In other words, Walmrath found little change in jurisprudence between Weimar and Nazi Germany up until the war's outbreak, but he did find drastic intensification of punishments after the war began.[1] This change, of course, was not accidental, and the watershed in jurisprudence had little to do with Nazi ideology.

The draconian nature of Wehrmachtjustiz, in fact, had been consciously planned well in advance of the Second World War. When Germany again took a stab at world domination in 1939, "decisive measures" had already been taken to prevent a repetition of the revolutionary events of 1918.[2] The Wehrmacht was determined that this time around the military administration of justice would be swift, severe, and equal to the demands of total war. Under the mantra of maintaining Manneszucht, commanding officers, with the aid of their jurists, ruthlessly purged those soldiers who obstructed the war effort. The Wehrgemeinschaft, the Wehrmacht's answer to total war, had to be maintained in order to avoid another stab in the back.

Scholars also agree that the intensification of punishments that began in September 1939 continued as the war progressed, with rapidly escalating severity after 1943 when the war turned against Germany. National Socialism provided an environment for the radicalization of all institutions and practices, yet the wartime intensification of Wehrmachtjustiz was a reaction to the war situation and remained relatively independent of the accompanying fascist circumstances.

It was not just the unprecedented number of death and penal servitude sentences that made Wehrmachtjustiz such a draconian tool for the war's prosecution. The associated penal and parole system, the means of carrying out the punishments, also was as a central factor in making Wehrmachtjustiz so brutal. The system of front-parole, which exposed soldiers to enemy fire for the duration, and the special penal formations, which employed prisoners for the most dangerous assignments, contributed greatly to the military judicial system's harshness and the Wehrmacht's reduction of men to human matériel.

Many Nazi fanatics undoubtedly entered the military judiciary and sat on the bench, using the courts as a forum for their National Socialist views. Many probably also hoped to implement the führer's will through the courts-martial. This, however, is neither surprising nor out of place in the chaotic Third Reich, where all institutions swelled with fanatics who attempted to create their own satrapies for the promotion of party (or their own personal) interests.

Yet there were too many countervailing forces, primarily the institution of the Gerichtsherr, for fanatics to dispense their own ideological brand of justice. The Gerichtsherren, despite critics' protestations to the contrary, controlled and indeed dominated the military judicial and penal system. As the individuals responsible for their units' cohesion, discipline, and military effectiveness, the Gerichtsherren took their legal power as an instrument of command authority very seriously. Harnessing the "law" to serve immediate military interests, the Gerichtsherren sacrificed the needs of the Volksgemeinschaft in favor of the needs of the Wehrgemeinschaft. In doing so, they fielded an effective force of motivated fighters despite a rapidly deteriorating military situation.

The willingness of these commanders to sacrifice thousands of deserters in pursuit of this goal is not being challenged here. As Ulrich Vultejus has pointed out, the execution of soldiers for military organizations is "unproblematic." If the Wehrmacht executed 13,500 servicemen out of an average effective strength of five million men, he explains, the total sacrificed amounted to only 0.27 percent. From a military perspective, the death sentence is the ideal punishment, according to Vultejus, because it provides the greatest possible deterrent with "unusual economy."[3]

Indeed, based on the German military's perceived lessons of the First World War and the Wehrmacht's perception of the total war that it had unleashed, the commanders and the courts subordinated to them went to any length to purge individuals who obstructed the war's prosecution. Designed and implemented by right-wing elites, the military administration of justice and its associated penal institutions under Hitler concerned themselves largely with three questions: Will this individual carry a weapon in good faith? Will this individual adversely impact the discipline and performance of his comrades? Will this individual hinder the Wehrmacht's prosecution of the war or occupation policies?

Single-minded and brutal, Wehrmachtjustiz allowed the political leadership to field an effective military force long after the beginning of the end. As explained in 1941 by Supreme Judge Advocate Martin Rittau, "Justice (*Recht*) for the armed forces is . . . only that which benefits it (*Nur das ist . . . für die Truppe Recht, was ihr nützt*) and maintains and increases its fighting power. Think always about the fact that the jurisdiction of the Wehrmacht courts is . . . also a means, and indeed a very important means, for the achievement of victory."[4]

For the Wehrmacht, deserters and recalcitrant soldiers posed the most serious threat to its "fighting power." Their kind had to be stifled in embryo in order to avoid a second stab in the back. The jurists made use of the draconian tools contained in the Wartime Penal Code, often appropriating the Nazi vernacular to justify their application. They did so, however, for their own ends—for the perpetuation of the Wehrgemeinschaft and the pursuit of the Endsieg, the final victory, not for societal purification. The cases of sex offenders demonstrate this point clearly. They also illustrate that German militarism and nationalism, as conceived by the right and given free reign, were a match for fascism in terms of brutality.

The case files also document vast differences in sentencing practices, which can be attributed largely to the different attitudes of the commanding officers functioning as Gerichtsherren. Attempts by the political leadership to steer jurisprudence to uniformity failed miserably. In the vast majority of the cases, it was the commander on the scene who dispensed "justice." He did so primarily on the basis of the prevailing strategic realities facing the Wehrmacht at the time and on the basis of his unit's immediate needs.

Although the Court of the Eighty-second Infantry Division dispensed relatively mild punishments for sexual assaults against Soviet civilians, many courts dealt severely with these offenses. They did so primarily to maintain discipline, ensure the orderly prosecution of occupation policy, and defuse the partisan threat. Yet such discrepancies in sentencing practices make sweeping generalizations on the basis of a single court's jurisprudence ill-advised and highlight the need to investigate Wehrmachtjustiz court by court and case by case.

Generalizations can be made safely, however, about the penal and parole system. Designed as a filtering mechanism, the system purged the unwilling while channeling the Wehrmacht's usable human matériel back to the front. Created, refined, and then brutalized in response to successive military crises, its purpose was to reorient men through the most extreme methods toward continued service, motivated to fight and determined never to risk punishment in the future.

The military's willingness to turn over its most recalcitrant soldiers (and those who from no fault of their own were unable to subordinate themselves to military order) to the horrors of the concentration camps stands as one more indictment of the Wehrmacht. In fact, the critics of Wehrmachtjustiz have missed a golden opportunity to further break down the myth of a noncomplicit Wehrmacht. By attempting to lay the blame for the military judiciary's crimes solely at the feet of the jurists, the critics fail to understand that the actual perpetrator was the Wehrmacht itself. The military administration of justice was just that: a military organization controlled by military officers. The Gerichtsherren dominated the process and military officers commanded the prisons and penal formations. They collectively bear responsibility for the deaths that occurred before the firing squads or in penal formations at the front where prisoners labored under fire without weapons.

Martin van Creveld, in *Fighting Power*, analyzes the organization and methods—the carrots and sticks, so to speak—of the U.S. and German armed forces during the Second World War in an attempt to explain the Wehrmacht's impressive performance against its numerically and materially superior Allied opponent. In his discussion of negative sanctions, van Creveld devotes only three pages to Wehrmachtjustiz. Although the Wehrmacht indeed employed many "carrots" to encourage its soldiers to fight, the military judicial "stick" may have been the most compelling factor behind the tenacity and stamina of the German *Landser*. With the Russians in the front, partisans all around, and a brutal military judicial system behind, the German soldier had no choice but to fight until the bitter end.[5]

Introduction

1. Seidler, *Prostitution, Homosexualität, Selbstverstümmelung*, 193–232.

2. During the publication process for this book, there was an important addition to the historiography of sexuality and the Wehrmacht. See Beck, *Wehrmacht und sexuelle Gewalt*.

3. Brownmiller, *Against Our Will*, 48–49.

4. Brownmiller, *Against Our Will*, 53–56.

5. Boog et al., *Attack on the Soviet Union*, 506.

6. Brownmiller, *Against Our Will*, 65.

1. The Historiography of Wehrmachtjustiz

1. Messerschmidt and Wüllner, *Wehrmachtjustiz im Dienste*, 79, 84, 87. When processes involving civilians, war prisoners, and legionnaires were considered, the authors estimate that the number of death sentences reached 50,000.

2. Schwinge attempts to "relativize" the number of death sentences by "manipulated international comparisons" to Germany's opponents in both World Wars. Schwinge, *Die deutsche Militärjustiz*, 265, 268–69; and Haase, "Aus der Praxis," 380–81. Based on the total number of soldiers who served in the respective armed forces, the per capita ratio is only marginally less. U.S. courts-martial imposed 736 death sentences during the Second World War, and only 146 were carried out. Messerschmidt and Wüllner, *Wehrmachtjustiz im Dienste*, 29.

3. Messerschmidt, "Deserteure im Zweiten Weltkrieg," 69.

4. Angermund, *Deutsche Richterschaft*, 12.

5. Messerschmidt and Wüllner, *Wehrmachtjustiz im Dienste*, 177–78. Otto Barwinksi's unpublished memoirs also characterize the Reich Supreme Military Court as a refuge of constitutionality. See Haase, "Aus der Praxis," 380–81.

6. Rudolf Lehmann, the highest-ranking jurist in the Wehrmacht (the Generaloberstrichter OKW), was the only military jurist convicted by the International Military Tribunal (IMT). The IMT convicted Lehmann for his participation in the formulation of laws contrary to international law (the Barbarossa Jurisdiction Decree and the Commissar Order) but not for his jurisprudence. Schwinge, *Die deutsche Militärjustiz*, 113–14. See also Schwinge, *Verfälschung und Wahrheit*, 18.

7. Rüdiger Schleicher, chief of the Air Force Legal Division before the war, was also executed for his resistance activities. Schleicher was convicted for high treason and executed in April 1945. See Schwinge, *Die deutsche Militärjustiz*, 113–14.

8. Hennicke, "Auszüge aus der Wehrmachtkriminalstatistik," 438–56. See also Hennicke, "Über den Justizterror," 715–20.

9. Amtsgruppe Heeresrechtswesen has no English equivalent. This department, however, united the agencies responsible for the administration of justice for both the reserve and field armies. Hence, the term "combined office" is used here to refer to the department.

10. This number includes all branches of service as well as retinue, civilians, war prisoners, and legionnaires.

11. Rösler comes to the same conclusion, stating that only judicial terror can explain why the German people conducted a hopeless battle to the very end against their own best interest. Rösler, "Die faschistische Gesetzgebung," 575.

12. Erdmann, "Zeitgeschichte," 131. See also Messerschmidt and Wüllner, *Wehrmachtjustiz im Dienste,* 10–20; and Schwinge, *Die deutsche Militärjustiz,* iv–x.

13. Messerschmidt and Wüllner, *Wehrmachtjustiz im Dienste,* 10–19.

14. Schwinge, *Die deutsche Militärjustiz,* 246–49, 382–84. Although punishments were often harsh for crimes that endangered military discipline, such as desertion, cowardice, and insubordination, Schwinge concludes that most punishments were still "legally defensible." See Schwinge, *Die deutsche Militärjustiz,* 255–58.

15. Schwinge, *Die deutsche Militärjustiz,* 159, 266, 382. Demonstrating his inversion of the war's origin and reality, Schwinge states, "If the courts and Gerichtsherren had taken a lax attitude, then that would have opened the way for the tank units rolling from Siberia to overrun all of Europe and gain a foothold after a few weeks on the Atlantic."

16. Schwinge, *Die deutsche Militärjustiz,* 218.

17. Schwinge fails to mention that only a fraction of the death sentences imposed against French soldiers in World War I were actually carried out, which makes his comparison meaningless and misleading.

18. Schwinge, *Die deutsche Militärjustiz,* 275–83, 303–4. Schwinge fails to inform the reader that "parole" was actually the deferment of punishment until after the war. See Wüllner, *Die NS-Militärjustiz,* 669.

19. Schwinge, *Die deutsche Militärjustiz,* 56–72, 114.

20. Messerschmidt and Wüllner, *Wehrmachtjustiz im Dienste,* 87–89. Naval courts were required to send case files for completed death sentences to a facility at Flensburg, not Potsdam. These files therefore survived the war.

21. Schwinge neglected the obvious geometric progression in the number of courts-martial during the war, instead factoring in a mathematical increase when extrapolating data for the last year of the war.

22. Messerschmidt and Wüllner, *Wehrmachtjustiz im Dienste,* 51.

23. In addition to the 30,000 soldiers condemned to death, the authors conclude that Wehrmacht courts condemned to death as many as 18,000 civilians,

war prisoners, and legionnaires. See Messerschmidt and Wüllner, *Wehrmacht-justiz im Dienste*, 77, 87, 91.

24. Messerschmidt and Wüllner, *Wehrmachtjustiz im Dienste*, 31–33, 78–79. More than 10,000 civilians, legionaries, and war prisoners also had their death sentences carried out.

25. Messerschmidt and Wüllner, *Wehrmachtjustiz im Dienste*, 31–32, 34, 93, 305. Schwinge, in a 1938 commentary appearing in *Zeitschrift für Wehrrecht*, lobbied for a "Gemeinschaft-oriented" military criminal law for the Volksge-meinschaft's purification. See Messerschmidt and Wüllner, *Wehrmachtjustiz im Dienste*, 45.

26. Staff, *Justiz im Dritten Reich*, 132. The Reich Justice Ministry's *Ausstat-tung der Bucherein mit NS-Schrifttum* (Equipment of libraries with National So-cialist literature) of July 29, 1936, for example, established standards for the agency's libraries.

27. Messerschmidt and Wüllner, *Wehrmachtjustiz im Dienste*, 34. See also Kammler, *Ich habe die Metzelei satt*, 15.

28. See, for example, jurist personnel file w10/1782.

29. Schwinge, *Verfälschung und Wahrheit*, 75.

30. Messerschmidt and Wüllner, *Wehrmachtjustiz im Dienste*, 72–73. In his rebuttal, *Verfälschung und Wahrheit*, Schwinge effectively challenges Mess-erschmidt and Wüllner's calculations. According to Schwinge, case files were shipped in bundles of thirty to fifty files. With death sentences imposed at a rate of less than 1 percent, it would have required the destruction of hundreds of thousands of files to have destroyed the thousands of death sentence case files that Messerschmidt and Wüllner claim were lost. Also, redundant sources en-sured that this vital information would have been registered in the official statis-tics. Schwinge, *Verfälschung und Wahrheit*, 75.

31. Messerschmidt and Wüllner, *Wehrmachtjustiz im Dienste*, 35.

32. Wüllner, *Die NS-Militärjustiz*, 679.

33. Wüllner, *Die NS-Militärjustiz*, 725–31. Wüllner uses the phrase "sword of Damocles" specifically to describe the practice of granting temporary stays of execution in order to give condemned men the opportunity to earn clemency through heroism. The "Damocles Method," as Wüllner describes it, is applicable to all paroled soldiers because they were required to serve at the perilous front while conducting themselves exceptionally.

34. The military judicial authorities used the term *Bewährung*, which trans-lates as "probation" or "rehabilitation," rather than the specific term for "pa-role," *Ehrenwort*, when releasing men early from detention for service at the front. The term "parole" is used here because it most accurately reflects the real-ity of the situation.

35. Bad conduct or another legal infraction were also grounds for having one's parole revoked.

36. Messerschmidt, "Justiz und Strafvollzug," 26–27.

37. Block, "Die Ausschaltung und Beschränkung," 3–5. See also Philipp, "Der Gerichtsherr," 534, 543. See also Hannemann, *Die Justiz der Kriegsmarine,* 186.

38. Messerschmidt, *Was damals,* 142–43. See also Vultejus, *Kampfanzug,* 117–18.

39. In addition, few scholars acknowledge the differences that existed in the purposes and methods between the Wehrmacht's centralized penal institutions, such as military prisons, and the Wehrmacht's decentralized penal institutions, such as the field penal battalions.

40. Wüllner, *Die NS-Militärjusitz,* 644–45.

41. Wüllner, *Die NS-Militärjusitz,* 646.

42. After January 1945, however, the Gerichtsherr was removed from the process of paroling those soldiers detained in prisons. See chapter 4.

43. Fahle, *Verweigern—Weglaufen—Zersetzen,* 177–78. In the civilian administration of justice the liberal concept of rehabilitation was replaced during the Third Reich by the earlier concepts of punishment and societal protection.

44. Most belligerents, including the United States, prosecuted homosexuals during the Second World War, and the military penal codes in Germany were therefore not exceptional. It should also be noted that homosexual behavior, like heterosexual behavior, can often produce "victims,"—for example, in cases that involve harassment or the abuse of a minor.

45. Kahle, *"Konservierung,"* 45.

46. Wüllner, *Die NS-Militärjusitz,* 648.

47. See, for example, Kammler, *Ich habe die Metzelei satt,* 15.

48. Messerschmidt, *Was damals,* 103–4.

49. Deist et al., *Build-up of German Aggression,* 16.

2. The Military Administration of Justice

1. Philipp, "Der Gerichtsherr," 535–36.

2. Haase, *"Gefahr für die Manneszucht,"* 40–41. The military and reactionary right agreed that the post–World War I political climate rendered the continuation of special military jurisdiction problematic. See Philipp, "Der Gerichtsherr," 542.

3. Philipp, "Der Gerichtsherr," 543. In the now-infamous meeting of February 3, 1933, Hitler informed high-ranking officers that the "construction of the Wehrmacht" was the "most important prerequisite in the struggle for export possibilities" and in the "conquest of *Lebensraum* in the east and its ruthless Germanization." Hitler also outlined the need for the political leadership to ensure that pacifism, Bolshevism, and Marxism had not poisoned conscripts before and during service. See Klausch, *Die Bewährungstruppe 500,* 13–14.

4. Garbe, "Im Namen des Volkes?!," 95.

5. Klausch, *Die Bewährungstruppe 500,* 13. See also Messerschmidt, *Was damals,* 98–99.

6. Thomas, *Wehrmachtjustiz und Widerstandbekämpfung*, 33, 39. See also Schwinge, *Die deutsche Militärjustiz*, 32.

7. Haase, *"Gefahr für die Manneszucht,"* 43. The military administration of justice did not wait until January 1, 1934, to begin its work, but operated under the Military Penal Code (Militärstrafgesetzordnung) of 1898 until the new penal code became effective in January 1934. See Philipp, "Der Gerichtsherr," 543.

8. Haase, *"Gefahr für die Manneszucht,"* 43. See also Garbe, "Im Namen des Volkes?!," 95; and Philipp, "Der Gerichtsherr," 540.

9. Garbe, "Im Namen des Volkes?!," 95. See also Philipp, "Der Gerichtsherr," 540.

10. Hannemann, *Die Justiz der Kriegsmarine*, 186.

11. Garbe, "Im Namen des Volkes?!," 95. See also Hannemann, *Die Justiz der Kriegsmarine*, 186.

12. According to Erich Schwinge, during the First World War the military administration of justice suffered from too much mildness, too much formality, and too much "slowness," the "exact opposite of what was required." See Schwinge, *Die deutsche Militärjustiz*, 32.

13. Haase, *"Gefahr für die Manneszucht,"* 41.

14. Haase, *"Gefahr für die Manneszucht,"* 42. Literature on military law began beating the drum again once the preparations for war got under way in 1936, explaining that during the First World War, due to the flood of general and executive pardons, every perpetrator could count fairly accurately on clemency. Leadership and legislation had failed, and the courts showed infinite mildness, proclaimed the critics. See Schwinge, *Die deutsche Militärjustiz*, 35.

15. Fritz, *Frontsoldaten*, 90.

16. Haase, *"Gefahr für die Manneszucht,"* 42

17. Kammler, *Ich habe die Metzelei satt*, 88.

18. Garbe, "Im Namen des Volkes?!," 96.

19. Messerschmidt, *Was damals*, 47.

20. Haase, *"Gefahr für die Manneszucht,"* 47. According to historian Just Block, "The maintenance of Manneszucht and military order is the task of every military administration of justice. It also serves, however, the security of the troops and military command authority and must protect the armed forces from attacks by a third party." See Block, "Die Ausschaltung und Beschränkung," 14.

21. Walmrath, *"Iustitia und disciplana,"* 155.

22. Deist et al., *Build-up of German Aggression*, 104. The military considered insufficient psychological preparation a contributing factor to Germany's defeat in World War I, and even before 1933 military leaders searched for a means of unifying the nation for the complete mobilization needed for a future total war.

23. Even the political left was determined to erase the stigma of the stab in the back. See Paul, *Ungehorsame Soldaten*, 21.

24. Messerschmidt and Wüllner, *Wehrmachtjustiz im Dienste*, 31–32. Even the

Barbarossa Jurisdiction Decree and Commissar Order were produced by leading military jurists, not by political leaders.

25. Deist et al., *Build-up of German Aggression*, 149.

26. Fritz, *Frontsoldaten*, 8.

27. Fahle, *Verweigern—Weglaufen—Zersetzen*, 59.

28. Thomas, *Wehrmachtjustiz und Widerstandbekämpfung*, 38–39.

29. Thomas, *Wehrmachtjustiz und Widerstandbekämpfung*, 40–42. The General Staff's directive on international law stipulated that "humanitarian requirements could only be considered to the extent permitted by the nature and objective of the war." Boog et al., *Attack on the Soviet Union*, 5.

30. Thomas, *Wehrmachtjustiz und Widerstandbekämpfung*, 40–41.

31. Thomas, *Wehrmachtjustiz und Widerstandbekämpfung*, 42.

32. Messerschmidt, *Was damals*, 166.

33. According to Norbert Haase, jurists did not apply "war necessity" as a criterion in sentencing until the second half of the war. He states that their use of the criterion nevertheless reveals how fully the jurists oriented themselves to "victory or defeat." See Haase, *"Gefahr für die Manneszucht,"* 60.

34. Block, "Die Ausschaltung und Beschränkung," 20. Even members of the Reich Supreme Military Court did not have to be "party comrades." The lack of a requirement of party membership is in striking contrast to the central role of the party in the screening and selection of jurists in the civilian sphere. See also Staff, *Justiz im Dritten Reich*, 131–32. See also Thomas, *Wehrmachtjustiz und Widerstandbekämpfung*, 43.

35. Sixteen jurists' personnel files were examined for this study. The particular jurists were selected from among all those who presided over numerous trials held before the Courts of the Sixth and 253rd Infantry Divisions as well as the Court of the Wehrmacht Commander–Berlin.

36. Thomas, *Wehrmachtjustiz und Widerstandbekämpfung*, 43–44.

37. Müller, *Hitler's Justice*, 6–8. See also Fieburg, *Justiz im nationalsozialistischen Deutschland*, 24; and Angermund, *Deutsche Richterschaft*, 41.

38. Fieburg, *Justiz im nationalsozialistischen Deutschland*, 25. See also Thomas, *Wehrmachtjustiz und Widerstandbekämpfung*, 26–27.

39. Walther, "Hat der positivismus," 264–65.

40. Block, "Die Ausschaltung und Beschränkung," 20. See also Thomas, *Wehrmachtjustiz und Widerstandbekämpfung*, 43.

41. In addition, at least one-third of the jurists claimed Prussian citizenship.

42. Absolon, *Die Wehrmacht im Dritten Reich, Band II*, 224.

43. Walmrath, *"Iustitia und disciplana,"* 293–99. The youngest one-quarter of the jurists had an average age of 26 in 1933. In 1944, nearly 60 percent of the senior presiding judges on the courts were older career military officers. According to Walmrath, the fourteen jurists not accepted into the Truppensonderdienst (TSD) in 1944 were not rejected on ideological or political grounds, but for their inability to integrate themselves into the "military judicial apparatus."

44. Eberlein et al., *Militärjustiz im Nationalsozialismus*, 53.

45. Hannemann, *Die Justiz der Kriegsmarine*, 110.

46. See, for example, Jurist personnel file W10/1452.

47. Eberlein et al., *Militärjustiz im Nationalsozialismus*, 16–17. See also Thomas, *Wehrmachtjustiz und Widerstandbekämpfung*, 43.

48. Haase, *"Gefahr für die Manneszucht,"* 54. See also Boog et al., *Attack on the Soviet Union*, 36.

49. The civilian Reich Ministry of Justice also had the prevention of November 1918 in mind, perceiving the task of justice during war as the "selection of criminal elements" that might attempt a stab in the back at a critical time. See Haase, *Das Reichskriegsgericht*, 12.

50. Thomas, *Wehrmachtjustiz und Widerstandbekämpfung*, 43. See also Vultejus, *Kampfanzug*, 48.

51. Germany was divided into defense districts for the purpose of raising, training, and administering the troops. Franz Seidler, "Das Justizwesen," 364.

52. Philipp, "Der Gerichtsherr," 543.

53. Haase, "Aus der Praxis," 84.

54. Block, "Die Ausschaltung und Beschränkung," 12.

55. Even the Reich Supreme Military Court was subordinated to a military officer who functioned as Gerichtsherr. See Block, "Die Ausschaltung und Beschränkung," 10–11.

56. Haase, "Aus der Praxis," 387.

57. The Reich Supreme Military Court also retained competence for attacks on the Führer and most crimes directed against the national defense establishment and war economy. See Haase, "Aus der Praxis," 384–85.

58. Haase, *Das Reichskriegsgericht*, 10, 18–19.

59. Another precedent that demonstrates the court's arbitrary jurisprudence is its affirmation of the retroactive application of the law. Haase, *Das Reichskriegsgericht*, 18.

60. Messerschmidt, *Was damals*, 33–34.

61. Klausch, *Die Bewährungstruppe 500*, 13, 348. After a brief reduction in terror between 1935 and 1936, the regime initiated a new wave of repression in 1937 and 1938 in preparation for war, targeting a wide spectrum of "asocial" elements. See Deist et al., *Build-up of German Aggression*, 146–47.

62. Deist et al., *Build-up of German Aggression*, 109.

63. The civilian Reich Ministry of Justice also believed in maintaining the Wehrgemeinschaft. According to a memo from the Reich Ministry of Justice to the Nazi party, the task of justice during war was the "selection of criminal elements" who could attempt a stab in the back "at a critical time." See Haase, *Das Reichskriegsgericht*, 12.

64. For information regarding the close cooperation between the police and Wehrmacht, see Klausch, *Die 999er*. See also Klausch, *Antifaschisten in ss-Uniform*; and Klausch, *Die Bewährungstruppe 500*.

65. Müller, *Hitler's Justice*, 196–97.

66. Subsequent changes to the National Defense Act made less heavily punished individuals eligible for service. See Klausch, *Bewährungstruppe 500*, 14.

67. Absolon, *Die Wehrmacht im Dritten Reich, Band III*, 14.

68. Rass, *Menschenmaterial*. Rass's title, which translates to "human matériel," aptly characterizes the Wehrmacht's perception and treatment of its soldiers.

69. Klausch, *Die Bewährungstruppe 500*, 14–15, 19.

70. Absolon, *Die Wehrmacht im Dritten Reich, Band IV*, 345.

71. Absolon, *Die Wehrmacht im Dritten Reich, Band IV*, 345–46. See also Klausch, *Die Bewährungstruppe 500*, 21. The navy's "education unit" was initially attached to army Disciplinary Unit I at Stablack but eventually was designated the Naval Disciplinary Unit (Kriegssonderabteilung der Kriegsmarine) and transferred to the Island of Hela. The education unit was dissolved in 1942 and replaced by the 30th and 31st *Schiffsstammabteilungen*, a term which has no English equivalent. See Absolon, *Die Wehrmacht im Dritten Reich, Band IV*, 346. See also Haase, *"Gefahr für die Manneszucht,"* 262. The air force's disciplinary unit was officially designated the *Prüfunglager*, which translates loosely as "examination" or "review camp." See Fahle, *Verweigern—Weglaufen—Zersetzen*, 187.

72. Klausch, *Die Bewährungstruppe 500*, 20–22, 25. Also suitable for these units were individuals who had committed crimes under the influence of alcohol and received the protection of the clauses governing diminished responsibility. See chapter 10. See also Wüllner, *Die NS-Militärjustiz*, 659–60. Politicals and conscientious objectors were not conscripted into the disciplinary units. They were not the designated repositories for these "nonconformists." See Klausch, *Die Bewährungstruppe 500*, 23.

73. Klausch, *Die Bewährungstruppe 500*, 21–22, 26.

74. Wüllner, *Die NS-Militärjustiz*, 660.

75. Klausch, *Die Bewährungstruppe 500*, 22, 36.

76. Klausch, *Die Bewährungstruppe 500*, 23, 25, 36. Klausch estimates that only 4 to 7 percent of disciplinary units' members were affiliated with the German Communist Party.

77. Klausch, *Die Bewährungstruppe 500*, 36.

78. Klausch, *Die Bewährungstruppe 500*, 36.

79. Absolon, *Die Wehrmacht im Dritten Reich, Band V*, 336. See also Klausch, *Die Bewährungstruppe 500*, 33.

80. Absolon, *Die Wehrmacht im Dritten Reich, Band V*, 336–37. See also Klausch, *Die Bewährungstruppe 500*, 33–38.

81. Wüllner, *Die NS-Militärjustiz*, 661–62. Wüllner sees racial-biological concepts in the various "education units" too. He nevertheless quotes the following from an efficiency report regarding a disciplinary unit detainee: "He possesses neither the capacity nor the will to be a valuable soldier. He is a danger for oth-

ers that are still capable of education. He is worthless as a soldier." Wüllner, *Die NS-Militärjustiz*, 665.

82. Seidler, *Die Militärgerichtsbarkeit*, 154–56.

83. Wüllner, *Die NS-Militärjustiz*, 664.

84. Klausch, *Die Bewährungstruppe 500*, 39–40. Klausch contradicts himself on this point. He later says that after February 2, 1942, members of the disciplinary units of the reserve army could not be transferred to police custody. Thus, it is not clear why he discusses transfers that took place up to September 1944.

85. Wüllner, *Die NS-Militärjustiz*, 661–62.

86. See chapter 4.

3. Wehrmachtjustiz at War

1. Messerschmidt and Wüllner, *Wehrmachtjustiz im Dienste*, 31–32, 38. See also Absolon, *Die Wehrmacht im Dritten Reich, Band V*, 328.

2. Walmrath, "*Iustitia und disciplana*," 535.

3. Garbe, "Im Namen des Volkes?!," 98.

4. Walmrath, "*Iustitia und disciplana*," 168–78.

5. Rabofsky and Oberkofler, *Verborgene Wurzeln der NS-Justiz*, 112.

6. Haase, *Das Reichskriegsgericht*, 12.

7. Walmrath, "*Iustitia und disciplana*," 168–72. See also Messerschmidt and Wüllner, *Wehrmachtjustiz im Dienste*, 131–32.

8. Messerschmidt and Wüllner, *Wehrmachtjustiz im Dienste*, 132.

9. Klausch, *Die Bewährungstruppe 500*, 15.

10. Absolon, *Das Wehrmachtstrafrecht*, 52.

11. Absolon, *Das Wehrmachtstrafrecht*, 57.

12. Klausch, *Die Bewährungstruppe 500*, 15.

13. Walmrath, "*Iustitia und disciplana*," 178–82.

14. Walmrath, "*Iustitia und disciplana*," 124.

15. Absolon, *Das Wehrmachtstrafrecht*, 61.

16. Absolon, *Das Wehrmachtstrafrecht*, 61.

17. Seidler, "Das Justizwesen," 368. Although Seidler describes the impact of changes made in 1944 to section 5 of the code, the changes made in 1943 were actually responsible for the impact of the changes he describes.

18. Absolon, *Das Wehrmachtstrafrecht*, 62–63.

19. The impact of fanatics on the bench, however, was tempered greatly by the powers of the Gerichtsherren, the military commanders with supreme legal authority over courts-martial. Punishments could only be carried out after these officers had confirmed the verdict.

20. Walmrath, "*Iustitia und disciplana*," 124.

21. Absolon, *Die Wehrmacht im Dritten Reich, Band V*, 329–30. See also Walmrath, 178.

22. Wüllner, *Die NS-Militärjustiz*, 40.

23. One hundred forty-eight defendants in the trials in Schwinge's thousand

case files were denied counsel when representation was required. See Messer-schmidt and Wüllner, *Wehrmachtjustiz im Dienste*, 41.

24. Walmrath, *"Iustitia und disciplana,"* 188.

25. In the case files, at least one soldier was exonerated after new evidence was discovered. See Court of the Wehrmacht Commder–Berlin RW55/2915.

26. See Walmrath, *"Iustitia und disciplana,"* 258. These petitions were granted for sex offenders only on rare occasions. See also Seidler, "Das Justizwesen," 389.

27. Walmrath, *"Iustitia und disciplana,"* 258. Walmrath discovered only one nonposthumous case in which a sailor had his record expunged.

28. Absolon, *Das Wehrmachtstrafrecht*, 69–70. Civilian courts cited the ordi-nance frequently when imposing death sentences for theft and plundering. Natu-rally, these crimes took place during blackout conditions, and most perpetrators therefore avoided apprehension. When an offender was caught, the authorities wanted to make an example of him. See Angermund, *Deutsche Richterschaft*, 211–12.

29. Schwinge, *Die deutsche Militärjustiz*, 24. According to Schwinge, this ar-rangement did not prejudice judicial independence. Most objective scholars dis-agree.

30. Philipp, "Der Gerichtsherr," 544.

31. Wüllner, *Die NS-Militärjustiz*, 100.

32. Jurist personnel file W10/1742.

33. Schwinge, *Die deutsche Militärjustiz*, 25. See also Seidler, "Das Justizwe-sen," 365.

34. Walmrath, *"Iustitia und disciplana,"* 295.

35. The presiding judge exercised judicial independence (in theory) according to section 7, paragraph 2, of the Wartime Judicial Procedure Code. See Thomas, *Wehrmachtjustiz und Widerstandbekämpfung*, 36.

36. If a commander as Gerichtsherr opposed a verdict, he sent the case and his assessment of the sentence and the defendant to his immediate military judicial superior. This officer could confirm the verdict or order a new trial. The case could be heard by the original court or handed over to an entirely different one.

37. For obvious reasons, these court officers also bent to the commander's will when representing his interests at court. Seidler, "Das Justizwesen," 365.

38. Absolon, *Das Wehrmachtstrafrecht*, 140–41.

39. Messerschmidt and Wüllner, *Wehrmachtjustiz im Dienste*, 40–41.

40. This was an important power and it provided the Gerichtsherr with even more influence over courts-martial. The soldiers selected as the lay judges, not surprisingly, would not want to displease their commander and thus voted as lay judges accordingly.

41. Udo Reifner criticizes the transcripts' format and contends that they read like police reports. In other words, the format led commanders to automatically accept their content as incontrovertible, leading to almost certain confirmation.

This criticism is rather shortsighted. Most likely, commanders desired concise summaries rather than a document full of legalese and long-winded technical assessments. Few courts represented in the case files provided in-depth analyses on subtle points of law. See Reifner and Sonnen, *Strafjustiz und Polizei*, 29.

42. For reserve divisions, the verdict in question was submitted to the reserve army commander. See Block, "Die Ausschaltung und Beschränkung," 13. See also Seidler, *Die Militärgerichtsbarkeit*, 34.

43. The power of mitigation did not extend to penal servitude and death sentences. See Philipp, "Der Gerichtsherr," 544.

44. See chapter 4.

45. Walmrath, "*Iustitia und disciplana*," 189.

46. Seidler, "Das Justizwesen," 365.

47. A jurist attached to the court but not involved with the case in question usually functioned as the staff adviser. If there were an insufficient number of jurists on a court to permit this distribution of labor, a judge from another court or an officer qualified for the bar as a civilian could submit the opinion.

48. The field penal battalions were one of the Wehrmacht's more draconian wartime forms of punishment. See chapter 4.

49. Philipp, "Der Gerichtsherr," 538.

50. Philipp, "Der Gerichtsherr," 542–43. The Law regarding Military Courts and the Military Judicial Process of September 22, 1926, established the punishment decree in order to permit speedy justice on board ship.

51. Philipp, "Der Gerichtsherr," 544.

52. Messerschmidt and Wüllner, *Wehrmachtjustiz im Dienste*, 49–50.

53. Messerschmidt and Wüllner, *Wehrmachtjustiz im Dienste*, 50. After minimizing the role of the Gerichtsherr in the judicial process, Messerschmidt and Wüllner go to great lengths to impress upon the reader that a large number of men were sent by heartless Gerichtsherren via the punishment decree to prison without any type of oral hearing. See also Wüllner, *Die NS-Militärjustiz*, 117–120.

54. Haase, "*Gefahr für die Manneszucht*," 51.

55. This is most applicable to repeat homosexual offenders. For rapists and child molesters, Gerichtsherren often cited a crime's "reprehensibility" as the reason for not supporting a clemency petition.

56. Thomas, "Nur das ist für die Truppe Recht," 40.

57. Walmrath, "*Iustitia und disciplana*," 132.

58. Seidler, "Das Justizwesen," 364.

59. All the courts, whether they were located in Germany or in an operational area during the war were designated as field courts (*Feldkriegsgericht*). Those with the navy were designated shipboard courts (*Bordgericht*). See Block, "Die Ausschaltung und Beschränkung," 11.

60. Schwinge, *Die deutsche Militärjustiz*, 20.

61. Examples of courts assigned to such geographic commands include the

Court of the Commanding Officer of Greater Paris, the Court of Military Government Area Headquarters 579–Lublin, and the Court of Air Force District (Luftgau) III.

62. Newly appointed jurists received their training with the reserve units. Therefore, the number of jurists with reserve units could fluctuate greatly.

63. Wüllner, *Die NS-Militärjustiz*, 106.

64. Seidler, "Das Justizwesen," 364. See also Schwinge, *Die deutsche Militärjustiz*, 20.

65. Walmrath, *"Iustitia und disciplana,"* 301–2.

66. Seidler, "Das Justizwesen," 364.

67. Garbe, "Im Namen des Volkes?!," 100.

68. Walmrath, *"Iustitia und disciplana,"* 270–75.

69. Thomas, *Wehrmachtjustiz und Widerstandbekämpfung*, 50. Thomas's conclusion regarding periodic reports may not be entirely correct. The personnel files show that reports on verdicts and sentences were submitted primarily during a jurist's ninety-day probation period before permanent appointment to the bench.

70. Walmrath, *"Iustitia und disciplana,"* 295.

71. Walmrath, *"Iustitia und disciplana,"* 269.

72. Late in the war, Admiral Karl Dönitz warned that he would refuse all clemency petitions for deserters who had been sentenced to death. The revolutionary disturbances that rocked the armed forces in 1918 began in the navy with the Kiel uprising of November 4, 1918. The navy carried this burden and became especially motivated to atone for 1918. Indeed, this became the navy credo. Walmrath, *"Iustitia und disciplana,"* 90–91.

73. Walmrath, *"Iustitia und disciplana,"* 187–88.

74. Schwinge, *Die deutsche Militärjustiz*, 270–71.

75. Walmrath, *"Iustitia und disciplana,"* 168. Messerschmidt and Wüllner are quite critical of the last criterion because nearly every soldier had to commit some illegal act, such as stealing civilian clothes and food or forging travel papers and other documents, in order to survive while on the run. Messerschmidt and Wüllner, *Wehrmachtjustiz im Dienste*, 95.

76. Walmrath, *"Iustitia und disciplana,"* 168–69.

77. Vultejus, *Kampfanzug*, 54–56. When a naval judge referred to Hitler's guidelines in order to grant a deserter mitigating circumstances after Dönitz's decree had been issued, the jurist received a rebuke from the OKM.

78. See, for example, Schwinge, *Verfälschung und Wahrheit*, 52–53.

79. The prison commandants and commanders of penal formations also demonstrate this orientation to military considerations. Their evaluations of prisoners being reviewed for parole address the individual's fitness and willingness for service, not his worthiness for reintegration into the Volksgemeinschaft. The phrase "he is (or is not) useful to the troops" appears frequently in these evaluations.

80. Not all case files contained information on the prosecution's requested sen-

tence. Regarding the 2:1 ratio, Lothar Walmrath arrived at a similar conclusion, with certain offense categories demonstrating an even higher ratio. For example, in cases involving offenses against military order (*Militärordnungsdelikte*) the ratio came to 10:1. See Walmrath, *"Iustitia und disciplana,"* 413.

81. Jurist personnel file W10/1766.

82. Seidler, "Die Fahnenflucht," 35.

83. Walmrath, *"Iustitia und disciplana,"* 187.

84. Walmrath, *"Iustitia und disciplana,"* 568–69. The remaining 8.5 percent were rejected on technical legal grounds.

85. Erich Schwinge also reports a high confirmation rate. In his case file sample, commanders refused to confirm only sixteen verdicts out of the 753 judgments passed by army courts. Upon retrial, eleven of the sixteen cases resulted in a higher sentence and five resulted in a lower sentence. Schwinge, *Die deutsche Militärjustiz*, 325.

86. These statistics represent the average length of prison sentences (i.e., excluding penal servitude punishments). These statistics are based only on case files that indicate that an individual definitely received parole.

87. For 1939–40 the average sentence was approximately eighteen months, while for 1941–42 the average was approximately twelve months and for 1943–45 the average was approximately twenty-two months. Again, these statistics are based on case files in which the documents leave no doubt about an individual's early release. The percentage of penal servitude sentences likewise decreased significantly during the war.

88. Seidler, "Das Justizwesen," 395–98. Other measures such as the OKW's Decree Regarding Communist Insurgent Movements in the Occupied Areas of September 16, 1941, limited military jurisdiction but was of minor importance. See Thomas, *Wehrmachtjustiz und Widerstandbekämpfung*, 51. The Night and Fog Decree, which deprived the military courts of jurisdiction over persons accused of resistance activities in occupied Western Europe, remains outside the purview of this book.

89. Schwinge, *Verfälschung und Wahrheit*, 69–71. See also Schwinge, *Die deutsche Militärjustiz*, 64–72.

90. Absolon, *Das Wehrmachtstrafrecht*, 137. See also Block, "Die Ausschaltung und Beschränkung," 13.

91. Boog et al., *Attack on the Soviet Union*, 501–2.

92. Schwinge, *Die deutsche Militärjustiz*, 64–65. See also Boog et al., *Attack on the Soviet Union*, 499, 502. Under section 1, paragraph 4, of the Wartime Judicial Procedure Code enemy civilians could not be punished without due legal processes. In the other theaters of war, crimes against civilians were indeed prosecuted if the authorities became aware of such offenses. See Block, "Die Ausschaltung und Beschränkung," 13. See also Absolon, *Das Wehrmachtstrafrecht*, 137; De Zayas, "Die Rechtsprechung der Wehrmachtsgerichtsbarkeit," 121.

93. Jacobsen, "The Kommissarbefehl," 180.

94. Boog et al., *Attack on the Soviet Union*, 498, 508, 510.

95. Jacobsen, "The Kommissarbefehl," 180. See also Boog et al., *Attack on the Soviet Union*, 503, 514–15.

96. Boog et al., *Attack on the Soviet Union*, 503–4. For the punishment of civilians committing acts that were less grave than "serious cases of rebellion," von Brauchitsch's guidelines called for "improvised measures" such as putting them to work.

97. Jacobsen, "The Kommissarbefehl," 181. See also Boog et al., *Attack on the Soviet Union*, 510.

98. Boog et al., *Attack on the Soviet Union*, 299.

99. Boog et al., *Attack on the Soviet Union*, 302–3.

100. Boog et al., *Attack on the Soviet Union*, 506.

101. Boog et al., *Attack on the Soviet Union*, 504.

102. Boog et al., *Attack on the Soviet Union*, 510–11.

103. Boog et al., *Attack on the Soviet Union*, 1251.

104. The difference, for example, between official requisitions and helping oneself to a farmer's eggs must have been quite confusing to many soldiers.

105. The bulk of the military judicial case files examined here were selected from the German Federal Archives Central Documentation Agency's Bestand Ost, or Eastern Collection. This special collection consists of documents that fell into Soviet hands at the end of World War II; thus these documents came largely from Wehrmacht units operating in the east. The statistic cited in the text is based on cases of rape, child molestation, homosexual offenses, and sexual offenses that were punished under diminished responsibility due to the consumption of alcohol.

106. Boog et al., *Attack on the Soviet Union*, 506.

107. See the strange saga of Josef M. in Snyder, "The Prosecution and Punishment," 328–29. The reference to the Jurisdiction Decree was not even made by a presiding judge or commanding officer. Rather, it was contained in a second opinion submitted by a staff legal adviser. See also Eastern Collection BO-S152. Birgit Beck reports the same phenomenon. Beck, *Wehrmacht und sexuelle Gewalt*, 183.

108. Beck, "Sexual Violence," 9.

109. Although many courts operating in the east were forced to destroy files when the Red Army overran Wehrmacht units, some documents should have survived, including punishment lists, which might yield information on the frequency of these processes.

110. Experts estimate that even in ideal victim-friendly environments the vast majority of rapes go unreported. See Brownmiller, *Against Our Will*, 175. For more on this question, see chapter 7.

111. For more on this point, see chapter 7.

112. Rass, *Menschenmaterial*, 243–44.

113. Rass, *Menschenmaterial*, 245–46.

114. Rass, *Menschenmaterial*, 247–48. Soviet citizens who assisted the Wehrmacht, such as *Hiwis* (volunteer auxiliaries), legionnaires, conscripted laborers, and other Soviet civilians who were officially part of the "institutional structures" of the military, did receive a certain degree of protection from mistreatment.

115. Snyder, "The Prosecution and Punishment," 99. Although occasional examples of bias against eastern inhabitants were encountered in the documents, specific racial slurs did not appear in any of the court transcripts. For more on this question, see chapter 7.

116. Block, "Die Ausschaltung und Beschränkung," 118.

4. The Wehrmacht's Penal and Parole System

1. Haase, *"Gefahr für die Manneszucht,"* 232.

2. Although Hans-Peter Klausch concludes that the use of penal and parole formations for the prevention of counter-selection is "self-evident," he states that this had been "nevertheless only openly expressed . . . by Himmler with regard to the Dirlewanger formation," the infamous ss parole unit. See Klausch, *Die Bewährungstruppe 500*, 61. The Special Formation Dirlewanger was subordinated to the ss and therefore falls outside the purview of this study.

3. Klausch, *Die Bewährungstruppe 500*, 53.

4. The parole battalions were armed. Trusted inmates in the field penal battalions were armed on occasion. These two formations, along with the Wehrmacht field penal camps, were all employed at the front, giving their members the best opportunity for crossing over to the enemy.

5. Klausch, *Die Bewährungstruppe 500*, 61.

6. Of course, all nations' armed forces "discard" their human matériel when they are no longer useful. The Wehrmacht, however, gladly turned its unusable human matériel over to the regime, knowing exactly what fate awaited the victims in the concentration camps.

7. Absolon, *Das Wehrmachtstrafrecht*, 166.

8. Absolon, *Das Wehrmachtstrafrecht*, 172. This did not apply to soldiers receiving penal servitude sentences. Individuals sentenced to penal servitude were automatically dismissed from service, handed over to the civilian judicial authorities, and, as a rule, incarcerated in the Emsland concentration camp.

9. Seidler, *Die Militärgerichtsbarkeit*, 56–57.

10. Wüllner, *Die NS-Militärjustiz*, 620–21. See Seidler, *Die Militärgerichtsbarkeit*, 57. The military leadership also wanted, in case of defeat, to prevent soldiers who committed crimes from being "lionized as resistance fighters." This issue is still being debated in Germany today. See Seidler, "Das Justizwesen," 362.

11. It is possible that many commanders initially misinterpreted section 104 as well. Just four weeks into the war, the Directive for the Completion of Prison Sentences during the War was issued. It clarified the purpose of parole and emphasized that prison sentences should be served during the war only in exceptional circumstances. See Wüllner, *Die NS-Militärjustiz*, 668, 711–12.

12. Haase, *"Gefahr für die Manneszucht,"* 233–34.

13. This also applied to detention in the Wehrmacht's field penal camps, which were introduced in 1942.

14. Wüllner, *Die NS-Militärjustiz,* 711, 782.

15. Seidler, *Die Militärgerichtsbarkeit,* 57. See also Auslander, "Vom Wehrmacht-zum Moorsoldaten," 175.

16. Absolon, *Das Wehrmachtstrafrecht,* 173.

17. Seidler, *Die Militärgerichtsbarkeit,* 57.

18. See case files of the Sixth Infantry Division, numbers 19, 28, 79, 117, 324, 349, 355, and 360.

19. Klausch, *Die Bewährungstruppe 500,* 62.

20. Hennicke and Wüllner, "Über die barbarischen Vollstreckungsmethoden," 90. See also Wüllner, *Die NS-Militärjustiz,* 780.

21. Wüllner, *Die NS-Militärjustiz,* 667–69. The term used by the Wehrmacht for describing a sentence's deferment for front-parole was *Bewährung,* which translates to "rehabilitation" or "testing," rather than the exact term for "parole," *Ehrenwort.*

22. Germany created penal units during the First World War to combat this problem. See Philipp, "Der Gerichtsherr," 541. A total of seventy-eight penal units were established before the end of the First World War, "a sign of the always-sinking morale in the army." See Absolon, *Die Wehrmacht im Dritten Reich, Band II,* 228.

23. Wüllner *Die NS-Militärjustiz,* 668–79, 710–11. See also Schwinge, *Die deutsche Militärjustiz,* 259, 303, 679.

24. Walmrath, *"Iustitia und disciplana,"* 189.

25. Seidler, *Die Militärgerichtsbarkeit,* 67. See also Klausch, *Die Bewährungstruppe 500,* 62.

26. From August 24, 1939, to June 30, 1940, more than twenty-seven thousand servicemen had been sentenced to imprisonment or penal servitude (*Zuchthaus*). One-third had their sentence fully suspended and one-third were paroled after partial atonement of the sentence. See Seidler, *Die Militärgerichtsbarkeit,* 58. See Wüllner, *Die NS-Militärjustiz,* 712.

27. Seidler, *Die Militärgerichtsbarkeit,* 58. By the end of 1941 there were probably "several divisions of men behind bars." See Wüllner, *Die NS-Militärjustiz,* 713.

28. Haase, *"Gefahr für die Manneszucht,"* 256–57. Lehmann has drawn extensive criticism for demanding that the courts rule not on the "degree of guilt or the personality of the perpetrator, but rather above all according to the requirements of Manneszucht." This quote demonstrates disregard for individual rights, but it also supports the thesis of a military judiciary geared toward maintaining discipline at all costs.

29. The OKH feared that if the parole units were very large, the formations would be an easy propaganda target for the enemy, which would damage the

reputation of the Wehrmacht. The OKH also feared that if the selected parolees proved to be undependable, a large formation might endanger an entire section of the front. The OKW initially had proposed that the parole units be regiment-sized, but eventually agreed to the smaller battalions. See Klausch, *Die Bewährungstruppe 500*, 66.

30. Haase, *"Gefahr für die Manneszucht,"* 258. See also Seidler, *Die Militärgerichtsbarkeit*, 58.

31. Klausch, *Die Bewährungstruppe 500*, 65–66. See also Haase, *"Gefahr für die Manneszucht,"* 257; Seidler, "Das Justizwesen," 390–91.

32. Haase, *"Gefahr für die Manneszucht,"* 258.

33. Haase, *"Gefahr für die Manneszucht,"* 257. The parole units were referred to as "500 troops" because the units were designated as Parole Battalions 500, 540, 550, 560, and 561.

34. Seidler, "Das Justizwesen," 391–92.

35. Haase, *"Gefahr für die Manneszucht,"* 258, 260–61. See also Seidler, *Die Militärgerichtsbarkeit*, 67–68.

36. The penal camp was the military version of the civilian concentration camp.

37. Klausch suggests that the harsh regimen also may have been designed to provoke resistance. The purpose, of course, was to weed out any "bad elements" that might have been inappropriately selected for service in the parole battalions. See Klausch, *Die Bewährungstruppe 500*, 111.

38. Klausch, *Die Bewährungstruppe 500*, 114–15. Klausch also addresses the ideological indoctrination undertaken during the fitness exam. According to the contemporary accounts, it was less effective than the physical aspect of the exam.

39. Klausch, *Die Bewährungstruppe 500*, 115.

40. Klausch, *Die Bewährungstruppe 500*, 128.

41. Klausch, *Die Bewährungstruppe 500*, 62. Fritz Wüllner, Norbert Haase, and Franz Seidler offer different versions of the timing and location of the parole formations' establishment. See Haase, *"Gefahr für die Manneszucht,"* 259; Seidler, *Die Militärgerichtsbarkeit*, 67–68; and Wüllner, *Die NS-Militärjustiz*, 713.

42. Klausch, *Die Bewährungstruppe 500*, 70–72. Only two companies could be deployed in November 1941. The third and fourth companies, as well as the staff, did not reach Army Group North until shortly after the New Year.

43. Seidler, *Die Militärgerichtsbarkeit*, 67.

44. Klausch, *Die Bewährungstruppe 500*, 71–72.

45. Seidler, *Die Militärgerichtsbarkeit*, 67. Only privates could serve in the parole battalions. Convicted officers and NCOs had to be stripped of rank and reenrolled at the lowest conscripted grade before they were sent to these units. See Seidler, *Die Militärgerichtsbarkeit*, 70.

46. Haase, *"Gefahr für die Manneszucht,"* 258–59.

47. Seidler, *Die Militärgerichtsbarkeit*, 71.

48. Walmrath, *"Iustitia und disciplana,"* 256–57.

49. Haase, *"Gefahr für die Manneszucht,"* 261. The penal camps were the most severe form of punishment in the Wehrmacht, and the fact that time in detention was not calculated as time served was a special deterrent. See also Seidler, *Militärgerichtsbarkeit,* 72.

50. Klausch, *Die Bewährungstruppe 500,* 63–64. See also Haase, *"Gefahr für die Manneszucht,"* 259.

51. Klausch, *Die Bewährungstruppe 500,* 64.

52. Klausch, *Die Bewährungstruppe 500,* 64–65. In addition to the timing, Klausch stresses that Hitler's use of the phrase "renewal of military operations" in his order for the parole units' creation is evidence of their role in the preparations for Barbarossa.

53. Wüllner, *Die NS-Militärjustiz,* 713.

54. Haase, *"Gefahr für die Manneszucht,"* 258.

55. Seidler, "Das Justizwesen," 392–93.

56. Klausch, *Die Bewährungstruppe 500,* 107–8. The fact that a large number of soldiers remained in the Emsland camps in 1945 demonstrates that, despite the extensive relaxation of selection criteria, selection still operated until the final days of the war.

57. Klausch, *Die Bewährungstruppe 500,* 71–72.

58. Wüllner, *Die NS-Militärjustiz,* 722. See also Auslander, "Vom Wehrmacht-zum Moorsoldaten," 187.

59. Klausch, *Die Bewährungstruppe 500,* 117–18, 256–57, 354.

60. Klausch, *Die Bewährungstruppe 500,* 351–55. According to Lothar Walmrath, the courts undertook "calculated decimation of the inner enemy" that was "unfit for inclusion in society." The case files, however, reveal that many of these "inner enemies" were reintegrated after they demonstrated their willingness to carry a weapon in good faith. Walmrath, *"Iustitia und disciplana,"* 255.

61. Wüllner, *Die NS-Militärjustiz,* 722–23. Parole battalion records were kept in Skierniewice after August 1943. It is unclear whether they were destroyed or fell into Soviet hands at the end of the war.

62. Wüllner, *Die NS-Militärjustiz,* 722. Wüllner neglects to mention that the Gerichtsherr, not the courts, made the final decision on how a sentence would be executed and which soldiers received parole.

63. Klausch, *Die Bewährungstruppe 500,* 87. See also Seidler, *Die Militärgerichtsbarkeit,* 73.

64. Seidler, *Die Militärgerichtsbarkeit,* 73.

65. Seidler, *Die Militärgerichtsbarkeit,* 73.

66. Seidler, "Das Justizwesen," 394. See also Klausch, *Die Bewährungstruppe 500,* 63–64. The parole battalions ultimately were employed at various times with over fifty different infantry divisions in twelve different armies. See Seidler, *Die Militärgerichtsbarkeit,* 73.

67. Klausch, "Erziehungsmänner und Wehrunwürdige, 67.

68. Seidler, "Das Justizwesen," 392.

69. Seidler, *Die Militärgerichtsbarkeit*, 156.

70. Also as a result of the blitzkrieg's failure, Hitler ordered in February 1942 the establishment of the 999 parole formation for civilian political detainees and antifascists. See Vultejus, *Kampfanzug*, 64.

71. Haase, *"Gefahr für die Manneszucht,"* 235.

72. Klausch, *Die Bewährungstruppe 500*, 40. By September 1942, German losses on the eastern front amounted to 1.6 million. See Wüllner, *Die NS-Militärjustiz*, 743.

73. Wüllner, *Die NS-Militärjustiz*, 743. See also Klausch, *Die Bewährungstruppe 500*, 40.

74. Klausch, *Die Bewährungstruppe 500*, 40.

75. Klausch, *Die Bewährungstruppe 500*, 41.

76. Klausch, *Die Bewährungstruppe 500*, 41. See also Wüllner, *Die NS-Militärjustiz*, 744.

77. Haase, *"Gefahr für die Manneszucht,"* 235.

78. Wüllner, *Die NS-Militärjustiz*, 808.

79. Wüllner, *Die NS-Militärjustiz*, 697. Section 104 also failed to provide options for the use of soldiers who were not fully fit for combat. The new penal formations mobilized even soldiers with very limited fitness ratings.

80. The Gestapo often petitioned in these cases to the Reich Main Security Office to take individuals into "protective custody" for their "sabotage of military service." See Walmrath, *"Iustitia und disciplana,"* 249.

81. Haase, *"Gefahr für die Manneszucht,"* 235.

82. These statistics include individuals convicted for rape, child molestation, incest, homosexual offenses, and all sexual offenders convicted for committing their crime under diminished responsibility due to alcohol consumption.

83. Klausch, *Die Bewährungstruppe 500*, 53.

84. Walmrath, *"Iustitia und disciplana,"* 244.

85. Wüllner, *Die NS-Militärjustiz*, 744. Other scholars also place great emphasis on the OKM clarifications of August 2, 1940, and July 1, 1942, which state that "prisoners should not be better off than the soldiers at the front," as proof of the role that the prevention of counter-selection had in the formations' establishment.

86. The German armed forces created field punishment units in 1916 to combat the defeatism and war weariness that was manifested in increasing desertion and insubordination rates. See Philipp, "Der Gerichtsherr," 541. See also Absolon, *Die Wehrmacht im Dritten Reich, Band II*, 228; and Dreetz, "Zur Bildung von Militärstrafkompanien," 462–64.

87. See, for example, the OKW's Directive for the Execution of Punishments in War and Special Operations of September 30, 1939, a similar OKH directive of October 10, 1939, and a subsequent OKW implementation decree of November 3, 1939. Seidler, *Die Militärgerichtsbarkeit*, 135. See also Haase, *"Gefahr für die Manneszucht,"* 252–53; and Wüllner, *Die NS-Militärjustiz*, 780, 785–86.

88. Wüllner, *Die NS-Militärjustiz*, 694. See also Seidler, *Die Militärgerichtsbarkeit*, 135.

89. Exempt from this order were penal camp inmates scheduled to be returned to a prison for the orderly completion of their sentence because of good conduct, those in the infirmary, those with legal hearings pending, and those "incorrigible" prisoners who were scheduled to be turned over to the police. Klausch, *Die Bewährungstruppe 500*, 41. Documents suggest that various Wehrmacht prisons continued to maintain penal camps after the creation of the field penal camps. See Wüllner, *Die NS-Militärjustiz*, 709.

90. Klausch, *Die Bewährungstruppe 500*, 41–42. See also Seidler, *Die Militärgerichtsbarkeit*, 136.

91. Wüllner, *Die NS-Militärjustiz*, 709. See also Seidler, *Die Militärgerichtsbarkeit*, 136. Field Penal Camp III also was initially sent to Norway and Finish Lapland.

92. Seidler, *Die Militärgerichtsbarkeit*, 136. See also Klausch, *Die Bewährungstruppe 500*, 41.

93. Haase, "*Gefahr für die Manneszucht*," 254. The camps often were employed on construction projects, and thus prisoners frequently were subordinated to divisional engineering battalions. See Seidler, *Die Militärgerichtsbarkeit*, 137.

94. Seidler, *Die Militärgerichtsbarkeit*, 138.

95. Walmrath, "*Iustitia und disciplana*," 247.

96. Klausch, *Die Bewährungstruppe 500*, 42. See also Seidler, *Die Militärgerichtsbarkeit*, 138.

97. Haase, "*Gefahr für die Manneszucht*," 253–54.

98. Klausch, *Die Bewährungstruppe 500*, 43.

99. Klausch, *Die Bewährungstruppe 500*, 42. Klausch cites "contemporary accounts by eyewitnesses." The commander was empowered by section 13 of the Wartime Judicial Procedure Code to convene summary courts at any time. See Wüllner, *Die NS-Militärjustiz*, 705.

100. Klausch, *Die Bewährungstruppe 500*, 44.

101. Seidler, *Die Militärgerichtsbarkeit*, 136, 140–41.

102. Klausch, *Die Bewährungstruppe 500*, 44–45.

103. Seidler, *Die Militärgerichtsbarkeit*, 141. See also Wüllner, *Die NS-Militärjustiz*, 693.

104. Klausch, *Die Bewährungstruppe 500*, 45.

105. Haase, "*Gefahr für die Manneszucht*," 255. See also Seidler, *Die Militärgerichtsbarkeit*, 141.

106. Wüllner, *Die NS-Militärjustiz*, 665.

107. Haase, "*Gefahr für die Manneszucht*," 255. See also Seidler, *Die Militärgerichtsbarkeit*, 143.

108. Seidler, *Die Militärgerichtsbarkeit*, 137.

109. Klausch, *Die Bewährungstruppe 500*, 41.

110. Klausch, *Die Bewährungstruppe 500*, 41. See also Wüllner, *Die NS-Mili-*

tärjustiz, 807–13. K.v., or *kriegsverwendungsfähig*, denotes "fit for combat"; g.v.F, or *garnisonsverwendungsfähig Feld*, denotes "fit for garrison duty in the field"; and g.v.H., or *garnisonsverwendungsfähig Heimat*, denotes "fit for garrison duty—homeland."

111. Klausch, *Die Bewährungstruppe 500*, 41.

112. Seidler, *Die Militärgerichtsbarkeit*, 144.

113. Wüllner, *Die NS-Militärjustiz*, 744.

114. Klausch, *Die Bewährungstruppe 500*, 47. Each field penal battalion eventually maintained one "penal servitude" company. Initially, only soldiers sentenced to imprisonment could be sent to a field penal battalion. See Wüllner, *Die NS-Militärjustiz*, 744.

115. Wüllner, *Die NS-Militärjustiz*, 744, 746.

116. Seidler, *Die Militärgerichtsbarkeit*, 148. See also Wüllner, *Die NS-Militärjustiz*, 748.

117. Haase, *"Gefahr für die Manneszucht,"* 255.

118. Walmrath, *"Iustitia und disciplana,"* 244.

119. Wüllner, *Die NS-Militärjustiz*, p. 698. See also Seidler, *Die Militärgerichtsbarkeit*, 148.

120. Klausch, *Die Bewährungstruppe 500*, 50.

121. Seidler, *Die Militärgerichtsbarkeit*, 146.

122. Klausch, *Die Bewährungstruppe 500*, 49. See also Walmrath, *"Iustitia und disciplana,"* 251.

123. Klausch, *Die Bewährungstruppe 500*, 49–50.

124. Wüllner, *Die NS-Militärjustiz*, 755.

125. Klausch, *Die Bewährungstruppe 500*, 42–46. See also Wüllner, *Die NS-Militärjustiz*, 705, 710.

126. After the war many prisoners may have felt compelled to characterize themselves as victims of an inhuman judicial system in order to avoid the shame that befell those who had failed to do their duty.

127. Wüllner, *Die NS-Militärjustiz*, 693. See also Klausch, *Die Bewährungstruppe 500*, 105.

128. Wüllner, *Die NS-Militärjustiz*, chapter 6 and 706–7.

129. During an interrogation one defendant declared that he was an old communist and defiantly told the investigator to "put me against a tree and shoot me." He was reintegrated into the regular troops after serving approximately seven months of a nine-month prison sentence for child molestation. See the case of Karl H. in Eastern Collection BO-S250.

130. Seidler, *Die Militärgerichtsbarkeit*, 141.

131. Seidler, *Die Militärgerichtsbarkeit*, 143.

132. See Wüllner, *Die NS-Militärjustiz*, 680–81, for a discussion of these provisions.

133. Hennicke and Wüllner, "Über die barbarischen Vollstreckungsmethoden," 90.

134. Of course, the parole would then be revoked and the sentence served at the conclusion of hostilities.

135. Wüllner, *Die NS-Militärjustiz*, 682.

136. Absolon, *Das Wehrmachtstrafrecht*, 205.

137. Wüllner, *Die NS-Militärjustiz*, 683. An additional problem for Wehrmachtjustiz proved to be the rapid increase in crime after the beginning of the Russian campaign. Speed was needed to process the large number of convicted soldiers.

138. Absolon, *Das Wehrmachtstrafrecht*, 208. The change probably also had been intended to aid the selection process for the soon to be established field penal camps and battalions.

139. Absolon, *Das Wehrmachtstrafrecht*, 208.

140. Seidler, *Die Militärgerichtsbarkeit*, 72–73. Many prison inmates had been sent into battle before Keitel's January 1945 order for the mobilization of prisoners. Prisoners held in Wehrmacht Prison Fresnes in Paris allegedly had been employed against the French resistance as early as August 1944, while four days before Keitel's order inmates in Anklam Prison had been sent against the advancing Russian troops. See Walmrath, *"Iustitia und disciplana,"* 243.

141. Haase, *"Gefahr für die Manneszucht,"* 255.

142. Seidler, *Die Militärgerichtsbarkeit*, 166–67.

143. See, for example, Court of the Wehrmacht Commander–Berlin RW55/1828.

5. Method and Selection of Case Files

1. The former Federal Republic's collection consists of approximately seventy-two thousand case files from naval courts, thirty-three thousand case files from army courts, and three thousand case files from air force courts. The Eastern Collection's fifty-five thousand case files are primarily from army courts, but the collection does include a small number of air force case files.

2. The Eastern Collection is officially designated as the "110 Ost Spezial." The sex offense subgroup is designated as "Sittlichkeit." For convenience the abbreviation "BO-S" is used to refer to the case files contained in the Eastern Collection's "Bestand Ost—Sittlichkeit" subgroup.

3. The archive is currently building a computer database that includes the offense, punishment, unit, and other pertinent information for each case; the completed database will facilitate the identification and retrieval of specific case files.

4. For example, both Erich Schwinge and Fritz Wüllner compare the number of "trivial" punishments that U.S. and German courts-martial imposed during the war in support of their opposing positions. However, this exercise is not very profitable and falls into the "apple and oranges" category. See Schwinge, *Die deutschen Militärjustiz*, 10–11, 31, 45, 243–58. See also Wüllner, *Die NS-Militärjustiz*, 80–84. Wüllner is successful, however, in demonstrating Schwinge's attempt to deceive the reader into believing that U.S. courts-martial imposed more severe punishments than Wehrmachtjustiz.

5. Air force case files were nevertheless scrutinized to discern differences in jurisprudence between service branches.

6. Compiling statistics from the contents of the case files is extremely problematic. For example, a case file could contain just a transcript and not the confirmation order, and in such a case it is impossible to determine whether that particular case represents a legally binding verdict. For this and other reasons, the decision about whether to include a particular case file in a particular statistic is extremely subjective.

7. The Sixth Infantry Division was included in this study because the number of case files that survived the war is much higher than the average for combat units. The 253rd Infantry Division, also with a large number of surviving case files, was included because the sex offense case files had already been identified by another scholar.

8. In addition to case files for sex offenses, case files for other offenses from the Sixth Infantry Division, such as desertion, subversion, and plundering, were examined in order to understand this court's jurisprudence. Overall, the court's jurisprudence was unremarkable.

9. The six thousand case files from the Court of Wehrmacht Commander–Berlin represent the single largest collection of case files from a single court held by the Central Documentation Agency.

10. These files, according to wartime provisions, were sent to the Potsdam archive, which was completely destroyed by an Allied bomb attack.

11. Schwinge, *Die deutschen Militärjustiz*, 289–90. The one death sentence was imposed in 1943 and is discussed in chapter 6.

12. Beck, "Sexual Violence," 6.

13. Hannemann, *Die Justiz der Kriegsmarine*, 353.

6. Homosexuality and Violations of Paragraph 175

1. Homosexuality was punishable during the Weimar Republic, but the liberal "climate of opinion" led to attempts to decriminalize homosexuality between consenting adults. The reform movement came to a halt with the Nazi seizure of power. Burleigh and Wippermann, *The Racial State*, 186.

2. Hitler ordered the murder of Ernst Röhm, a well-known homosexual and head of the SA, and other top SA officials in June 1934. Publicly proclaimed by Hitler as a necessary measure to remove homosexuals from the movement, the real purpose of the murders was to remove the SA as a potential rival to Hitler's authority and win Hitler the support of the army, which likewise felt threatened by the SA.

3. Seidler, *Prostitution, Homosexualität, Selbstverstümmelung*, 193. See also Plant, *The Pink Triangle*, 15.

4. Burleigh and Wippermann, *The Racial State*, 184. See also Mosse, *Nationalism and Sexuality*, 28.

5. Anal, oral, and intra-crural sex were usually all subsumed under this interpretation.

6. Giles, "Nazi Masculinity and the Persecution of Homosexuality," 12.

7. Seidler, *Prostitution, Homosexualität, Selbstverstümmelung*, 195.

8. In practice, both the criminal police and the judges became the arbiters of "public morality." See Burleigh and Wippermann, *The Racial State*, 191. See also Plant, *The Pink Triangle*, 110.

9. Plant, *The Pink Triangle*, 112–13. The Reich Ministry of Justice issued guidelines in December 1934, six months before the changes in the criminal code, which established that an offense did not have to take place for an individual to be punishable: intent was sufficient.

10. Plant, *The Pink Triangle*, 110.

11. Seidler, *Prostitution, Homosexualität, Selbstverstümmelung*, 196. See also Burleigh and Wippermann, *The Racial State*, 190–92.

12. Mosse, *Nationalism and Sexuality*, 64, 165. In 1937 Himmler secretly ordered that all ss members and policemen convicted for homosexuality were to be shot "while escaping." In 1941 he dropped the pretense, convincing Hitler to promulgate the Ordinance for the Purity of the ss and Police, which threatened violations of paragraphs 175 with death.

13. Jellonnek, *Homosexuelle unter dem Hakenkreuz*, 327–28. According to Jellonnek, it was possible for individuals to confess their homosexuality, yet escape punishment if they could convince the Gestapo that they practiced abstinence. See also Grau, "The Final Solution," 340.

14. Mosse, *Nationalism and Sexuality*, 164.

15. Giles, "Nazi Masculinity and the Persecution of Homosexuality," 5–6. According to Giles, a clear parallel existed between Himmler's thinking and Hitler's perception that German women were permanently defiled if they had sex with Jews. See also Maiwald and Mischler, *Sexualität unter dem Hakenkreuz*, 171.

16. Mosse, *Nationalism and Sexuality*, 143.

17. Giles, "Nazi Masculinity and the Persecution of Homosexuality," 15. See also Jellonnek, *Homosexuelle unter dem Hakenkreuz*, 329. According to Mosse, only if homosexuals failed to reform were they to be exterminated like the Jews. Mosse, *Nationalism and Sexuality*, 144.

18. Seidler, *Prostitution, Homosexualität, Selbstverstümmelung*, 228.

19. Jellonnek, *Homosexuelle unter dem Hakenkreuz*, 284–85. Before 1900 only about five hundred convictions per year were recorded for the entire German Reich. Burleigh and Wippermann, *The Racial State*, 184, 197.

20. Intent became punishable with the changes to paragraph 175 in 1935. Sixteen percent of the individuals taken into custody by the Gestapo in Düsseldorf had only attempted "to make contact." See Jellonnek, *Homosexuelle unter dem Hakenkreuz*, 313.

21. Touching a comrade's genitals through the clothing sufficed for a charge of homosexual activity. Kissing and hugging likewise were often pursued as violations of paragraph 175.

22. Plant, *The Pink Triangle*, 146. See also Seidler, *Prostitution, Homosexu-*

alität, Selbstverstümmelung, 206; and Hennicke, "Auszüge aus der Wehrmacht-kriminalstatistik," 453.

23. Giles, "Nazi Masculinity and the Persecution of Homosexuality," 16. As reflected in the case files, the effort expended to prosecute men for violations of paragraph 175 suggests that homosexuals were not summarily shot, as some have suggested. See Rector, *The Nazi Extermination of Homosexuals*, 112.

24. According to Jellonnek, "ideological outbursts" were rare in the Düsseldorf civilian courts. He suggests that this may be attributed to desensitization on the part of the judges. See Jellonnek, *Homosexuelle unter dem Hakenkreuz*, 310. However, considering the low number of homosexual cases coming before the military courts, desensitization probably does not explain the low frequency of ideological outbursts in the case files examined.

25. Seidler, *Prostitution, Homosexualität, Selbstverstümmelung*, 228–29. See also Plant, *The Pink Triangle*, 144–45. In the case files, the courts refer to the following decrees as the basis of the habitual offender process: AHM 1943 Ziffer 623 [and/or] 721; Chef OKW 14n 19 WWR(II)/58/43g von 19.5.43; OKW von 11.8.43 nr. 213/413; OKH von 8.6.43 AgHR Wes (IV b/1)/653/43g. The United States also introduced a three-category classification for homosexual offenders during World War II. See Berube, *Coming Out under Fire*, 136–40.

26. See OKW 14 n 19 WR (II)—58/43g and OKH/ Chef H. Rust. U. BdE of 8.6.43—Az. Ag HR Wes (4b/1)—653/43g.

27. Plant, *The Pink Triangle*, 146.

28. Despite leading Nazis' "pathological hate" for homosexuals, those convicted for homosexual offenses were not automatically excluded from service for two reasons. First, many of the convicted had simply committed a one-time blunder, and second, by dismissing men from service automatically for a homosexual offense, the Wehrmacht would have established an "easily imitated precedent" for individuals unwilling to serve. See Klausch, *Die Bewährungstruppe 500*, 24.

29. Schwinge, *Die deutsche Militärjustiz*, 224–25.

30. Schwinge, *Die deutsche Militärjustiz*, 289–90. In Lothar Hannemann's sample of death sentences, naval courts imposed 296 death sentences between May 1944 and May 1945. Of these, 256 were carried out. Only one of the completed death sentences had been imposed for a homosexual offense. See Hannemann, *Die Justiz der Kriegsmarine*, 348, 353,

31. The death sentence was imposed in July 1943 (see the case of Friedrich A.) and therefore should be in the Wehrmacht Criminal Statistics. Schwinge, however, only reports up to the end of 1942. See Schwinge, *Die deutsche Militärjustiz*, 289–90. The Eastern Collection also contains one death sentence imposed by an SS court for a homosexual offense. The SS, however, falls outside the purview of this study. See Eastern Collection BO-S315.

32. Himmler feared that the deaths of two million German men during the Great War, when added to the estimated two million German homosexuals, would upset Germany's "sexual balance sheet," threatening the future of the Ger-

man nation and race. See Burleigh and Wippermann, *The Racial State*, 192–93.

33. For examples of repeat homosexual offenders being reintegrated, see Eastern Collection BO-S173, BO-S168, BO-S367, BO-S383; and Court of the Wehrmacht Commander–Berlin RW55/936.

34. Due to wartime conditions, civilian records could not always be checked thoroughly. Thus the number with civilian convictions could be even higher.

35. See Eastern Collection BO-S173 and RW55/2913.

36. See, for example, Eastern Collection BO-S173, 367, 168, and 383; and Court of the Wehrmacht Commander–Berlin RW55/936.

37. Eastern Collection BO-S173. Note that the remainder of the six-month prison sentence was deferred until after the war, not waived.

38. Intensified arrest consisted of solitary detention on short rations.

39. Court of the Wehrmacht Commander–Berlin RW55/936.

40. Eastern Collection BO-S168. Karl W. was sentenced to eighteen months and incarcerated at the Emsland complex. Because time in detention for Emsland inmates was not calculated as time served, Karl W. was incarcerated for twenty months before his reintegration.

41. Eastern Collection BO-S268. For examples, see Eastern Collection BO-S235 and BO-S305.

42. In each case the Gerichtsherr is the unit commander unless otherwise indicated. For example, in this case, the Gerichtsherr of the Court of the Fifty-second Infantry Division is the officer commanding that division.

43. The phrase "the court" is the most convenient way to refer to "the three-judge panel" or "the court members" that presided over courts-martial.

44. Eastern Collection BO-S383.

45. OKH of 18 December 1940 Az.469Gr.R.Wes/Nr.213/40 and OKW 9 January 1941 54e10-AHA/Ag/HStra./Str.102/41.

46. The change in jurisdiction is most likely explained by the Fifty-second Infantry Division's deployment for Operation Barbarossa, the attack on the Soviet Union.

47. For a prime example of the "one-time blunder," see Eastern Collection BO-S171.

48. Eastern Collection BO-S245.

49. Eastern Collection BO-S192.

50. For another curious example of a court's rejection of paragraph 175a, see Eastern Collection BO-S217.

51. Compounding Fritz E.'s misfortune was the fact that he was a civilian administrator, not a soldier, and thus not regarded as an instrument of war in the first place.

52. Eastern Collection BO-S104. For another example of a severe punishment for a violation of paragraph 175a, number 3, see Eastern Collection BO-S339.

53. Subordinates who engaged in homosexual acts, even if coerced by a superior officer, could also be prosecuted under paragraph 175a, number 2.

54. Eastern Collection BO-S100. Technical Sergeant A.'s two victims received short prison sentences for violating paragraph 175. The Gerichtsherr confirmed the sentences and ordered the punishments served as four and three weeks' intensified arrest respectively. The younger of the two soldiers was killed in action on the eastern front in 1944.

55. Divisional commanders functioning as Gerichtsherren did not have the authority to confirm death sentences or prison and penal servitude (Zuchthaus) sentences of more than five years. For the death sentence, confirmation power lay with the supreme commanders of the three service branches and, during the war, also with the reserve army commander. Hitler, as the Wehrmacht's supreme commander, reserved to himself the power to confirm death sentences imposed against officers. For prison and penal servitude sentences in excess of five years, the power of confirmation rested with a division commander's immediate military judicial superior, normally the commander of an army.

56. See Eastern Collection RW55/1304 for another example of harsh punishments for violations of paragraph 175a, number 2.

57. All plaintiffs and victims were regarded with a certain degree of mistrust, regardless of nationality. An example of overt prejudice can be seen in Eastern Collection BO-S386. In that case, the presiding court refrained from severely punishing a German soldier under paragraph 175a, number 3, because it was "a matter of a Russian youth."

58. Eastern Collection BO-S197. For other examples, see Eastern Collection BO-S288, BO-S116, BO-S292, and BO-S386.

59. Plant, *The Pink Triangle*, 99–100. Himmler extended this principle to abortion. In contrast to German women, Slavic women were encouraged to undergo abortions and were not punished.

60. Rass, *Menschenmaterial*, 247–48.

61. Eastern Collection BO-S292 and BO-S386.

62. Eastern Collection BO-S288.

63. Eastern Collection BO-S116.

64. For other examples see Eastern Collection BO-S288 and BO-S386.

65. See Court of the Wehrmacht Commander–Berlin RW55/3454 and RW55/415.

66. Eastern Collection BO-S306. The region's judge advocate did not question the application of paragraph 175a, number 3, in the entrapment incident; instead he questioned the use of entrapment as a tool of law enforcement. In a scathing letter to the division, the judge advocate characterized entrapment as a dangerous practice, one that he considered unworthy of a German soldier. He demanded that the sergeant and the "victim" be warned against any repetition of their behavior as "agents provocateur."

67. In Frankfurt and Koblenz, Adolf H.'s former places of residence, the police did extensive background checks and reported in the late summer of 1944 that they could find no evidence to support dismissing him as a homosexual. The pe-

nal battalion physician also reported that he did not appear to be a homosexual and attributed his crimes to the excessive use of alcohol.

68. Court of the 253rd Infantry Division, no. 131.

69. The Berlin court conducted approximately forty-four thousand legal processes during the war. About six thousand case files survived.

70. Seidler, *Prostitution, Homosexualität, Selbstverstümmelung*, 219. According to Seidler, the Berlin court had jurisdiction over all homosexual cases against members of the reserve army. The case files examined suggest otherwise. Seidler also maintains that the Berlin garrison's commander, General von Hase, was just as lenient in homosexual cases as he was in political cases. The basis for this claim is not clear.

71. The Berlin court sentenced one soldier to penal servitude, but the Gerichtsherr rejected the verdict in favor of a retrial that produced a prison sentence. This rejected penal servitude punishment is not included in the statistics. See Court of the Wehrmacht Commander–Berlin RW55/2910.

72. Due to the sparse paper trails for individuals sentenced to penal servitude, it has been assumed that individuals who are not listed as paroled, transferred to a penal formation, or deceased must have remained in detention until the end of the war. However, the possibility that these eleven individuals were reintegrated or mobilized for militarily useful purposes should not be ruled out.

73. One soldier was declared to be an incorrigible homosexual at trial. However, no documentation could be found to show whether or not the reserve army commander indeed ordered him turned over to the civilian authorities. See Eastern Collection BO-S279. One soldier dismissed from service as an incorrigible homosexual offender was reenrolled and sent to a field penal battalion after his civilian attorney intervened. Franz H. apparently preferred the dangers of a penal formation to being under the auspices of the civilian authorities. If this assumption is correct, it is a revealing fact. See Eastern Collection BO-S403.

74. In the case files examined, perhaps as many as 85 to 90 percent of the individuals sent to a special penal formation upon conviction rejoined a regular unit or parole battalion. See chapter 4.

75. This figure does not include individuals sentenced to penal servitude.

76. Court of the Wehrmacht Commander–Berlin RW55/1826. Touching an individual's genitals through the clothing was regarded as a violation of paragraph 175.

77. The penal camp was the Wehrmacht's most draconian form of punishment. It sat at the apex of the Wehrmacht's graduated penal chain. Failure here meant dismissal from service and transfer to the state police.

78. Time spent in penal camp detention was not calculated as time served. The phrase "transfer for the orderly completion of the punishment" meant sending a prisoner to a penal facility or formation in which time in detention was calculated as time served and credited to the prisoner's account.

79. Jellonnek, *Homosexuelle unter dem Hakenkreuz*, 311. For violations of

paragraph 175, Jellonnek calculated that Düsseldorf civilian courts imposed an average prison sentence of eight months, while the Würzburg courts' average sentence came to twenty-one months. The case file sample for this study yielded an average sentence of approximately eleven months.

80. Jellonnek, *Homosexuelle unter dem Hakenkreuz*, 314. For violations of paragraph 175a, Jellonnek's regional averages ranged from sixteen to twenty-four months. The average sentence in the case file sample for this investigation was thirty-seven months.

81. The Eastern Collection contains a number of case files devoted to correspondence with civilian attorneys representing soldiers dismissed as incorrigible homosexuals. Thus the number of men in the sample who were discharged as habitual homosexuals might be artificially inflated.

82. Berube, *Coming Out under Fire*, 33, 147. See also Seidler, *Prostitution, Homosexualität, Selbstverstümmelung*, 206. If the individuals who were sentenced to penal servitude and more than likely not reintegrated were included, the number would be approximately 900. In addition, if the 6.4 percent rate were applied only to the *Heer*, or German army (that is, excluding sailors and airmen), the number dismissed would be 320.

7. Sexual Assault

1. Due to the comparatively small number of relevant case files for sexual assaults, statistics are featured much less prominently in this chapter than in chapter 6.

2. Mosse, *Nationalism and Sexuality*, 10, 133, 150, 160, 186.

3. Mosse, *Nationalism and Sexuality*, 160.

4. See, for example, Maiwald and Mischler, *Sexualität unter dem Hakenkreuz*, 154. See also Brownmiller, *Against Our Will*, 48–49.

5. Cases leading to acquittal were also examined to obtain a sense of the burden of proof for sexual assault as well as to uncover any bias toward victims. These files reveal that the military courts did not conduct show trials. Substantial evidence was required to bring a case to trial and obtain a conviction.

6. Under section 2, the Antisocial Parasite Ordinance threatened crimes that exploited blackout conditions with severe punishments, including death. See Absolon, *Wehrmachtstrafrecht*, 69.

7. The decision by the various Gerichtsherren to not include this charge in indictments most likely explains this phenomenon.

8. Maiwald and Mischler, *Sexualität unter dem Hakenkreuz*, 152–55. See also Evans, *In Hitler's Shadow*, 62.

9. Maiwald and Mischler, *Sexualität unter dem Hakenkreuz*, 194.

10. The Wehrmacht also hoped the brothels would prevent instances of homosexual activity between soldiers, a common by-product of the wartime experience, even for heterosexual men.

11. Even with severe rubber shortages plaguing the Nazi war machine, the

Wehrmacht never ran out of government issue condoms. See Seidler, *Prostitution, Homosexualität, Selbstverstümmelung,* 167.

12. Maiwald and Mischler, *Sexualität unter dem Hakenkreuz,* 152, 155.

13. Evans, *In Hitler's Shadow,* 62.

14. For an example of the former, see Eastern Collection BO-S228; for an example of the latter, see Eastern Collection BO-S149.

15. The decree ended the obligatory prosecution of crimes committed by German soldiers against civilians in the Barbarossa operational area.

16. See the strange saga of Josef M. The reference to the decree was not even made by a presiding judge or Gerichtsherr but was contained in a second opinion submitted by a staff legal adviser. See Snyder, "Prosecution and Punishment," 328–29. The document is contained in Eastern Collection BO-S152. Birgit Beck reports similar findings. Beck, *Wehrmacht und sexuelle Gewalt,* 183.

17. Seidler, *Prostitution, Homosexualität, Selbstverstümmelung,* 141.

18. Even in victim-friendly environments, experts estimate that perhaps as many as 95 percent of all rapes go unreported. Thus it should not be surprising if the inhabitants of an occupied country (especially the Soviet Union during World War II) chose not to report rape crimes committed by the enemy soldiers of a conquering army. See Brownmiller, *Against our Will,* 175.

19. Even in civilian courts where nationality and ethnicity are not an issue, convictions for rape are exceptionally hard to obtain. This is especially true when the only witness is the victim herself. The conviction rate, in fact, can be as low as "a shocking 3 percent." See Brownmiller, *Against Our Will,* 175.

20. One document suggests German soldiers were cognizant that sexual assaults against Soviet civilians were pursued as such by the military judicial authorities. A court transcript recounts a conversation among several comrades regarding the recent punishment of a soldier for sexual assault. See Eastern Collection BO-S317.

21. These statistics are based on those cases in the Eastern Collection that ended in convictions for completed acts of rape and exclude cases of attempted rape. Also excluded are cases in which the perpetrators were punished under section 330a, the code governing crimes committed while completely intoxicated. If multiyear prison sentences are considered "severe" punishments, then the rate approaches 90 percent in the east.

22. Beck, "Sexual Violence," 2, 11–13. Beck does concede, however, that the authorities dealt ruthlessly with individuals convicted for rape crimes against Soviet civilians if the crimes threatened to exacerbate the partisan problem.

23. Beck, "Sexual Violence," 10.

24. The "mild" prison sentences seen in the east were well within the normal spectrum of severity encountered in cases involving west European victims.

25. Eastern Collection BO-S334.

26. Eastern Collection BO-S243. The court imposed two years for the rape charge. Alfred M. was also convicted for coercion (*Nötigung*) and plundering.

27. Eastern Collection BO-S283. Evidence suggested that the defendant shot the girl on the street, dragged her into a house, and attempted to have intercourse with the corpse. The court, however, rejected this hypothesis. Whether the court intentionally was shielding the defendant from a murder charge is not clear, but the possibility does exist. Under German law, the burden of proof for murder is very high. Malicious intent and premeditation must be clearly established. If not, the provisions for manslaughter are frequently applied.

28. The authorities occasionally did express considerable sympathy toward Slavic rape victims. See Eastern Collection BO-S411.

29. Eastern Collection BO-S258.

30. ObdH Az. 458 Gen Qu (III) GenStdH Nr. 169098/40 vom 5.7.40.

31. Eastern Collection BO-S254, BO-S313, and BO-S355.

32. Eastern Collection BO-S355.

33. Eastern Collection BO-S254.

34. The Court of the 253rd Infantry Division likewise imposed comparatively mild punishments. Three case files for assaults against eastern inhabitants survived the war. See Rass, *Menschenmaterial*, 289–91.

35. Birgit Beck reports similar findings. Beck, *Wehrmacht und sexuelle Gewalt*, 196.

36. See, for example, Eastern Collection BO-S269 or BO-S317.

37. The courts frequently questioned the credibility of even west European victims. See, for example, Eastern Collection BO-S167 or Court of Wehrmacht Commander-Berlin RW55/1088.

38. Beck, "Sexual Violence," 2, 11–12. Michael Fellman suggests that the low frequency of rapes against white women is explained by the fact that both armies in the Civil War shared common cultural values that emphasized the protection of women and family.

39. Nationality in many ways proved to be far less important to the authorities than the reputation and credibility of the victims and their families. This was also true in child molestation cases. See chapter 8.

40. The majority of convicted rapists in the east served only a fraction of their sentences before returning to the regular troops. However, this was not unique to the eastern front.

41. For examples, see Eastern Collection BO-S208, BO-S233, BO-S379, and BO-S213.

42. Eastern Collection BO-S248. Christian S. reportedly suffered repeated lapses of discipline while incarcerated. His inability or unwillingness to conform prevented his reintegration. He nevertheless served the war effort; he was mobilized in 1944 for service in an arctic construction battalion. His ultimate fate was not documented in the case file.

43. Eastern Collection BO-S233.

44. Eastern Collection BO-S213.

45. The coercion and breaking and entering charges brought an additional eight months' imprisonment.

46. The individual sentences were ten years of penal servitude for rape and one year's imprisonment for coercion and breaking and entering.

47. The army's commander-in-chief was Walther von Brauchitsch.

48. Eastern Collection BO-S167.

49. Eastern Collection BO-S161, 190, 249, 263, 349, and 122.

50. Mitcham, *Hitler's Legions*, 404.

51. The tenth prisoner was in fact incarcerated, but only briefly. Convicted in March 1944 by the labor-saving punishment decree, he received a six-month prison sentence. The Gerichtsherr, however, ordered only three months served followed by front-parole with his unit.

52. Eastern Collection BO-S190.

53. Eastern Collection BO-S161.

54. Eastern Collection BO-S349.

55. Eastern Collection BO-S249.

56. The one exception was Herbert N., who was sentenced via a punishment decree and incarcerated for three months by order of the Gerichtsherr. The remainder of the six-month sentence was suspended for front-parole. See Eastern Collection BO-S122.

57. See Court of the Wehrmacht Commander–Berlin RW55/4224 for an example of a paternalistic display by the court. In this case the court blamed the young victim for her misfortune.

58. Eastern Collection BO-S265.

59. Eastern Collection BO-S172.

60. No documentation could be found indicating which authority granted the parole.

61. The 251st Infantry Division participated in the Western Offensive, driving through Belgium as part of Army Group B. Mitcham, *Hitler's Legions*, 183.

62. Court of the 253rd Infantry Division, no. 424.

63. Court of the Wehrmacht Commander–Berlin RW55/443.

64. Stanislaus B. had been fined for "offending a woman's sexual honor" and fathering an illegitimate child.

65. Court of the Wehrmacht Commander–Berlin RW55/558.

66. In late 1942, Wilhelm R.'s wife filed suit against the women who testified against him for perjury. They were acquitted. The Berlin court subsequently informed Frau R. to discontinue her attempts at intervention and warned her that her continued criticism of the court would "definitely not help [her] husband."

67. Court of the Wehrmacht Commander–Berlin RW55/4226.

68. For an example of "nazified" verbal abuse, see Eastern Collection BO-S188.

8. Child Molestation and Incest

1. Not all of the incest victims were minors. However, the majority were under the age of consent, rendering their inclusion in this chapter methodologically acceptable.

2. As in rape cases, the courts endeavored greatly to ascertain the reputation and thus the "credibility" of victims and their families.

3. Eastern Collection BO-S97.

4. Hans L. had one disciplinary punishment of three days' confinement for sleeping on watch.

5. Hans L. had ten days added to his sentence for "violating military order and discipline" while he was incarcerated.

6. Gerichtsherren could impose legal punishments without conducting a trial through the use of the punishment decree (*Strafverfügung*). This device allowed commanders with military judicial authority to sentence servicemen to a maximum of three months in prison without resort to an oral hearing. The initially established maximum was raised to six months in 1942 in order to speed up the legal process.

7. Eastern Collection BO-S143. The pregnancy was terminated. Documents indicate the civilian authorities were debating whom to indict for the abortion.

8. Eastern Collection BO-S358. The civilian authorities requested Paul B.'s file in order to prosecute the sister, Anneliese.

9. Eastern Collection BO-S195.

10. The significantly higher punishment in this case is primarily attributed to the multiple charges lodged against Franz H., with the sentence for child molestation amounting to six months and each incident of intercourse bringing ten months' imprisonment.

11. As a parolee, Franz H. was of course subject to the sword of Damocles, which apparently had its intended effect. After returning to his unit, he subsequently received praise for his performance. On September 24, 1944, his regiment reported that he had conducted himself flawlessly, had again been decorated, and had received the Iron Cross after being wounded in September 1943.

12. Court of the Wehrmacht Commander–Berlin RW55/2914.

13. The camp superintendent also reported that Siegfried H. was fit for combat, so he might have been paroled at a later time.

14. See, for example, Court of the Wehrmacht Commander–Berlin RW55/2997, RW55/4814, and RW55/1694.

15. Court of the Wehrmacht Commander–Berlin RW55/2915.

16. Court of the Wehrmacht Commander–Berlin RW55/1088.

17. After being delivered to a mobile prison unit, Otto G. immediately petitioned for front-parole. His petition apparently was rejected. He was released after serving the entire sentence and sent to the appropriate reserve unit.

18. Court of the Wehrmacht Commander–Berlin RW55/1539.

19. Court of the Wehrmacht Commander–Berlin RW55/1694.

20. General von Hase commanded the Berlin garrison from shortly after the beginning of the war until the July 20, 1944, assassination attempt against Hitler. Von Hase was arrested and executed on August 8, 1944, for his role in the failed coup. See Hoffmann, *The History of the German Resistance*, 528.

21. For another example of a relatively mild punishment, see Court of the Wehrmacht Commander–Berlin RW55/12.

22. Court of the Wehrmacht Commander–Berlin RW55/1828. Specifically, Franz J. violated Reich Criminal Code section 174, paragraph 1, in coincidence with section 176, paragraph 3.

23. See, for example, Eastern Collection BO-S222, BO-S346, and BO-S294.

24. Eastern Collection BO-S294. Additional documents can be found in BO-S412.

25. Eastern Collection BO-S205 and BO-S144.

26. See Eastern Collection BO-S222, BO-S346, and BO-S294. In the first two case files, the detainees, both potentially "usable" and "dependable" soldiers, were reintegrated. In the latter case, the detainee was forty-two years old and had never been a soldier. He remained in detention at least up until the fall of 1944 when the paper trail ends.

27. See, for example, Eastern Collection BO-S294 and BO-S412. The defendant in this case is characterized as a "stubborn corrupter of youths" (*Jugendverderber*) by a staff legal adviser.

28. Court of the 253rd Infantry Division, no. 394.

29. Note that in this situation the "penal camp" in question was actually "safely" behind the lines. The "field penal camps" were not created until 1942.

30. Court of the 253rd Infantry Division, no. 394.

31. Heinrich T. apparently suffered from some form of pulmonary disease.

32. See Eastern Collection BO-S156, 344, 220, and 380; and Court of the 253rd Infantry Division, no. 107.

33. Eastern Collection BO-S156. Copies of the verdict and transcript are also contained in Eastern Collection BO-S360. The court transcript contains a typographical error, misdating the crime as having taken place in April 1943. The incident actually occurred in April 1942, which can be verified in the police interrogation record.

34. Court of the 253rd Infantry Division, no. 107.

35. Eastern Collection BO-S380.

36. See Eastern Collection BO-S156, 344, 220, and 380; and Court of the 253rd Infantry Division, no. 107.

9. Racial Defilement and Bestiality

1. Ley, *"Zum Schutze des deutchen Blutes,"* 82.

2. Ley, *"Zum Schutze des deutchen Blutes,"* 101–2, 120.

3. Ley, *"Zum Schutze des deutchen Blutes,"* 120–24. According to Ley, in the

few acquittals he found, the court had very little choice because the accusations were "so misguided." See Ley, *"Zum Schutze des deutchen Blutes,"* 120.

4. Eastern Collection BO-S13.

5. Case file RH69/908. The relationship came to light when Josef L. contracted gonorrhea. He was disciplined for not immediately reporting that he had contracted a sexually transmitted disease. See Ley, *"Zum Schutze des deutchen Blutes,"* 120.

6. Court of the Wehrmacht Commander–Berlin RW55/7232. The documents do not indicate whether or not Karl S. was in fact executed. The case file ends with his application for clemency.

7. Court of the Wehrmacht Commander–Berlin RW55/3554.

8. The girl's fate is unknown. She was interrogated by the state police on November 6, 1943.

9. In several of the cases, soldiers either sexually or economically exploited Jews. See, for example, Court of the Wehrmacht Commander–Berlin RW55/4815.

10. Eastern Collection BO-S391.

11. One document reported that the infant was buried immediately and therefore the gendarme could not determine the cause of death, which perhaps explains why no charges were lodged. This explanation seems unlikely, however.

12. German Federal Archives RM123/71638. The defendant was also convicted for military theft for giving his lover curtains taken from his quarters.

13. While still in active service, Anton B. received the War Service Cross and other citations for heroic action in extinguishing a blazing fuel tank in 1940.

14. German Federal Archives RM123/15751. Karl D. experienced "monetary difficulties" as a result of the affair and allegedly stole 50 RM from a unit member.

15. Two case files from the 253rd Infantry Division survived the war and were included in the sample.

16. Another recurring theme in such cases is the question of whether this form of sexual expression also represents animal cruelty. Soldiers often found themselves charged with this crime in addition to the sodomy charge if they had wounded an animal during their sexual act.

17. Eastern Collection BO-S363.

18. August S. was disciplined no less than seven times for offenses ranging from theft to unauthorized absence. He also received six weeks' confinement in 1939 for a traffic violation and four weeks' arrest in early 1944 for wearing an unauthorized decoration.

19. Eastern Collection BO-S212.

20. Delivered to a local detention facility in Lublin, Franz N. served his four weeks and was released for parole on May 6, 1942.

21. Eastern Collection BO-S264.

22. Eastern Collection BO-S357.

23. Note that the court did not use the defendant's mental weakness against

him, a phenomenon reported by scholars in cases of desertion and subversion. Many defendants in the sample who were accused of sodomy were also described as possessing little intelligence, and the courts likewise did not use it against them. See Eastern Collection BO-S102 for another example. For more on this phenomenon, see chapter 10.

24. Eastern Collection BO-S106.

25. Other perpetrators of sodomy crimes made the same mistake, frequently leaving behind clothing or identification papers, usually as a result of drunkenness.

26. Eastern Collection BO-S365.

10. Intoxication and Diminished Responsibility

1. Fritz, *Frontsoldaten*, 113.

2. Schwartz, *Strafgesetzbuch*, 527. According to section 2 of the provision, the punishment could not exceed that established in the normal provisions for the crime that was committed.

3. See, for example, German Federal Archives, Other Files, RH69/2644, Eastern Collection BO-S51, or Court of the Wehrmacht Commander–Berlin RW55/5847.

4. See Eastern Collection BO-S379 or BO-S213.

5. See, for example, Eastern Collection BO-S253.

6. There was, however, at least one exception: one repeat offender punished under section 330a was discharged as a habitual homosexual offender. See Eastern Collection BO-S178 below.

7. See, for example, Eastern Collection BO-S130 and BO-S214.

8. Ferdinand B.'s persistence is rather surprising, considering that six of his prospective partners resisted his advances firmly, with two soldiers punching him in the face.

9. Court of the Wehrmacht Commander–Berlin RW55/316. Fragments of this case can also be found in Court of the Wehrmacht Commander–Berlin RW55/5801.

10. Although the defendant made inappropriate contact with four individuals, two were Russian *Hiwis*. The court considered his actions with them as a unified act, and thus he faced only three counts.

11. Eastern Collection BO-S178.

12. Hans S. had been convicted for engaging in anal sex, among other things, by the civilian court.

13. According to the defendant, he began abusing alcohol after receiving word that all three of his sisters had been the victims of Allied bomb attacks.

14. Eastern Collection BO-S353.

15. The staff legal adviser supported the application of section 330a, and based on the "repulsive vulgarity" of Karl H.'s offenses, he characterized the punishment as appropriate.

16. The 293rd Infantry Division had participated in the Barbarossa campaign

since its beginning as part of Army Group Center. See Mitcham, *Hitler's Legions*, 210.

17. An itemized list of the prisoners in question could not be found in the case file, but according to the formation's report, eighteen prisoner personnel files had been lost, so it can be assumed that there were at least eighteen men being considered for parole.

18. Here the documents are fragmentary, but at some point during the next twelve months Karl H. was severely wounded, losing one eye and suffering reduced vision in the other. No longer fit for combat, Karl H. should have had his parole revoked as per the established guidelines. Evidence nevertheless suggests that he remained free. In September 1944, Karl H. reported to the Court of Division Number 409 that he had been transferred on August 31, 1944, to Grenadier Regiment 105.

19. The commander and Gerichtsherr of Wehrkreis IX rejected his request for clemency on the issue of rank restoration in a document dated August 31, 1944.

20. Eastern Collection BO-S224.

21. The court conceded that a "condition of disrupted consciousness" (*Bewußtseinsstörung*) could not be refuted. Citing the Reich Supreme Military Court's jurisprudence, the court explained that an individual need not be senselessly drunk for the application of 330a, but rather it sufficed if a "considerable disruption of the conscious" existed.

22. As per HM 8.6.1942 Ziffer 469.

23. In addition to the Purple Heart and Iron Cross (first and second class) he possessed the Armored Assault Badge.

24. Eastern Collection BO-S105.

25. It appears that the court stenographer misspelled the German term *Narkolepsie*. The expert testimony on this point was highly technical in nature and reads as follows: "In dem besonderem Fall kommt hinzu, dass [Wilhelm B.] an der Erscheinung einer Narkolysie [sic] in Form von anfallsreichen Schlafzuständen aber ohne affectiven Turnusverlust d.h. eine völlige Muskelerschlaffung im Affekt leidet."

26. Presumably involved in the trial as one of the lay judges, an officer contacted party officials in a letter dated November 7, 1940. In his opinion, the defendant should not have been granted the protection of section 51. His complaint was rejected with reference to the expert medical opinion. However, based on this letter, the party began an investigation into whether or not Wilhelm B. should be expelled from the party and Hitler Youth.

27. OKH 54e 10AHA/Ag/H Str. a—St 102/41. Although dismissed from detention on April 29, Wilhelm B. did not report to a regular unit, but remained in the area as a free soldier employed in arms production as per an OKH decree. Eventually released from arms work, Wilhelm B. was sent to the appropriate reserve formation in February 1942.

28. AHM 1941, number 362 and AHM 1942, number 240. The Federal Railway

authorities opened a disciplinary process against Wilhelm B. as a career federal railway civil servant after his conviction. Apparently he was cleared and recalled to the Reichsbahn under the two aforementioned decrees.

29. Eastern Collection BO-S247.

30. He was recalled to active duty in 1939.

31. Eastern Collection BO-S361.

32. Called up in 1938, Peter G. served in the Polish and French campaigns. He participated in the eastern campaign until he was wounded in December 1941. He possessed the Purple Heart, the Iron Cross, the Armored Assault Badge, and the Eastern Campaign Medal.

33. Eastern Collection BO-S335.

34. Based on his belief that the Allies would have to take the Channel Islands before invading Fortress Europe, Hitler began reinforcing the 319th in 1943 until it reached a total strength of 40,000 men, making it the largest German division during the war. Although this build-up began months after Gerhard D.'s parole, it may nevertheless explain the employment of a parolee in a noncombat area. Mitcham, *Hitler's Legions*, 219.

35. Mitcham, *Hitler's Legions*, 219.

36. Eastern Collection BO-S44.

37. Messerschmidt and Wüllner, *Wehrmachtjustiz im Dienste*, 227–37.

38. Wüllner, *Die NS-Militärjustiz*, 348–60.

39. Eastern Collection BO-S359. The court transcript notes that it was due to his mother's alcoholism, but the 1944 performance evaluation notes that it was due to his feeble-mindedness.

40. Court of the Wehrmacht Commander–Berlin RW55/1821.

41. Court of the Wehrmacht Commander–Berlin RW55/1709.

42. Messerschmidt and Wüllner, *Wehrmachtjustiz im Dienste*, 227–38.

11. Conclusion

1. Walmrath, "*Iustitia und disciplana*," 317–34.

2. Klausch, *Die Bewährungstruppe 500*, 13, 348. See Deist et al., *Build-up of German Aggression*, 146–47.

3. Vultejus, *Kampfanzug*, 60–61. According to Vultejus, one could hardly expect that the military leaders responsible for the deaths of millions of soldiers and civilians would have moral doubts about these particular deaths.

4. Haase, *Das Reichskriegsgericht*, 13.

5. Van Creveld, *Fighting Power*. If Messerschmidt and Wüllner are correct, crime was more rampant in the Wehrmacht than is reflected in the official Wehrmacht Criminal Statistics. This finding, in conjunction with this study's final conclusion, also raises doubt about Omer Bartov's conclusions regarding "Hitler's Army." See Bartov, *Hitler's Army*, 179–86.

Bibliography

Unpublished Documents

These archival collections contain hundreds and in some cases thousands of individual military judicial case files. Only a fraction of these files were sampled for this book. Thus, all case files that are cited in the notes or that have otherwise informed this book are specifically identified here. The one exception is the Eastern Collection Sex Offense Subgroup. All 418 case files from this collection were sampled. "Other Files" refers to military judicial documents from various military units and institutions.

German Federal Archives Central Documentation Agency (Bundesarchiv-Zentralnachweistelle), Aachen-Kornelimünster

Court of the Sixth Infantry Division. Case file numbers 19, 28, 36, 42, 62, 78, 79, 100, 111, 113, 117, 140, 158, 205, 211a, 212, 243, 244, 254, 270, 295, 302, 304, 309, 320, 324, 337, 345, 349, 355, 360, 370, 411, 465, 468.

Court of the 253rd Infantry Division. Case file numbers 106, 107, 125, 126, 131, 155, 268, 243, 334, 361, 387, 394, 424, 459, 460, 489.

Court of the Wehrmacht Commander–Berlin (RW55). Case file numbers 12, 49, 134, 174, 292, 293, 316, 360, 387, 413, 415, 443, 477, 558, 590, 651, 709, 936, 1088, 1095, 1184, 1198, 1236, 1237, 1304, 1317, 1327, 1453, 1539, 1694, 1702, 1709, 1821, 1822, 1823, 1824, 1826, 1828, 1999, 2188, 2214, 2582, 2852, 2909, 2910, 2912, 2913, 2914, 2915, 2981, 2982, 2991, 2992, 2996, 2997, 2998, 3446, 3454, 3554, 4222, 4224, 4225, 4226, 4814, 4815, 4853, 5801, 5847, 6415, 7232.

Eastern Collection (*Bestand Ost Spezial* 110). Sex Offense Subgroup (Group *Sittlichkeit*). "BO-S" Case File Numbers 1–418.

Jurist Personnel Files. Case file numbers W10/1440, W10/1441, W10/1452, W10/1706, W10/1733, W10/1742, W10/1766, W10/1782, W10/1944, W10/2085, W10/2167, W10/2609, W10/2610, H2/8235, H2/14243, H2/32056, H2/32072, H2/36297, H2/39832.

Other Files. Case file numbers RM123/1918, RM123/8476, RM123/15751, RM/71638, RM123/83078, RW55/7232, RH69/908, RH69/1584, RH69/2644.

U.S. National Archives and Records Administration, College Park, Maryland

Miscellaneous German Records Collection. Microfilm T-84; reels 176–82.

Records of Headquarters of the German Army High Command. Microfilm T-78; reel 69.

Secondary Works

Absolon, Rudolf. *Das Wehrmachtstrafrecht im 2. Weltkrieg.* Kornelimünster, Germany: Bundesarchiv-Zentralnachweistelle, 1958.

———. *Die Wehrmacht im Dritten Reich. Band II, 30. Januar 1933 bis 2. August 1934.* Boppard am Rhein, Germany: Harald Boldt Verlag, 1969.

———. *Die Wehrmacht im Dritten Reich. Band III, 3. August 1934 bis 4. Februar 1938.* Boppard am Rhein, Germany: Harald Boldt Verlag, 1975.

———. *Die Wehrmacht im Dritten Reich. Band IV, 8. Februar 1938 bis 31. August 1939.* Boppard am Rhein, Germany: Harald Boldt Verlag, 1979.

———. *Die Wehrmacht im Dritten Reich. Band V, 1. September 1939 bis 18. December 1941.* Boppard am Rhein, Germany: Harald Boldt Verlag, 1988.

———. *Die Wehrmacht im Dritten Reich. Band VI, 19. Dezember 1941 bis 9. Mai 1945.* Boppard am Rhein, Germany: Harald Boldt Verlag, 1995.

———. *Wehrgesetz und Wehrdienst, 1933–1945: Das Personalwesen in der Wehrmacht.* Boppard am Rhein, Germany: H. Boldt, 1960.

Angermund, Ralph. *Deutsche Richterschaft, 1919–1945: Krisenerfahrung, Illusion, politische Rechtsprechung.* Frankfurt: Fischer Taschenbuch Verlag, 1990.

Auslander, Fietje. "Vom Wehrmacht- zum Moorsoldaten: Militärstrafgefangene in dem Emslandlagern 1939 bis 1945." In *Bremsklötze am Siegeswagen der Nation: Erinnerungen eines Deserteurs an Militärgefangnisse, Zuchthäuser und Moorlager in den Jahren 1941–1945,* edited by Fietje Auslander and Norbert Haase, 165–93. Bremen, Germany: Edition Temmen, 1989.

Auslander, Fietje, ed. *Verater oder Vorbilder? Deserteure und ungehorsame Soldaten im Nationalsozialismus.* Bremen, Germany: Edition Temmen, 1990.

Bartov, Omer. *The Eastern Front, 1941–1945: German Troops and the Barbarization of Warfare.* London: MacMillan Press, 1985.

———. *Hitler's Army: Soldiers, Nazis, and War in the Third Reich.* Oxford: Oxford University Press, 1992.

Beck, Birgit. "Sexual Violence, Racism and the German Army on the Eastern Front." Paper presented at the German Historical Institute meeting, "A World at Total War: Global Conflict and the Politics of Destruction, 1937–1945." Hamburg, Germany, August 29–September 1, 2001.

———. *Wehrmacht und sexuelle Gewalt: Sexualverbrechen vor deutschen Militärgerichten, 1939–1945.* Paderborn, Germany: Ferdinand Schöningh, 2004.

Bennhold, Martin. "Ein Volk in Wehr und Waffen." In *Verater oder Vorbilder? Deserteure und ungehorsame Soldaten im Nationalsozialismus,* edited by Fietje Auslander, 41–64. Bremen, Germany: Edition Temmen, 1990.

Berube, Allan. *Coming Out under Fire: The History of Gay Men and Women in World War II.* New York: Free Press, 1990.

Bleuel, Hans Peter. *Sex and Society in Nazi Germany.* New York: Lippincott, 1973.

Block, Just. "Die Ausschaltung und Beshränkung der deutschen ordentlichen Militärgerichtsbarkeit während des Zweiten Weltkrieges." PhD diss., Würzburg University, 1967.

Boog, Horst, Jürgen Förster, Joachim Hoffman, Ernst Klink, Rolf-Dieter Müller, and Gerd R. Ueberschär. *The Attack on the Soviet Union*. Vol. 4 of *Germany and the Second World War*, edited by The Research Institute for Military History. Translated by Dean S. McMurry, Ewald Oser, and Louise Wilmong. Oxford: Clarendon Press, 1998.

Bracher, Karl Dietrich. *The German Dictatorship: The Origins, Structure, and Effects of National Socialism*. New York: Praeger Publishers, 1971.

Bredemeier, Karsten. *Kriegsdienstverweigerung im Dritten Reich: Ausgewählte Beispiele*. Baden-Baden: Nomos Verlagsgesellschaft, 1991.

Breitman, Richard. *Architect of Genocide: Himmler and the Final Solution*. New York: Knopf, 1991.

Brockling, Ulrich, and Michael Sikora, eds. *Armeen und ihre Deserteure*. Göttingen, Germany: Vandenhoeck & Ruprecht, 1998.

Broszat, Martin. *The Hitler State: The Foundation and Development of the Internal Structure of the Third Reich*. Translated by John W. Hinden. London: Longman, 1981.

———. "Siegerjustiz oder Strafrechtliche 'Selbstreinigung': Aspekte der Vergangenheitsbewältung der deutsche Justiz während der Besatzungszeit, 1945–1949." *Vierteljahrshefte für Zeitgeschichte* 4 (1981): 477–544.

———. "Zur Perversion der Strafjustiz im Dritten Reich." *Vierteljahrshefte für Zeitgeschichte* 4 (1958): 390–443.

Browning, Christopher. *Ordinary Men: Reserve Police Battalion 101 and the Final Solution in Poland*. New York: HarperCollins, 1992.

Brownmiller, Susan. *Against Our Will: Men, Women, and Rape*. New York: Simon and Schuster, 1975.

Burliegh, Michael, and Wolfgang Wippermann. *The Racial State: Germany 1933–1945*. Cambridge: Cambridge University Press, 1991.

Cocks, Geoffrey. *Psychotherapy in the Third Reich: The Göring Institute*. New York: Oxford University Press, 1985.

Cooper, Mathew. *The German Army, 1933–1945: Its Political and Military Failure*. New York: Stein and Day, 1978.

Deist, Wilhelm, Manfred Messerschmidt, Hans-Erich Volkmann, and Wolfram Wette. *The Build-up of German Aggression*. Vol. 1 of *Germany and the Second World War*, edited by The Research Institute for Military History. Translated by P. S. Falla, Dean S. McMurry, and Ewald Osers. Oxford: Clarendon Press, 1990.

De Zayas, Alfred. "Die Rechtsprechung der Wehrmachtsgerichtsbarkeit zum Schutze der Zivilbevölkerung in besetzten Gebieten 1939–1945." *Humanitäres Volkerrecht* 3 (1994): 118–24.

————. *The Wehrmacht War Crimes Bureau, 1939–1945*. Lincoln: University of Nebraska Press, 1989.

Dreetz, Dieter. "Zur Bildung von Militärstrafkompanien im deutschen Heer während des Ersten Weltkrieg." *Zeitschrift für Militärgeschichte* 6 (1967): 462–68.

Eberlein, Michael, Roland Müller, Michael Schöngarth, and Thomas Werther. *Militärjustiz im Nationalsozialismus: Die Marburger Militärgericht*. Marburg, Germany: Die Geshichtswerkstaatt Marburg, 1994.

Eberlein, Michael, Roland Müller, and Günter Saathoff, eds. *Dem Tode Entronnen: Zeitzeugeninterviews mit Überlebenden der NS-Militärjustiz*. Köln: Heinrich Boll Stiftung, 1993.

Eckert, Joachim. "Hitler und die Juristen." *Recht und Politik* 29 (1993): 34–50.

Erdmann, Karl Dietrich. "Zeitgeschichte, Militärjustiz und Völkerrecht." *Geschichte in Wissenschaft und Unterricht* 30, no. 3 (1979): 129–39.

Evans, Richard. *In Hitler's Shadow*. London: I. B. Tauris & Company, 1989.

Fahle, Günter. *Verweigern—Weglaufen—Zersetzen: Deutsche Militärjustiz und ungehorsame Soldaten, 1939–1945*. Bremen, Germany: Edition Temmen, 1990.

Fieburg, Gerhard. *Justiz im nationalsozialistischen Deutschland*. Köln: Bundesanzeiger Verlagsgesellschaft, 1984.

Frese, Hans. *Bremsklötze am Siegeswagen der Nation: Erinnerungen eines Deserteurs an Militärgefängnisse, Zuchthäuser und Moorlager in den Jahren 1941–1945*, edited by Fietje Auslander und Norbert Haase. Bremen: Edition Temmen, 1989.

Friedrich, Jörg. *Freispruch für die Nazi-Justiz: Die Urteile gegen NS-Richter seit 1948. Eine Dokumentation*. Hamburg: Rowohlt Taschenbuch Verlag, 1983.

Fritz, Stephen. *Frontsoldaten: The German Soldier in World War II*. Lexington: University Press of Kentucky, 1995.

Garbe, Detlef. *"Im jedem einzelnfall . . . bis zur Todesstrafe": Der Militärstrafrechtler Erich Schwinge. Ein deutsches Juristenleben*. Hamburg: Hamburg Stiftung für Sozialgeschichte des 20th Jahrhundert, 1989.

————. "Im Namen des Volkes?!" In *Verater oder Vorbilder? Deserteure und ungehorsame Soldaten im Nationalsozialismus*, edited by Fietje Auslander, 90–129. Bremen, Germany: Edition Temmen, 1990.

————. *Zwischen Widerstand und Martyrium: Die Zeugen Jehovahs im Dritten Reich*. Munich: R. Oldenbourg Verlag, 1994.

Gaspar, Andreas, H. Rotheweiler, and E. F. Ziehlke, eds. *Sittengeschichte des Zweiten Weltkrieges: Die tausend Jahre von 1933–1945*. Hanau, Germany: Komet, 1990.

Giles, Geoffrey. "Nazi Masculinity and the Persecution of Homosexuality: Sexual Otherness in the Third Reich." Paper presented at the University of Nebraska–Lincoln, Harris Center for Judaic Studies, Wald Lecture Series, April 19, 1999.

Grau, Fritz. "Das Gnadenrecht der Wehrmacht." *Zeitschrift für Wehrrecht* 3 (1938–39): 388–95.

Grau, Gunter. "The Final Solution of the Homosexual Question? The Antihomosexual Policies of the Nazis and the Social Consequences for Homosexual Men." In *The Holocaust and History: The Known, the Disputed, and the Reexamined*, edited by Michael Berenbaum and Abraham J. Peck, 338–44. Bloomington: Indiana University Press, 1998.

———, ed. *Hidden Holocaust?: Gay and Lesbian Persecution in Germany, 1933–1945*. Translated by Patrick Camiller. Chicago: Fitzroy Dearborn, 1995.

Gruchmann, Lothar. "Ausgewählte Dokumente zur deutschen Marinejustiz im Zweiten Weltkrieg." *Vierteljahrshefte für Zeitgeschichte* 3 (1978): 433–98.

———. *Justiz im Dritten Reich 1933–1940: Anpassung und Unterwerfung in der Ära Gürtner*. Munich: R. Oldenbourg Verlag, 1988.

Grunberger, Richard. *Twelve Year Reich: A Social History of Nazi Germany, 1933–1945*. New York: Holt, Rinehart, and Winston, 1971.

Gustrow, Dietrich. *Tödlicher Alltag: Strafverteidiger im Dritten Reich*. Berlin: Siedler Verlag, 1981.

Haase, Norbert. "Aus der Praxis des Reichskriegsgericht: Neu Dokumente zur Militärgerichtsbarkeit im Zweiten Weltkrieg." *Vierteljahrshefte für Zeitgeschichte* 39 (1991): 379–411.

———. *Das Reichskriegsgericht und der Widerstand gegen die nationalsozialistische Herrschaft*. Berlin: Gedenkstätte Deutscher Widerstand, 1993.

———, ed. *Die anderen Soldaten: Wehrkraftzersetzung, Gehorsamsverweigerung und Fahnenflucht im Zweiten Weltkrieg*. Frankfurt: Fischer Taschenbuch Verlag, 1995.

———. *"Gefahr für die Manneszucht": Verweigerung und Widerstand im Spiegel der Spruchtätigkeit von Marinegerichten in Wilhelmshaven (1939–1945)*. Hanover: VHB, 1996.

Hamburg Institute for Social Research, ed. *The German Army and Genocide: Crimes Against War Prisoners, Jews, and Other Civilians, 1939–1945*. New York: The New York Press, 1999.

Hannemann, Ludwig. *Die Justiz der Kriegsmarine, 1939–1945*. Regensburg, Germany: S. Roderer Verlag, 1993.

Heck, Bruno. *Hans Filbinger—Der 'Fall' und die Fakten: Eine historische und politologische Analyse*. Mainz, Germany: V. Hase & Koehler Verlag, 1980.

Hennicke, Otto. "Auszüge aus der Wehrmachtkriminalstatistik." *Zeitschrift für Militärgeschichte* 5 (1966): 438–56.

———. "Über den Justizterror in der deutschen Wehrmacht am Ende der Zweiten Weltkrieg." *Zeitschrift für Militärgeschichte* 4 (1965): 715–20

Hennicke, Otto, and Fritz Wüllner. "Über die barbarischen Vollstreckungsmethoden von Wehrmacht und Justiz im Zweiten Weltkrieg." In *Deserteure der Wehrmacht: Feiglinge—Opfer—Hoffnungsträger?*, edited by Wolfram Wette, 74–94. Essen, Germany: Klartext, 1995.

Hirsch, Martin, Diemut Majer, and Jürgen Meinck, eds. *Recht, Verwaltung und Justiz im Nationalsozialismus: Ausgewählte Schriften, Gesetze und Gerichtsentscheidigungen von 1933 bis 1945*. Köln: Bund Verlag, 1984.

Hirschfeld, Magnus, and Andreas Gaspar. *Sittengeschichte des Ersten Weltkrieges*. Hanau, Germany: Komet, 1990.

Hoffmann, Peter. *The History of the German Resistance, 1933–1945*. Cambridge: MIT Press, 1977.

Hürten, Heinz. "Im Umbruch der Normen: Dokumente über die deutsche Militärjustiz nach der Kapitulation der Wehrmacht." *Militärgeschichtliche Mitteilungen* 28 (1980): 137–56.

Jacobsen, Hans-Adolf. "The Kommissarbefehl and Mass Executions of Soviet Russian Prisoners of War." In *Anatomy of the ss State*, edited by the Research Institute for Military History, 505–34. New York: Walker and Company, 1968.

Jasper, Gotthard, and Hansgeorge Loebel. *Justiz und Nationalsozialismus*. Rosdorf, Germany: Dieterichsche Universitäts-Buchdruckerei, 1985.

Jellonnek, Burkhard. *Homosexuelle unter dem Hakenkreuz: Die Verfolgung von Homosexuellen im Dritten Reich*. Paderborn, Germany: Ferdinand Schöningh, 1990.

Kahle, Hans-Jürgen. . . . *dessen "Konservierung" in Zuchthaus sinnlos ware!: Todesurteile der Militärjustiz in Cuxhaven und Wesermünde 1939–1945*. Cuxhaven, Germany: Wilhelm Heidsiek Verlag, 1991.

Kammler, Jorg. *Ich habe die Metzelei satt und laufe über . . . : Kasseler Soldaten zwischen Verweigerung und Widerstand, 1939–1945*. Fuldabrück, Germany: Hesse, 1985.

Kater, Michael H. "Die Ernsten Bibelforscher im Dritten Reich." *Vierteljahrshefte für Zeitgeschichte* 2 (1969) 181–218.

Kershaw, Ian. *The Nazi Dictatorship*. London: Edward Arnold, 1989.

———. *Popular Opinion and Political Dissent in the Third Reich: Bavaria 1933–1945*. Oxford: Clarendon Press, 1983.

Klausch, Hans-Peter. *Antifaschisten in ss-Uniform: Schicksal und Widerstand der deutschen politischen kz-Häftlinge, Zuchthaus und Wehrmachtstrafgefangenen in der ss-Sonderformation Dirlewanger*. Bremen, Germany: Edition Temmen, 1993.

———. *Die Bewährungstruppe 500: Stellung und Funktion der Bewährungstruppe 500 im System von ns-Wehrrecht, ns-Militärjustiz und Wehrmachtstrafvollzug*. Bremen, Germany: Edition Temmen, 1995.

———. *Die 999er. Von der Brigade Z zur Afrika-Division 999: Die Bewährungsbataillone und ihr Anteil am antifaschistischen Widerstand*. Frankfurt: Röderberg-Verlag, 1986.

———. "Erziehungsmänner und Wehrunwürdige: Die Sonder- und Bewährungseinheiten der Wehrmacht." In *Die Anderen Soldaten: Wehrkraftzersetzung, Gehorsamsverweigerung, und Fahnenflucht im Zweiten*

Weltkrieg, edited by Norbert Haase and Gerhard Paul, 66–84. Frankfurt: Fischer Taschenbuch Verlag, 1995.

Knippschild, Dieter. "Deserteure im Zweiten Weltkrieg: Der Stand der Debatte." In *Armeen und ihre Deserteure: Vernachlässigte Kapitel einer Militärgeschichte der Neuzeit*, edited by Ulrich Bröckling and Michael Sikora, 222–51. Göttingen, Germany: Vandenhoeck & Ruprecht, 1998.

Koch, H. W. *In the Name of the Volk: Political Justice in Hitler's Germany*. London: Tauris, 1989.

Ley, Michael. *"Zum Schutze des deutschen Blutes . . . ": "Rassenschandegesetze" in Nationalsozialismus*. Mainz, Germany: Philo Verlagsgesellschaft, 1997.

Lukas, Richard. *The Forgotten Holocaust: The Poles under German Occupation, 1939–1944*. Lexington: University Press of Kentucky, 1986.

Maier, Klaus A., Horst Rohde, Berno Stegemann, and Hans Umbreit. *Germany's Initial Conquests in Europe*. Vol. 2 of *Germany and the Second World War*, edited by The Research Institute for Military History. Translated by Dean S. McMurry and Ewald Osers. Translation editor, P. S. Falla. Oxford: Clarendon Press, 1991.

Maiwald, Stefan, and Gerd Mischler. *Sexualität unter dem Hakenkreuz: Manipulation und Vernichtung der Intimsphäre im NS-Staat*. Hamburg, Germany: Europa Verlag, 1999.

Majer, Diemut. *"Fremdvölkische" im Dritten Reich: Ein Beitrag zur nationalsozialistischen Rechtsetzung und Rechtspraxis in Verwaltung und Justiz unter besonderer Berücksichtigung der eingegliederten Ostgebiete und des Generalgouvernements*. Boppard am Rhein, Germany: Harald Boldt Verlag, 1981.

Meinen, Insa. "Wehrmacht und Prostitution—Zur Reglementierung der Geschlechterbeziehungen durch die deutsche Militärverwaltung im besetzten Frankreich 1940–1944." *Zeitschrift für Sozialgeschichte des 20. und 21. Jahrhunderts* 2 (1999): 35–55.

Messerschmidt, Manfred. "Deserteure im Zweiten Weltkrieg." In *Deserteure der Wehrmacht: Feiglinge—Opfer—Hoffnungsträger?*, edited by Wolfram Wette, 58–73. Essen, Germany: Klartext, 1995.

———. *Die Wehrmacht im NS-Staat: Zeit der Indoktrination*. Hamburg, Germany: R. v. Decker Verlag, 1969.

———. "German Military Law in the Second World War." In *The German Military in an Age of Total War*, edited by Wilhelm Deist, 323–35. Leamington Spa, UK: Berg Publishers, 1985.

———. "Justiz und Strafvollzug der Wehrmacht im Dienste des Nationalsozialismus." In *Die anderen Soldaten: Wehrkraftzersetzung, Gehorsamsverweigerung und Fahnenflucht im Zweiten Weltkrieg*, edited by Norbert Haase and Gerhard Paul, 19–36. Frankfurt: Fischer Taschenbuch Verlag, 1995.

———. *Was damals Recht War . . . : NS-Militär- und Strafjustiz im Vernichtungskrieg*. Essen, Germany: Klartext, 1996.

Messerschmidt, Manfred, and Fritz Wüllner, *Die Wehrmachtjustiz im Dienste des Nationalsozialismus: Zerstorung einer Legende*. Baden-Baden: Nomos Verlagsgesellschaft, 1987.

Mitcham, Samuel W. Jr. *Hitler's Legions: The German Order of Battle in World War II*. New York: Stein and Day, 1985.

Möhler, Rainer. "Strafjustiz im 'Dritten Reich.'" *Neue Politische Literatur* 39 (1994): 423–41.

Mörbitz, H. *'Hohes Kriegsgerichts!' Ein Tatsachenbericht nach den Erlebnissen eines Kriegsgerichtsverteidiger*. Wien, Germany: CFH Verlag, 1988.

Mosse, George. *Nationalism and Sexuality: Respectability and Abnormal Sexuality in Modern Europe*. New York: Howard Fertig, 1985.

Müller, Ingo. *Hitler's Justice: The Courts of the Third Reich*. Translated by Deborah L. Schneider. Cambridge: Harvard University Press, 1991.

Müller, Klaus Jürgen. *Armee, Politik, und Gesellschaft in Deutschland, 1933–1945: Studien zur Verhältnis von Armee u. NS-System*. Paderborn, Germany: Ferdinand Schöningh, 1981.

O'neill, Robert. *The German Army and the Nazi Party, 1933–1939*. New York: James H. Heineman, 1966.

Paul, Gerhard. *Ungehorsame Soldaten: Dissens, Verweigerung und Widerstand deutscher Soldaten*. St. Ingbert, Germany: Röhrig Universitätsverlag, 1994.

Peukert, Detlev. *Inside Nazi Germany: Conformity, Opposition, and Racism in Everyday Life*. Translated by Richard Deveson. New Haven CT: Yale University Press, 1982.

Philipp, Joachim. "Der Gerichtsherr in der deutschen Militärgerichtsbarkeit bis 1945." *Zeitschrift für Militärgeschichte* 27 (1988): 533–47.

Plant, Richard. *The Pink Triangle: The Nazi War against Homosexuals*. New York: Henry Holt, 1986.

Rabofsky, Eduard, and Gerhard Oberkofler. *Verborgene Wurzeln der NS-Justiz: Strafrechtliche Rüstung für zwei Weltkriege*. Wien, Austria: Europaverlag, 1985.

Rass, Christoph. *Menschenmaterial: Deutsche Soldaten an der Ostfront. Innenansichten einer Infanteriedivision, 1939–1945*. Paderborn, Germany: Ferdinand Schöningh, 2003.

Rector, Frank. *The Nazi Extermination of Homosexuals*. New York: Stein and Day, 1981.

Reifner, Udo, and Bernd-Rüdiger Sonnen, eds. *Strafjustiz und Polizei im Dritten Reich*. Frankfurt: Campus Verlag, 1984.

Robinson, Hans. *Justiz als politische Verfolgung: Die Rechtsprechung in Rassenschandenfällen beim Landgericht Hamburg, 1936–1943*. Stuttgart: Deutsche Verlags-Anstalt, 1977.

Rösler, Ingo. "Die faschistische Gesetzgebung und Rechtsprechung gegen Wehrkraftzersetzung." *Zeitschrift für Militärgeschichte* 10 (1971): 561–75.

Rüthers, Bernd. *Entartes Recht: Rechtslehren und Kronjuristen im Dritten Reich.* Munich: Verlag C. H. Beck, 1989.

Saathoff, Günter, Franz Dillmann, and Manfred Messerschmidt. *Opfer der Militärjustiz: Zur Notwendigkeit der Rehabilitierung und Entschädigung.* Köln: Bundesverband Information & Beratung für ns-Verfolgte, 1994.

Säcker, Franz J., ed. *Recht und Rechtslehre im Nationalsozialismus: Ringvorlesung der Rechtswissenschaften Fakultät der Christian-Albrechts-Universität zu Kiel.* Baden-Baden: Nomos Verlagsgesellschaft, 1992.

Scherer, Klaus. *'Asozial' im Dritten Reich: Die vergessenen Verfolgten.* Münster, Germany: votum Verlag, 1990.

Schoeps, Julius H., ed. *Justiz und Nationalsozialismus: Bewältigt—Verdrängt—Vergessen.* Stuttgart: Burg Verlag, 1987.

Schorn, Hubert. *Der Richter im Dritten Reich: Geschichte und Dokumente.* Frankfurt: Vittorio Klostermann, 1959.

Schulte, Theo. *German Army and Nazi Policies in Occupied Russia.* Oxford: Berg Publishers, 1989.

Schwartz, Otto. *Strafgesetzbuch.* München: C.H. Beck Verlag, 1939.

Schwinge, Erich. *Die deutsche Militärjustiz in der Zeit des Nationalsozialismus.* 2d ed. Marburg, Germany: N. G. Verlag, 1978.

———. *Verfälschung und Wahrheit: Das Build der Wehrmachtgerichtsbarkeit.* Tübingen, Germany: Hohenrain-Verlag, 1988.

Seaton, Albert. *The German Army, 1933–1945.* London: Weidenfeld & Nicolson, 1982.

Seidler, Franz. "Das Justizwesen der Wehrmacht." In *Die Soldaten der Wehrmacht,* edited by D. H. Poeppel, 361–403. Munich: Herbig, 1998.

———. "Die Fahnenflucht in der deutschen Wehrmacht während des zweiten Weltkrieg." *Militärgeschichtliche Mitteilungen* 22 (1977): 23–42.

———. *Die Militärgerichtsbarkeit der deutschen Wehrmacht 1939–1945: Rechtsprechung und Strafvollzug.* Munich: Herbig, 1991.

———. *Prostitution, Homsexualität, Selbstverstümmelung: Probleme der deutschen Sanitätsführung, 1939–1945.* Neckargemünd, Germany: Kurt Vowinkel Verlag, 1977.

Snyder, David Raub. "The Prosecution and Punishment of Sex Offenders in the Wehrmacht, 1939–1945." PhD diss., University of Nebraska, 2002.

Staff, Ilse. *Justiz im Dritten Reich.* Frankfurt: Fischer Bücherei, 1964.

Stokesbury, James L. *A Short History of World War II.* New York: William Morrow, 1980.

Stollies, Michael. *The Law under the Swastika.* Chicago: University of Chicago Press, 1998.

Streit, Christian. *Keine Kameraden: Die Wehrmacht und die sowjetischen Kriegsgefangenen, 1941–1945.* Bonn: Verlag J. H. W. Dietz Nachf., 1997.

Suhr, Elke. *Die Emslandlager. Die politische und wirtschaftliche Bedeutung der*

Emslandischen Konzentrations- und Strafgefangenenlager, 1933–1945. Bremen, Germany: Donat Temmen Verlag, 1985.

Thomas, Jürgen. "Nur das ist für die Truppe Recht, was ihr nützt . . . ." In *Die anderen Soldaten: Wehrkraftzersetzung, Gehorsamsverweigerung und Fahnenflucht im Zweiten Weltkrieg*, edited by Norbert Haase and Gerhard Paul, 37–49. Frankfurt: Fischer Taschenbuch Verlag, 1995.

———. *Wehrmachtjustiz und Widerstandbekämpfung: Das Wirken der ordentlichen deutschen Militärjustiz in den besetzen Westgebieten 1940–45 unter rechtshistorischen Aspekten*. Baden-Baden: Nomos Verlagsgesellschaft, 1990.

Valentin, Rudolf. *Die Krankenbataillone: Sonderformationen der deutsche Wehrmacht im Zweiten Weltkrieg*. Düsseldorf: Droste Verlag, 1981.

Van Creveld, Martin. *Fighting Power: German and U.S. Army Performance, 1939–1945*. Westport CT: Greenwood Press, 1982.

Vultejus, Ulrich. *Kampfanzug unter der Robe: Kriegsgerichtsbarkeit des zweiten und dritten Weltkrieges*. Hamburg: Buntbuch, 1984.

Walmrath, Lothar. *"Iustitia et disciplana": Strafgerichtsbarkeit in der deutschen Kriegsmarine, 1939–1945*. Frankfurt: Peter Lang, 1998.

Walther, Manfred. "Hat der positivismus die deutschen Juristen wehrlos gemacht?" *Kritische Justiz* 21, no 3 (1988): 263–80.

Wette, Wolfram, ed. *Deserteure der Wehrmacht: Feiglinge—Opfer—Hoffnungsträger?* Essen, Germany: Klartext, 1995.

Wiebke, Steffen. "Grenzen und Möglichkeiten der Verwendung von Strafakten als Grundlage kriminologischer Forschung: Methodische Probleme und Anwendungsbeispiele." In *Die Analyse prozeßproduzierter Daten*, 89–108. Stuttgart: Klett-Cotta, 1977.

Wüllner, Fritz. "Der Wehrmacht 'strafvollzug' im Dritten Reich: Zur zentralen Rolle der Wehrmachtgefängnisse in Torgau." In *Das Torgau Tabo*, edited by Norbert Haase, 29–44. Leipzig, Germany: Forum Verlag, 1993.

———. Die NS-Militärjustiz und das Elend der Geschichtsschreibung. Baden-Baden: Nomo Verlagsgesellschaft, 1991.

diminished responsibility, 228–30, 242n72
disciplinary units, 32–35
Dönitz, Karl, 50–51

eastern occupied territories: homosexuality
among soldiers in, 118–19; intoxicated soldiers in, 212–17; sexual assault in, 135–148,
264nn20–21
Eberlein, Michael, 27
entrapment and homosexuality, 119–23
expert medical testimony, 217–19, 226–27

field courts, sentencing by, 123–29, 182–89
field penal camps: child molesters in, 185–86;
creation of, 78–82, 254n89; the Gerichtsherr
and, 91–92; homosexuals sentenced to, 111–
14, 115–16, 125–26, 129, 131–32; illness and
mortality in, 84–85, 88; intoxication convictions and, 213–14, 221; rapists sentenced
to, 147, 156–57, 159–60; structure, 85–86,
262nn77–78; work performed by soldiers sent
to, 82–84, 87–88
Fighting Power, 234
fighting power, subversion of, 37–38
Förster, Jürgen, 58–59
France, military justice, 20–21, sexual assaults
in, 148–55
Freisler, Roland, 4
Fritz, Stephen, 206
front-parole, 67–70, 231–32; for rapists, 164–66

Gerichtsherr, the, 12–15, 40; confirmation
of verdicts by, 51–55, 120–21, 244n36,
244–45nn40–41, 247n85; field penal camps
and, 84–85; inconsistency in punishments ordered by, 115–16; parolee transfers by, 91–92;
power of, 41–47, 93–94, 232, 243n19,
267n6; reinstatement of sentences by, 75;
sentencing of homosexuals, 111, 112; suspension and deferment of sentences by, 67–68,
186–87. *See also* courts
Germany and the Second World War, 58

Haase, Norbert, 22, 29–30, 94–95
habitual offender status, 110–14, 120–21, 128–
29, 159–62, 168, 209–12
Halder, Franz, 78–79
Hannemann, Ludwig, 27, 101
Hennicke, Otto, 5
Himmler, Heinrich, 35, 54; persecution of homosexuals by, 103–6, 108, 109, 118, 126, 130,
258n12

Hitler, Adolf: apologists for, 3, 55–56; attitude
toward Wehrmachtjustiz, 55–56, 238n3;
Barbarossa Jurisdiction Decree of, 55, 56–62;
clemency petitions judgment decree, 40;
Commissar Order, 56–62; on the death sentence and military justice, 21; death sentence
criteria established by, 50; field penal camps
ordered by, 78–79, 85–86; foreign political
goals of, 4; jurisdictional limitations imposed
by, 55; on negative selection, 66; and recruitment of jurists, 25–26, 28; response to the
blitzkrieg's failure, 78–79; special parole formations ordered by, 71–72; transfer of jurists
into Military Special Services by, 48; view of
homosexuals, 103, 107; war aims of, 24–25;
war of annihilation against the Soviet Union,
57–58; Wartime Penal Code and Wartime Judicial Procedure Code signed by, 36
Hitler Youth, 31, 170–71
homosexuality: among soldiers in occupied
eastern territories, 118–19; civilians courts
treatment of, 129–32; court-martials for, 131;
death sentence for, 116–17, 259nn30–31;
entrapment and, 119–23; Heinrich Himmler's
persecution of, 103–6, 108, 109, 118, 126,
130, 258n12; intoxication and, 212–13, 214,
217–18; paragraph 175 addressing, 103–10;
parole for those convicted of, 112–14; perceived threats of, 105–6; persons under 21
and, 114–17, 127; punishments for, 111–14,
115–16, 125–26, 129, 131–32, 257n1; repeat
offenders and reintegration, 110–14, 120–21,
128–29, 207, 210–11; sentences in different
military courts, 123–29; U. S. military's handling of, 130–31, 238n44

Imperial German Military Criminal Code of
1898, 20
incest: cases, 170–74; intoxication and, 173;
National Socialism philosophy and, 170–72;
punishments for, 169–82; Wehrmacht Commander–Berlin sentencing for, 173–82
independence, judicial, 48–49
Institute for Contemporary History, 6
Institute for Military Historical Research, 58
International Military Tribunal (IMT), 5, 235n6
intoxication: bestiality and, 201, 203, 226–27;
child molestation and, 222–23; courts concern with levels of, 208; diminished responsibility and, 228–30, 242n72; in the eastern
occupied territories, 212–17; expert medical
testimony and, 217–19, 226–27; habitual

New Ordinance for the Execution of Punishments, 80; lessons of World War I and, 36–41, 48–50, 239n14, 239n20; parole and deferment of sentences, 67–70

Studies in War, Society, and the Military

Lightning Source UK Ltd.
Milton Keynes UK
14 July 2010

157025UK00001B/68/P